Pure Evil

ALSO BY JACLYN WELDON WHITE

Whisper to the Black Candle: Voodoo, Murder, and the Case of Anjette Lyles (1999)*

The Empty Nursery: The Disappearance of Haley Hardwick (2001)*

A Very Special Gift: The Story of the Legacy of Emily Fisher Crum and Remer Hamilton Crum (2002)*

Distant Hearts (a novel, 2004)*

Bestest: The Biography of Peyton Anderson, Jr. (2005)*

Mockingbird in the Moonlight (a novel, 2007)

The Greatest Champion That Never Was: The Life of W. L. "Young" Stribling (2011)*

A Southern Woman's Guide to Herbs (2013)*

Sidetracked: Two Women, Two Cameras, and Lunches on Sherman's Trail (with Milam Propst, 2016)*

The Witch of Ben Hill County (a mystery, 2017)

The Fairy Crosses of Fannin County (a mystery, 2019)

* Published by MERCER UNIVERSITY PRESS

Pure Evil

The Machetti Murders of Macon, Georgia

JACLYN WELDON WHITE

MERCER UNIVERSITY PRESS
Macon, Georgia
2020

MUP/ P602
ISBN 9780881467598

Published by Mercer University Press
1501 Mercer University Drive
Macon, Georgia 31207

25 24 23 22 21 20 9 8 7 6 5 4 3 2 1

Books published by Mercer University Press are printed on acid-free paper that meets the requirements of the American National Standard for Information Sciences—Permanence of Paper for Printed Library Materials.

Printed and bound in the United States.

This book is set in Adobe Caslon Pro,
display Georgia and American Typewriter.

Cover/jacket design by Burt&Burt.

Names: White, Jaclyn Weldon, author.
Title: Pure evil : the Machetti murders of Macon, Georgia /
Jaclyn Weldon White.
Description: Macon, Georgia : Mercer University Press, 2020.
Includes index.
Identifiers: LCCN 2020024272 | ISBN 9780881467598 (paperback)
Subjects: LCSH: Machetti, Rebecca, 1938- | Akins, Ronny (Joseph Ronald), 1936-1974.
| Murder—Georgia—Macon—Case studies.
Classification: LCC HV6534.M124 W45 2020 | DDC 364.152/3092 [B]—dc23
LC record available at https://lccn.loc.gov/2020024272

This book is dedicated to

Victoria Akins, Valerie Akins, and Vanessa Akins.

Mercer University Press

Endowed by

Tom Watson Brown
and
The Watson-Brown Foundation, Inc.

Acknowledgments

I want to thank the following people for graciously sharing their time and recollections with me: Valerie Akins, Alan Barfield, Bob Boren, Emmett Goodwin, Ann McElroy, Bobby McElroy, Superior Court Judge C. Cloud Morgan, and Ray Wilkes.

Many thanks to Marsha Luttrell for providing the title for this book.

Pure Evil could never have been written without these resources: *The Athens Banner-Herald*, the Bibb County Clerk of Superior Court's office, the Bibb County District Attorney's office, the Georgia Archives, *The Gwinnett Daily News*, *The Macon Telegraph*, and the Washington Memorial Library.

PURE EVIL

Prologue

No one knows exactly what happened during the last few minutes of Coy Turpin's life and no one ever will. While there is no question that he and his three-year-old son Michael were shot and killed shortly after noon on November 9, 1955, the reasons for their deaths died with them on that cold autumn day in Athens, Georgia.

Nothing in Coy's life foreshadowed the events of that afternoon. He and his wife, Sara, were products of solid working class families, the sort of folks described as the salt of the earth. They owned their own home and both held full-time jobs—he as an electrician at a textile mill and she at a local department store.

Their daughter Rebecca, known as Becky, had been born in 1938 and lived her first fourteen years as an only child. That status suddenly changed with the birth of her brother, Anthony Michael, in 1952. Although unexpected, the baby was joyously welcomed into the family. Coy, especially, delighted in his new son.

When Sara returned to work a few months after Michael was born, a local woman named Janie Goolsby was hired to keep house for them and look after the baby.

That Wednesday in early November in 1955, Coy Turpin left work just before noon and drove home. The Turpin house at 230 Nacoochee Avenue was a craftsman-style bungalow built several decades before, but it was freshly painted and as attractive as the other homes on the narrow street off Prince Avenue. Coy parked his car in the drive and walked across the carpet of fallen leaves to the back door.

Janie Goolsby was on her hands and knees, scrubbing the kitchen linoleum, and young Michael played on the floor nearby. The television in the living room was blaring. Janie liked to be able to hear her soap operas, or "stories," when she was working.

She wasn't surprised when Coy Turpin opened the back door. He often came home for lunch. He adored his son and spent as much time as possible with him. In fact, people said he spoiled the boy.

After he ran to greet his father, Michael announced he had to go to the bathroom. His toilet training had gone well, but at three years old, he still needed some help. Janie started to get to her feet, but Coy stopped her.

"No," he told her, raising his voice over the sound of the television, "I'll take him."

The two left the kitchen and went to the bathroom at the other end of the house. Coy closed the hall door behind them and Janie went on with her work. It was only when she'd finished the floor that she began to wonder what was keeping them. The kitchen clock showed it was past 12:30.

She called out, "Mr. Turpin!" but there was no answer. She wouldn't have been able to hear one anyway above the noise of the television. Wiping her hands on her apron, she turned it off and went to investigate.

The bathroom door was closed and no voices could be heard from inside the room. Her knock sounded very loud.

"Mr. Turpin! Is everything okay?"

She knocked again. When there was still no answer, she slowly opened the door.

~~~
~~~

Michael Turpin lay motionless at her feet. Blood still ran from a wound to his head. Coy was slumped beside him, a similar wound in his face. A rifle lay loose in his limp hands. The man's blood joined that of his son, spreading across the tile floor Janie had cleaned only hours before.

News of the two deaths shocked the quiet university town. By the time the story hit the front page of the *Athens Banner-Herald* that evening, the police had already concluded it was a case of murder and suicide. But they could offer no motive. Turpin had never shown any indications of instability. He hadn't been drinking. In fact, there was no evidence of any alcohol or drugs in the house. While it was curious that the maid hadn't heard the shots, they believed that was explained by the fact that two closed doors separated her from the bathroom and the television had been turned up quite loud.

Coroner S. C. Cartledge chose not to call an inquest because he agreed with the police finding that Turpin had killed himself and his son. Without evidence of anything else, the coroner blamed the crime on Turpin's suffering a "sudden mental crack up."

Sara Turpin's life was shaken to the core. She found it difficult to comprehend what had happened and moved through the following days like a sleepwalker. In a state bordering on shock, she made the necessary arrangements for her son and husband.

Friday, November 11, was a golden autumn day. The sun shone down on trees that glowed with fall colors under a deep blue sky. The town itself was festively decked out in red and black, gearing up for Saturday's football game, when the University of Georgia would play Auburn University. And that afternoon, a double funeral service was held at the Oconee

Street Methodist Church.

Sara and Becky were surrounded by family members and friends. Becky's boyfriend, Joseph Ronald Akins, served as one of Michael's pallbearers. From the church, the long procession of cars made its way to Oconee Hill Cemetery where, just after 3:30, Coy Turpin and his son were buried side by side.

Becky Turpin kept a diary, as did many girls her age, and was faithful about making daily entries. On Wednesday night, she had written, "I came home from school today and my dad had killed my little brother."

Chapter 1

The oak-shaded house on Nacoochee Avenue was a dreary place to live after the deaths of Coy and Michael Turpin. Sara Turpin could hardly speak of the tragedy, but the fact of it hung over their home like a toxic cloud. When Becky turned seventeen on November 25, there was no celebration. Isolated and confused, she looked more and more to her boyfriend, Ronny Akins, for comfort.

Ronny, one of four sons born to Thelma and Raymond Akins, was a tall, dark-haired boy. He'd never been the boisterous sort. He was quiet and loved to tinker with machines of any kind. He spent hundreds of hours taking them apart and reassembling them. Airplanes especially fascinated him. He'd become so interested in them that, in his early teens, he went to the Clarke Flying Service at the local airport. He and the management there came to an agreement—Ronny would do odd jobs in exchange for flying lessons. He soloed at age sixteen.

Three years older than Becky, Ronny had attended the University of Georgia for one year but dropped out to pursue his real love—electronics. In 1955, he was working as a television repairman.

When Becky graduated from high school in 1956, she was pregnant with Ronny's child. For two youngsters in love, this didn't seem to be a terrible problem. But they knew their families wouldn't be happy. So, in early June, when Ronny's parents were on vacation, the two young people eloped. They were married in South Carolina. Becky was seventeen and

Ronny was twenty.

Sara Turpin, still reeling from the deaths of her husband and son, accepted her daughter's marriage. Ronny's parents, however, were disappointed. They'd hoped their son would establish himself in a career before taking on the responsibility of a wife. But the pregnancy changed all that, and there was nothing to be done but to make the best of the situation.

Once the shock began to fade, both Sara and the Akinses began looking forward to the birth of their grandchild. They all expected to spend a lot of time with the baby, but that wasn't to be. The new grandparents hardly had a chance to get to know their granddaughter. Victoria Ramona was born on February 18, 1957, and in March, Ronny and Becky moved 100 miles away to the Middle Georgia town of Macon. There, Ronny quickly found work in television repair.

Within only a few months, Becky was pregnant again. Their second daughter was due in March of 1958 but was born prematurely on January 2. They named her Valerie Rhonda. The couple completed their young family two years later with the birth of Vanessa Rebecca on October 13, 1960.

The early sixties were a time of turmoil for Macon and the rest of the South. Integration was inevitable, but its coming was slow and difficult. In 1961, twelve young black men boarded a Macon city bus and defiantly took the forbidden front seats. Ordered to move to the back of the vehicle, they refused and were arrested. That began a round of demonstrations culminating in a three-week bus boycott. Sporadic violence erupted from time to time and relations between the races grew even more tense than usual.

Ronny and Becky weren't directly affected by the furor downtown, although they and their neighbors talked about it all the time. The couple had recently bought a small frame house at 4924 York Place in the suburban area of Bloomfield and didn't go into the city very often. Ronny worked long hours and Becky was busy caring for the children.

In addition to his full-time job as a television repairman, Ronny took on other projects as well. He moved a one-room, prefab outbuilding into their backyard and turned it into a workshop. He took any part-time work that came along, including the installation of television antennas during his off hours. But no matter how hard or how much he worked, he still had a difficult time keeping up with Becky's demands for more money. She wanted the most fashionable clothes, the newest appliances, and all the other products she saw advertised on television.

Television was still a novelty in the early sixties, but because of his job, Ronny could give his family the best technology available. A huge, state-of-the art console television held the place of honor in the Akins living room. The enormous antenna on the roof of the small house guaranteed them the clearest possible picture. Ronny had also upgraded the set with a magnifying device that made the picture larger and installed a glass cover that was supposed to transform the black-and-white images into color. The color wasn't very accurate, but no one seemed to care.

For a while, the Akins family had the only TV on York Place. Sunday nights became major events for the children in the neighborhood. Dressed in pajamas, robes, and slippers, they crowded into the Akins's living room and sat on the floor to watch *The Wonderful World of Disney* and *The Ed Sullivan Show*. There were often fifteen or twenty children in the room, several accompanied by their parents. Becky and Ronny never seemed to tire of the company. Sometimes Becky would make hot chocolate or popcorn for the crowd. The Akins girls got their first glimpse of Elvis Presley and, later, the Beatles, sitting in front of the television in the York Place house.

In 1963, the Akins's television became a neighborhood draw for a more serious reason. Five-year-old Valerie was playing outside one sunny November afternoon, waiting for her sister Vicki to come home from school. If she noticed several of the neighborhood women entering her house, she didn't place any significance on it. Neighbors were in and out of each other's houses all the time on York Place. The little girl wasn't prepared for what she found when she went inside. Seven or eight women crowded around the television in the living room. All of them were crying and the voices on the television were somber.

"What's wrong?" Valerie asked fearfully.

"Kennedy's been shot," her mother told her.

Valerie didn't know who Kennedy was, but she began crying, too.

Most summers, the Akins family managed to get away for a week's vacation in Florida. Their favorite destination was Venice Beach. Reasonably priced and family friendly, it seemed the ideal spot for them. But one summer something happened that made them think they might have to find another place to vacation.

The long, white beach was, of course, the main attraction of Venice Beach. And Becky loved it as much as the children did. She spent hours, covered in suntan oil, stretched out on a towel. She never seemed to get enough sun. But one afternoon, with the children playing in the surf while she and Ronny relaxed on the sand, Becky spotted black fins in the water, some distance out beyond the swimmers.

She was convinced she'd seen a shark. Although Ronny

recognized it for what it was and tried to assure her that she'd only seen a dolphin, Becky went into full panic mode.

"Shark!" she began screaming as loud as she could. "There's a shark!"

She raced to the shore and started physically pulling people, including her now-terrified children, from the water. The lifeguards joined her and eventually cleared the surf. The frightened swimmers stood in small dripping groups on the sand, fearfully watching the water.

Then the cause of the commotion became apparent. A school of dolphin rolled playfully in the waves fifty yards from the beach. The lifeguards scolded Becky for jumping to conclusions. A few people laughed, but most of the crowd glared at her and shook their heads.

The Akins girls were miserable for the rest of the trip. Everywhere they went in Venice Beach, people recognized them as the children of "the crazy woman" who'd imagined seeing sharks.

The Florida vacation wasn't the only time that Becky overreacted. Her behavior was growing more erratic all the time. Her reactions were extreme, and any little thing could set her off.

All three of the children attended Morgan Elementary School in Macon, walking the short distance from their house every day. In the spring of 1967, Vanessa was in the first grade. She and her sisters had received baby chicks as Easter gifts that year, and Vanessa insisted on taking hers to school the next day.

The call from the principal's office came about ten that morning. The woman on the phone told Becky that Vanessa was hysterical.

"We've done everything we can, but we can't get her to stop crying."

"Let me talk to her," Becky said. A few seconds later, she could hear her daughter sobbing. "Nessie." Becky had to speak loudly to be heard over Vanessa's crying. "Nessie! What's wrong?"

There were a few anguished gulps, then Vanessa blurted out, "My teacher died!"

At least that's what Becky thought she said. Vanessa had a slight speech impediment which was worsened by her hysterical tears.

"Your teacher died? Is that what you said? Where is she?"

"She's in a box in my room."

Becky was horrified. How could the school even consider displaying a teacher in her coffin in a classroom? She told Vanessa she was coming to get her. Then she called several other mothers, announcing the horror that was taking place at Morgan Elementary. They, in turn, made more phone calls. In no time at all, the neighborhood was in turmoil.

Most families in Bloomfield had only one car that the husbands drove to and from work, but transportation wasn't a problem for these outraged parents. Less than an hour after Becky made her first call, a mob of angry mothers walked to Morgan Elementary School, ready to rescue their children from a morbid display of death.

When the truth came out, that it was a pet chicken, not a teacher, that was dead in a box in the classroom, Becky was humiliated, but she got over it quickly and just laughed about the misunderstanding. It wasn't quite that easy for Vicki, Valerie, or Vanessa, though. For weeks, the other students talked and laughed about their mother.

~~~
~~~

Becky Akins's life was full of all the things that should have made her happy, but she was never really satisfied. When new clothes and new appliances weren't enough, she looked for other diversion and found it with the man who lived across the street. The affair lasted several months before Ronny grew suspicious. He confronted her, but she denied that she'd done anything wrong.

Becky's denial didn't dispel Ronny's suspicions, and he believed he knew how to find out exactly what was going on. An expert in electronics, it was easy for him to rig their home telephone so that all conversations on the line were recorded. Soon afterwards, he told Becky what he'd done.

Once again, she denied having an affair. So, while his horrified children listened from the hallway, he played the tapes of several conversations between the lovers. As Becky stared at the floor, the room was filled with her voice and the neighbor's, laughing and brimming with sexual innuendo.

"You can't deny it now!" Ronny shouted. "I've got proof!"

That initial confrontation was followed by days of fighting, shouting, and destruction. Accusations and counter-accusations flew, as did dishes and pots and pans. The children's new Olan Mills portraits fell victim to the fury when, one night, at the height of one of the arguments, Becky snatched the photos from the wall and threw them across the room where they crashed to the floor. The next day, Valerie and Vicki picked up the shattered glass and ruined photos.

Finally, Ronny packed a bag and left.

With their father gone, life was difficult for the Akins girls. Becky's fury was awful, and she took it out on the children. Shouting became her most common form of communication, and she could be provoked to violence by almost anything.

The girls began trying to avoid any conversation with her. When that wasn't possible, they tried to stand out of reach.

Every time Ronny picked them up for a day out, the girls begged him to come home. Crying, they told him their lives weren't the same with him gone. Typical of so many children caught in their parents' problems, they promised never to misbehave again. Even Becky swallowed enough of her pride to ask him back.

Ronny's feelings for his wife had irrevocably changed, but the love of his children wouldn't let him leave for good. In the end, he relented and returned home.

Becky promised there'd be no more trouble, and, for a while, she kept her word. But she eventually returned to her old ways. The difference this time was that she grew more skilled at deceit. The girls never knew the name of the next man, but they had no doubt he existed.

Becky would take her daughters to a park in downtown Macon to play on the swings and slides, warning them not to leave the playground. Then she'd disappear for a while with a man who'd been waiting near the street. Although they glimpsed him from a distance several times, the girls never got a good look at their mother's new lover.

"You better not tell you father," she warned them after one of their outings. "If you do, he'll leave again and this time he won't come back. And it'll be all your fault."

So, her three young daughters, believing they were responsible for keeping the family together, became Becky's unwilling accomplices.

Chapter 2

Ronny Akins committed himself to keeping his family together. He focused all his energy on supporting his wife and children and spent as much time as possible with the girls. Becky liked nice things, and he tried hard to keep his income equal to her spending. After putting in several years at the TV repair store, he took a job with Southern Natural Gas at a significant increase in salary.

His main responsibility with the long-distance pipeline company was setting up and maintaining their communication towers. It was more than a full-time job, requiring him to be on call many nights and weekends, but he still squeezed in time to do some television repair and antenna installation on the side. From time to time, he also did occasional engineering jobs for a local radio station. He even took a turn or two behind the microphone as a country music disc jockey.

Ronny had always dreamed of living and raising his family in the country. And when he was promoted at Southern Natural Gas, he had the opportunity to do just that. Around the time Richard Nixon was elected president, Ronny and Becky started looking for a place to build a house. They found ten acres of rolling land on Hartley Bridge Road in a rural area on the south side of Macon. It was the perfect building site.

The new house would be a big place, with six bedrooms, three baths, and an enormous family room. Designed to be built on a slope, it would appear to be a modest brick ranch from the front. All the size would be in the back, where the house grew to two stories.

In the summer of 1969, the family sold the house on York Place and moved to a small rental house less than a mile from the property on Hartley Bridge Road. At the same time, construction began on their new house. Even though it was a bit cramped, the family settled comfortably into the rental house. There were only two bedrooms, but one of them was so large that all three of the girls' beds fit easily into it. They spent the summer learning their way around their new neighborhood, and in the fall Vicki, Valerie, and Vanessa enrolled at Porter Elementary School.

Well after midnight one January night, eleven-year-old Valerie awoke to extreme heat. Her feet felt like they were on fire. She threw back the covers to discover her electric blanket was smoldering. Screaming, she ran to her parents' room. By the time Ronny and Becky came back with her, there were actual flames leaping up from the bed.

Ronny ripped off the covers, ran through the house with the blazing mass of fabric, and threw it out the back door. Then he grabbed the garden hose, which was attached to an outside spigot, and struggled frantically to pull it through the house until he could hose down Valerie's bed.

About the time he'd doused the flames, Becky came running into the room. "The car!" she screamed. "You threw the covers under the car! It's going to blow up!"

When Ronny had tossed the burning blanket and sheets out the door, they'd landed partly underneath the family car. Now, he hurriedly dragged the hose back outside and directed the stream of water under the car until the flames had been defeated.

When the excitement was over, all the Akinses were exhausted, but safe. The night's only casualties were the bedclothes and a wet mattress.

Living as close by as they did, the family checked in at the building site several times a week. Although he contracted many jobs out, Ronny did much of the actual work on the house himself. As the work progressed, the Akinses got to know their future neighbors, Luther and Betty Barfield, who owned the property next door and were also in the process of building a house. Their son, Alan, was a high school student whose teenager status made him quite interesting to Vicki and Valerie. He was a nice boy, and they were flattered when he occasionally took time to talk with them.

Money was tight and Ronny was always on the lookout for ways to generate extra income. Just such an opportunity presented itself when he was driving home from work one afternoon. Traffic on the interstate slowed and then came to a stop. As the cars inched forward, an overturned chicken truck came into view. Chickens were running loose all over the place. The truck driver was too busy trying to explain the accident to the officers on the scene to be interested in retrieving his cargo. So, with the driver's blessing, Ronny picked up two of the birds and took them home. By the time he reached Hartley Bridge Road, the back seat of his company car was a mess, but he thought the chickens would be worth the trouble of cleaning it.

The two hens were established on the screened-in front porch where they continued making a mess of things, but they were soon nesting and laying eggs, which the family sold. This extra income lasted about three months before the egg-laying stopped and the chickens found their way to the family's dinner table.

Even though the hens weren't a great success, Ronny liked the idea of keeping livestock. And now, with ten acres of land, he had the chance to do just that. He fenced off a small portion of the acreage and turned a few calves out into the pasture. With the family living just up the road, caring for the animals presented no hardship. In fact, they all enjoyed feeding the cattle and watching them grow.

Then, one Saturday afternoon in late summer, they drove the short distance to the pasture and discovered the calves were missing. It didn't take Ronny long to find the place where the fence had been cut. He was furious. He called the sheriff's office and angrily reported that his herd of cattle had been stolen.

Within half an hour, lawmen, including the sheriff himself, were swarming all over the Akins's property. Neighbors were interviewed and photographs were taken of the pasture and the cut fence. While Ronny was gratified that the authorities were taking the theft so seriously, he was still devastated by the loss.

He shook his head, saying over and over, "They took my whole herd!"

The sheriff asked how many head of cattle were in the herd.

"Five," Ronnie said.

"Are you sure of that number? It would take an awful long time to load 500 head onto trucks."

"Not five *hundred*," Ronny said. "*Five*. There were five cows."

The sheriff just stared at him for a moment, then he quietly sent his men on their way. He wrote the report on the theft himself and was gone in ten minutes.

The Akins family never saw their cows again. Although they'd be able to laugh about it later, at the time, they considered the cattle theft a major crime.

~~~

Amid the next year's early summer green, the family left the little rental house and moved into their new home down the road. At first, the spaciousness almost overwhelmed them. Each of the girls had her own room. The bathrooms were roomy and the kitchen big and open. But soon everybody's favorite spot was the family room, which took up one whole end of the house.

Furnished with oversized couches and chairs, red carpet, and Tiffany-style lamps, the girls thought it was the grandest room they'd ever seen. The family spent most of their free time there. At Becky's urging, Ronny found not one, but two jukeboxes for the room. The first was stocked with music by Frank Sinatra, Frankie Avalon, the Platters, Nat King Cole, and Dean Martin. The second one was just for the children and had an ever-changing selection of the current Top 40 music.

Ronny was determined to make life as perfect as possible for his daughters. He constructed a tree house in one of the big oaks at the end of the driveway near the road and equipped it with a Tarzan-style rope swing. In the late afternoon, his daughters would wait there for him to come home from work. When he rounded the corner, they'd swing down, one by one, then pile into the car with him. Then, together they'd all ride up to the house.

Her father's homecoming soon became Valerie's favorite time of the day. All three girls adored him, and Ronny never tired of spending time with them. He was always up for a game of baseball in the big yard. He taught them to make gourd birdhouses to hang in the trees to attract purple martins. He danced with each of his girls to the music on their jukebox, and, when he held them close, smelling faintly of
~~~

cigarettes and Aqua Velva, they were sure no harm could ever come to them.

Ronny made Saturday nights special. He had built a brick barbecue grill in the backyard and loved to cook on it. When the weather wouldn't permit that, he and the girls gathered in the kitchen to make corndogs or oyster stew.

Becky was more reserved. She preferred watching television or reading a book to activities with the children. And she was more than happy to let her husband do as much cooking as he wanted.

Becky had battled weight gain most of her adult life. And the number on the scale colored how she saw her life. When she gained weight, she lost interest in most everything. She'd let her appearance go and would rarely leave the house. Then she'd force herself to diet—sometimes to the point of near starvation—and lose all the weight she'd gained. Once she was slim, she'd again pay attention to her appearance, putting up her long dark hair and using makeup that had been untouched in the drawer for months.

Soon after moving into their new house, Ronny and Becky came up with another idea for making extra money: they'd sell Georgia peaches to the tourists traveling to and from Florida. Ronny had become friends with a couple who ran the Texaco station at Hartley Bridge Road and Interstate 75. He told them his plan, and they were glad for him to set up a small wooden stand on the edge of their parking lot. Ronny and Becky then purchased bushels of peaches from a nearby orchard.

For four summers, Vicki and Valerie Akins were dropped off most mornings at the Texaco station with the peaches, a cash box, and sack lunches. Under the watchful eyes of the station owners, the girls sold their fruit all day long. With their pretty blond looks and sweet Southern accents, they did so well that they earned enough money to pay for the annual family vacation in Venice Beach.

Working at the fruit stand was an adventure for the sisters. It also gave them a certain amount of independence and a welcome respite from their mother. Becky was growing more difficult to live with every day. Although she could still be pleasant and upbeat on occasion, her good days became fewer and fewer. She was quick to anger and almost as quick to strike out at them physically. The worst of it was that they never knew what might set her off. Just about anything could bring on an explosion. It was like living beside a big balloon in a house full of pins.

When physical punishment wasn't enough, she'd take one of the girls aside and whisper that she was going to send her to a children's home.

"You'll never see your sisters again," she'd promise. "You'll never be a part of this family again."

And then there were the days when her mood was melancholy. Becky blamed her husband for all her dissatisfaction. Portraying herself as the victim and Ronny as the villain, she'd tell the children that he didn't care about them or her. He was, she'd declare, a really bad father. The girls knew that wasn't true. They had no doubt that their father loved them. But they also knew better than to ever argue with their mother.

In the early 1970s, the Watergate scandal was being revealed on the national front and the desegregation of the Macon schools was slowly being accomplished, but the Akins children were, for the most part, removed from the upset. Vicki,

Valerie, and Vanessa loved the outdoors and spent a lot of their time outside. By the time the two eldest girls entered Southwest High School, Ronny had acquired horses for all three of his daughters.

The horses were kept in the Akins's pasture, but every weekday morning, the girls rode them two miles up the road to catch the buses to school. The Miller family, who lived near the bus stop, let the girls turn the horses out in their pasture during the day. When school was over and the bus dropped off Valerie and Vicki, they'd wait until the elementary school bus arrived with Vanessa. Then, the three would retrieve their horses and ride home together.

The horses were exciting enough, but one Christmas their gifts were even better—the Akins girls were given minibikes. Ronny had painted the bikes three different colors and lettered them with each girl's name. As a final touch, Becky gave them scarves and caps in colors that matched their bikes. From then on, the minibikes took the place of the horses for the rides to the bus stop.

Southern Natural Gas required that Ronny be available for emergencies some nights and weekends. Once in a while, when the phone in the Hartley Bridge house rang at two or three in the morning and there was no school the next day, he'd wake one of his daughters and take her along. He took great pains to show no favoritism, choosing each one in turn.

The middle-of-the-night callouts were great treats for the girls. There was something exciting about going out into the night where few other people stirred and driving off into the darkness. Sometimes Ronny would stop at a service station and buy them Pepsis and peanuts. Before restarting the car, he'd help them pour the peanuts into the bottle.

While waiting for their father to fix whatever problem had called him out could be boring, they didn't complain.

They knew that after the work was done, he'd take them to eat in some all-night diner before heading home. The girls usually fell asleep during the drive back to Hartley Bridge Road, but they never forgot those late-night adventures with their father.

Ronny Akins never lost his love of flying. When he could afford to, he would rent a plane for a few hours. Becky wasn't interested in going with him, but he often took the children. One Christmas, his employer had him fly over some of Macon's most disadvantaged neighborhoods. While Ronny piloted the plane, Vicki and Valerie dropped Christmas stockings filled with candy and small toys to the children below.

Although Macon was only 100 miles from Athens, Becky and Ronny didn't see much of their own families. When the girls had been very young, they'd spent a couple of weeks each summer with Becky's mother, but the visits dwindled and finally stopped. Sara Turpin had remarried John Zuber, an electrical engineer who worked with Georgia Power. They had a son and were building a life of their own.

Becky had never been close to Ronny's family. Over the years of their marriage, she actively tried to prevent him from even taking the girls to visit them, but in this matter, he didn't give in to her. Ronny would lay down the law and declare that he was taking his children to see his parents whether she liked it or not. He believed the girls needed a relationship with their grandparents, uncles, and cousins, and he tried to nurture that relationship.

Any time a trip was planned—usually once or twice a year—it was preceded by a huge argument between husband

and wife, but he never changed his plans. When the shouting was over, Ronny and his daughters would then drive off alone for the two-hour trip to Athens.

Those visits were never very successful. During the first couple of hours in their grandparents' house, Vicki, Valerie, and Vanessa were stiff and self-conscious. They visited so rarely that the location and even the people seemed strange to them. After the big meal was over and pictures had been taken, the girls would gradually begin to relax and start to actually enjoy the visit. But by then, it was time to leave.

Visits to Ronny's family weren't the only things that triggered Becky's outbursts. And when Ronny wasn't home, her full attention turned to the children. While Vanessa's age somewhat protected her, Vicki and Valerie were frequent targets of their mother's rage. Anything, no matter how unimportant, could provoke her. A grade of B instead of A or failure to clean a room quickly enough could bring a quick slap or punch. And even when she wasn't punishing them physically, Becky heaped verbal abuse on them. It was a bad situation, but the sisters didn't know it wasn't normal.

With every passing year, their relationship with their mother seemed to worsen. When Vicki was sixteen and Valerie fifteen, they made friends with two sisters at Southwest High School. Donna and Linda Sherwood were friendly and fun-loving and immediately clicked with the Akins girls. But then Becky learned that her daughters' new friends were Jehovah's Witnesses. She, her family, and her friends were all Baptist, and she didn't approve of a lot of other religions, including the Jehovah's Witnesses. She didn't forbid her daughters to see the Sherwoods but demanded that there was no religion involved.

When the sisters invited them to a church party being held one Saturday night, Vicki and Valerie really wanted to go, but they knew their mother would never allow them to attend anything at the Kingdom Hall. So they concocted a more acceptable story. They told Becky that their friends had invited them to go to a movie that night.

"Their dad will take us and bring us home," Valerie said.

To their surprise, Becky gave her permission for them to go. "But I want you to come straight home after the movie."

Mr. Sherwood, accompanied by his daughters, arrived at the Akins house at 7:00, and Valerie and Vicki quickly ran out and got in the car. They drove straight to the church, where the party was already underway. It turned out to be a lot of fun, so much so that the Akins girls lost track of time.

They'd told their mother that the movie ended at 9:00. When the girls still weren't home by 10:00, Becky was growing angry. She'd *told* them to come straight home after the movie and they'd defied her. She was home alone with Vanessa because Ronny was out of town on business. Every few minutes she looked out the front window, but no headlights cut through the darkness. Finally, she called the Sherwood home and was surprised when Mr. Sherwood answered.

"I thought Vicki and Vanessa would be home by now," she said.

"Oh, the party doesn't end until 11:00," he told her. "But you don't have any reason to worry. They're all safe at the church and there are plenty of adults there. I'll pick them up at 11:00 and bring them straight home."

If they'd been face-to-face, Mr. Sherwood would have been alarmed at the fury that suffused Becky's features. But he didn't see that. So, when he drove to the church and waited in the parking lot, he had no idea of the events he'd set in motion. The four girls came out of the church building promptly at 11:00 and piled in the car, giggling and chattering about the party. But all that stopped as soon as Mr. Sherwood spoke.

"I just talked to your mother," he told the Akins girls. "She was worried. She thought you'd be home by 10:00. But everything's fine. I told her the party wasn't over until 11:00."

Valerie's and Vicki's high spirits vanished. They exchanged frightened looks and started to cry, knowing what was waiting for them at home. Mr. Sherwood was astonished by their reaction.

"Hey, girls, it's okay. I'm sure your mom understood once I told her when the party ended."

The sisters exchanged another look but didn't try to explain. How could they explain their mother?

When they arrived at the Hartley Bridge Road house, he walked with the two girls to the front door. Becky opened it before they reached the porch.

"Mrs. Akins, I want you to know that your daughters have been safe at all times. It was a chaperoned church event—"

Becky didn't even acknowledge his words. "You can go now."

She yanked her daughters inside the house and slammed the door in the man's face.

Becky swung at Vicki first, but her oldest daughter ducked and her fist connected squarely with Valerie's face. Valerie cried out and Becky turned back to Vicki, beating her with fists, a belt, and anything else she could pick up. Valerie stood by helplessly as her sister tried to defend herself against the attack by dropping to the floor and covering her face and stomach. She begged her mother to stop, but Becky was beyond reason. Then it was Valerie's turn. Although Becky had spent much of her fury on Vicki, Valerie's beating was no less severe.

Afterwards, the girls ran sobbing to their rooms, both of them so badly bruised that they missed the next week of school. Valerie promised herself she'd never, ever cross her mother again, no matter what.

Ronny came home sometime during the night. When he saw Valerie and Vicki the next morning, he was horrified. Becky was matter of fact about what had happened. She told him what the girls had done.

"I had to teach them a lesson."

"Not like this!" Ronny said. "You have to stop hitting them. You have to get control of yourself. I won't let you keep hurting them."

But she wasn't swayed. "They have to learn to behave."

Later that morning, while Becky's attention was occupied by a movie on television, he took Vicki and Valerie into his bedroom and closed the door. He sat with them on the bed, an arm around each one. They cried again and he did what he could to comfort them, but he knew he couldn't always be home with them.

"I'll do my best to protect you," he said, "but I can't always be here. And you know how your mother is. Just please try to stay out of trouble until I can figure out what to do."

They promised they would, but no matter how hard the girls tried to behave, Becky still found fault with them. Messy rooms, too much noise—anything was now an excuse for violence. But Becky never hit her children in front of other people, and none of the girls were ever allowed to bring friends to the house. So, no one outside the family knew what was happening.

Although they could have told someone—a neighbor, a teacher, or a counselor—the girls didn't dare. Becky had promised them that if they ever complained to anyone, they'd be taken away from both their parents and sent to separate foster homes.

"You'll never see each other again," she said.

And they believed her.

The Akins girls became adept at hiding their bruises and making excuses not to dress out for gym class. It got to be almost automatic to say, "I have my period" or "I have cramps today." They came up with a number of reasons for their bruises. They told people they walked into doors, fell down, or got hit with a ball playing softball. They even learned to hide the marks from their father or give him the same excuses they offered everyone else. They didn't want to be responsible for their parents' fighting.

When Valerie was fifteen years old, she and her next door neighbor, Alan Barfield, began dating. By then, Alan had graduated from high school, spent a year in the army, and returned to live with his parents and attend technical school. The fact that he was nearly six years older than Valerie didn't cause her parents concern. They'd known Alan and his family for years and believed they could trust him. As for Alan, he was just happy to spend time with Valerie. He would later describe himself as socially immature at that age. To him, Valerie seemed like a contemporary.

The two did very little actual dating because Alan stayed so busy. He worked seven days a week, mostly nights, at the Kroger supermarket, and studied electronics at Macon Technical College during the day. But he and Valerie spent time together at his house watching television and visiting with his mother, and most days he picked her up from school. His last class at Macon Tech was over about 3:00. That gave him just enough time to drive to Southwest High, pick up Valerie, and take her home before he reported to work. Even though their time was limited, the young couple formed a strong, loving bond.

During this time, Alan gave Valerie a puppy—an apricot-colored toy poodle they named Shannon. He was a lively little dog and Valerie adored him. The Akinses already had another toy poodle, a black female named Bridget, who was technically Vicki's dog. The two animals were well matched and were soon romping together.

In the late summer of 1972, Valerie and Alan planned a real date—dinner and a movie. They set the time for a Friday night, some two or three weeks in advance, and both were excited, anticipating candlelight and romance. But a few days before their date, Alan brought Valerie home from school five or ten minutes later than usual. It wasn't the first time it had happened, but it was enough to set Becky off. She met them in the driveway, screaming abuse at the two young people. Alan wasn't accustomed to being called names and instinctively shouted back. The resulting confrontation was a bitter one and the couple wasn't allowed to see each other for several months afterwards.

Chapter 3

Just as the lives of his children were becoming more and more stressful, Ronny Akins's was also beginning to unravel. He worried constantly about his daughters and their mother's treatment of them. And Becky's demands for more and more never stopped. In late 1972, she decided she wanted a bigger house in a new subdivision. Ronny tried to argue against the idea. He believed their marriage was on the verge of falling apart. But she was adamant and, in the end, he agreed. He hoped that she might be happier if she had a new house to occupy her time.

They found a suitable lot in Fulton Hills Estates, a subdivision off Fulton Mill Road, in the small Bibb County community of Lizella. The girls didn't want to move. They loved where they lived and didn't want to give up their horses, but Becky was determined. And Ronny just wanted to keep the peace.

Building a new house was an expensive undertaking. Ronny stepped up his work schedule. He put in more hours at Southern Natural Gas and took as many odd jobs as he could fit into his crowded schedule. He also spent a lot of time working on the new house. He did all the wiring and painting but had to contract out for the plumbing, roofing, and other jobs.

But no matter how busy he was, Ronny still managed to spend time with his children. He tried to reserve Saturdays for family activities—movies, taking rides, or shopping—but on Sundays, Ronny and his daughters went out alone for the day.

Although these excursions were designed to give Becky a break, the truth was that they were even greater breaks for Ronny and the girls.

In early 1973, the Akinses moved into the new house. Located in a cul-de-sac, it was built of red brick with a steeply pitched center roof and white columns flanking the front door. The interior was even larger than the Hartley Bridge Road house. Although their own familiar furnishings were moved into it, the new house never felt like home to the family.

Their next-door neighbors, Bea and Abram Watkins, were a friendly couple, known to their friends as "A and Bea." While they were a bit older than Ronny and Becky, Bea tried to be a good neighbor. She went over to meet them as soon as they moved in, but found that Becky was very standoffish. And the girls were no friendlier. They'd say hello, but never stopped to chat. She didn't know, of course, that they'd been told not to talk to outsiders.

On the other hand, Abram Watkins quickly became friends with Ronny. The two men both enjoyed working with their hands and were immediately comfortable in each other's company. Ronny became a frequent visitor to the workshop Abram had built behind his house.

Living in the new house felt wrong from the beginning. Ronny and Becky seemed to argue constantly, and the air was always thick with tension. Becky decided to go back to school and started taking nursing courses in the evenings, working toward her license as a practical nurse. She'd gotten a government grant to pay for the tuition and books, so it cost the family nothing.

However, she was dismissed from the program before

graduation for cheating. It was months before she told Ronny what had happened and broke the news to him that they had to repay all the tuition the grant had covered.

In the late spring, Vicki and Valerie found themselves in trouble again. They knew, of course, that their mother would punish them for disobeying her rules, but they were teenagers and had the same instincts for mischief and pushing limits as other kids their age. And sometimes they followed those instincts.

Vicki had a boyfriend now, but Becky wouldn't let her spend as much time with Mark as she wanted. So, one warm April day, she decided to do something about that. She and Valerie would "miss the bus" and then ask him for a ride home.

Valerie was reluctant. If Becky found out, it would be terrible. But Vicki convinced her their mother would never know. Their afternoon bus ride took an hour and a half, with the two older girls arriving at their home stop ten or fifteen minutes ahead of Vanessa, who now rode the middle school bus. Vicki was sure Mark could get them to the bus stop in plenty of time to meet Vanessa. Then, the three would walk home together and their mother wouldn't know a thing.

So, the two sisters intentionally missed their bus, and Mark obligingly offered to drive them home in his new Ford Mustang. Vicki and Valerie crowded into the car with the driver and three other people. It was a tight fit, but they didn't care. Rock music blared from the radio, and Vicki sat close beside Mark.

Before taking anyone home, Mark made a stop at McDonald's for Cokes and horseplay. They were having so much fun that time got away from them. Then Vicki saw that it was nearly 4:30.

"We have to get home!" Vicki told Mark. "We're going

to be late!"

The urgency in her voice was infectious. They all jumped back into the car, and Mark took off, driving faster than he should have. Then, somehow, on Pio Nono Avenue near the Interstate 75 intersection, he lost control of his new car. He fishtailed across several lanes of traffic and then flipped the Mustang. It came to rest on its crumpled top on the asphalt.

It could have been a tragedy, but somehow, even though a few of the passengers suffered minor mishaps, no one was seriously injured. Within minutes, two police cars and an ambulance were on the scene. The officers moved among the young people, getting names, addresses, and telephone numbers. Then, one of them went to a nearby pay phone and started calling, looking for parents to come pick up their teenagers.

Valerie was horrified—she knew she had to act fast. She ran to a nearby store, begged the use of a telephone, and called her father. In a panic, she explained what happened.

"We're okay," she told him, "but they're calling mom. She's going to kill us! Please come get us!"

He assured her he was on the way, and she returned to the accident scene, where some of the parents had already begun arriving. She sat on the curb beside her sister. Vicki, who was holding a piece of gauze over a cut on her head, began sobbing, saying she was sorry.

"It's all my fault," she said through the storm of tears. "It's all my fault."

But Valerie knew they were both to blame. She tried to comfort her sister, all the while keeping an eye on the busy street. Suddenly, she spotted her mother in the family car—easily recognizable by its bright yellow color. And at almost the same moment, from the opposite direction, her father's company car came into view. It was a race to the girls, but

Ronny pulled into the parking lot thirty or forty seconds ahead of his wife. His daughters ran to him.

"Get in!" he told them. "And lock the doors."

They did so just in time. Seconds later, Becky was out of her car and running toward them. The locked doors infuriated her. She beat on the windows with her fists and screamed at them.

"Open this goddamned door! Open the door!"

Vicki's and Valerie's friends and their parents turned to stare at the scene, along with police officers and bystanders.

Ronny rolled down his window just enough so Becky could hear him.

"Calm down, Becky. They're upset."

"Open this door!" She kept pounding the car with her fists.

"Everything is going to be okay," he said, trying to reason with her. "I'll take them home and we'll discuss it there."

After another few seconds of futile banging on the windows, she stalked back to her car. Moments later, she tore out of the parking lot, tires squealing in protest.

The girls cried all the way home. In between sobs, they told Ronny the truth, that they had missed the bus by design.

He tried to reassure them. "Everything will be okay. But I think it'll be better if you stick to the story that you missed the bus by accident and it wasn't your fault Mark stopped at McDonald's. I'll take care of your mother."

The moment that they walked in the door, Ronny sent the girls to their rooms. They were not allowed to come out, even for dinner. Her husband assured Becky that he would take care of everything and see that the girls were severely punished.

After dinner, he met with both girls in Vicki's room. He was disappointed with their behavior and let them know it.

That made them more miserable than any other punishment that might have been visited on them. They'd let him down and were so grateful to him for saving them from Becky.

"You're both grounded for a month," he told them.

They nodded, then apologized and promised to never do that sort of thing again.

When he went back to Becky, Ronny told her, "I've taken care of it. They're grounded for a month. You leave them alone."

Becky had recovered her composure by then and nodded as if she accepted what he'd said. They didn't discuss the girls' misbehavior any more that night.

But Ronny couldn't be with his children all the time. He left for work before seven the next morning, and Becky came after Vicki and Valerie. Armed with a belt and the fury that had built all night long, she beat them so badly that they again missed over a week of school. And this time, they were forbidden to come out of their rooms if their father was anywhere around.

"If you tell him about this, the next time will be worse."

When Ronny returned home that night, Becky told him the girls still were being punished and couldn't leave their rooms. At dinnertime, she fixed plates for them and they ate in their rooms. It was almost a week before Ronny saw his two oldest daughters. By then, those bruises that hadn't completely faded could be concealed by long sleeves and makeup.

Chapter 4

Although she possessed a fearsome temper, Becky Akins still could surprise her family with sudden acts of kindness. Just such a thing happened in August of 1973. It had been a difficult summer. The girls were still trying to win back their mother's favor after the car wreck. Then Ronny was diagnosed with the early stages of emphysema and spent several weeks in the hospital. He missed almost a full month of work and, in August, was just getting back to his regular routine. But he still tired easily and had trouble sleeping through the night.

One evening, as the family sat around watching television, Becky surprised them by serving the girls bowls of ice cream and making Ronny a milkshake.

"It's to build your health back up," she told him. "The ice cream will help you sleep."

The ice cream treats became a weeknight tradition, one to which everyone looked forward. And the milkshakes did seem to help Ronny to sleep. In fact, he was going to bed earlier than he ever had before. It seemed like real thoughtfulness on Becky's part until the evening of October 15, when Vicki shared some disturbing information with Valerie.

It had been an unusually hot, humid day for the third Monday in October, and the girls were sitting outside after dinner enjoying the cool evening air. Valerie was wondering if they'd get to go to the Georgia State Fair in Macon that week, but Vicki had more serious things on her mind.

"Mom sent me to the store to by Contac and mildew remover this afternoon," she told her sister.

"Who has a cold?"

"Nobody." She waited a few seconds, then continued. "She put them in Dad's milkshake. She's been putting Nyquil in his shakes. And Contac."

"That's crazy," Valerie said, dismissing her sister's statements as a bad joke.

She got up and went into the kitchen, where her mother was dishing up ice cream for the family. The milkshake made for her father was sitting on the kitchen counter, and, as Valerie watched in shocked horror, Becky sprayed the mildew remover into the glass. When her mother looked up and saw her standing there, she just glared. Valerie knew better than to say anything.

She watched fearfully as her father sipped his drink. Valerie ached to say something, but fear of her mother was greater than fear for her father. Ronny finished the milkshake. He hadn't seemed to find anything wrong with it, but later that evening he became incoherent. He acted as if he was drunk. He got to his feet, mumbled something unintelligible, and stumbled down the hall to his bed. Valerie and Vicki still didn't say anything, but they knew now that Becky was intentionally making him sick.

When she noticed the girls staring at each other, she reacted angrily.

"Go to bed right now," she said. "It's late. Go to bed."

They did as she ordered, but Valerie lay awake for quite a while, trying to decide what to do. She finally realized that she had to act, and once she'd made up her mind to tell her father what was going on, she was able to go to sleep. But her resolution came too late.

In the deepest part of the night, Vicki and Valerie were awakened by noises from their parents' bedroom. There was moaning, angry shouting, and something that sounded like vomiting. Then their mother began yelling out their names. They ran to her. What they saw stopped them in the doorway. Ronny was thrashing violently on the bed and Becky was lying across him, using her body weight to hold him down.

"He's out of control," she shouted at the frightened girls. "You've got to help me. Hold his legs down!"

They obeyed, one on either side of the bed, pressing down on his legs with their hands. Then Becky grabbed a pillow and pressed it over his face. The girls let go.

"You're hurting him," Vicki said, crying, but their mother screamed at them again.

"I said hold his legs!"

They put their hands back on their father, but neither pushed down very hard.

"Stop!" Valerie begged. "You'll kill him!"

"I'm just trying to calm him down," she told them, not lifting the pillow.

After a short time, the thrashing slowed and stopped. Ronny was still and the terrified girls thought he must be dead.

"Go to bed." Becky got to her feet, not giving even a glance to Ronny. "Go on. Go to bed right now!"

Hearts pounding and still crying, Vicki and Valerie returned to their beds, where they lay awake, staring into the darkness. It seemed like hours, but it probably wasn't that long before their mother called them again. They met her in the hallway.

"Get dressed."

"But..." Valerie protested.

"I don't want to hear a word out of you. Get dressed! If anyone asks you anything, you tell them your father went crazy and we had to leave!"

They hurried to do what she asked then joined her in the kitchen. Vanessa, who had evidently slept through all the commotion, was dressed and sitting at the table, yawning. Through the window they could see darkness was giving way to faint early morning light. Becky was on the telephone.

"Just please come get us," she said, sounding as if she were crying. The girls didn't see any tears. "You're the only one I knew to call."

Just after 7:00, Becky sent Vanessa out to catch the elementary school bus. The high school bus wasn't due for another half hour, so the older girls sat waiting at the table. A few minutes later, Julie Baldwin pulled into their driveway. Becky had met Julie while attending nursing school and the two had become casual friends.

The girls waited inside while their mother went out to talk to the woman. Then she called them and they hurried out of the house. Becky told them to get in the car, and she climbed in after them. Julie backed out of the drive and sped away.

With a convincing show of distress, Becky described having to flee her house because her husband had been drinking and become violent.

"He was throwing things and even hit me, but I think he finally passed out," she declared tearfully. "I was afraid he'd hurt the children. That's why we had to leave."

Julie took them to her home. They left the girls watching TV, and then the two women drove to a nearby convenience store to buy milk and doughnuts for breakfast.

Bea and Abram Watkins were the first to notice there might be something wrong at the Akins house that Tuesday morning. Ronny's white company car was parked in the same place it had been the night before. Becky's car hadn't been moved either. Even though it was a school day, no one seemed to be stirring at the house next door.

"I hope nothing's wrong," Abram told his wife, looking out the window. "I've never known Ronny to be late for work before. I sure hope he's not sick again."

Across town at the Southern Natural Gas offices on Bass Road, Ronny's coworkers were also beginning to worry. Theirs was a small office with only six employees in two divisions. They'd worked together for years and were more like family than fellow employees.

Their workday started every morning at 7:30. It was now past 8:30 and Ronny Akins still hadn't shown up. His boss, Ernest Doss, tried calling him at home as well as on the radio of his company car, but got no answer. Around 9:00, he walked from the communications section over to the corrosion office. There, he found Julian Jenkins, known as J. J., and his supervisor, J. W. Banks.

"Have either of you heard from Ronny this morning?"

They hadn't and agreed with Doss that it wasn't like Ronny to stay away from work without calling. After a few more fruitless phone calls, they grew concerned enough that they went to his house to see if they could find him.

J. J. Jenkins knew Ronny well. They'd worked together for a number of years and also installed television antennas together on weekends. Several times a year, Southern Natural Gas sent the two of them out of town together. After working all day, they'd have dinner in some local restaurant and spend their time talking. Jenkins figured he knew Ronny better than anyone else in the company. In fact, Ronny had recently confided in him that he and Becky were having serious problems, in part because she had been dismissed from the nursing program. Ronny had been furious when he learned he'd have to repay the grant.

During the half-hour ride to Fulton Drive, Jenkins wondered what the problem might be. He hoped no one was sick. But a family emergency was the only circumstance he could imagine that would keep Ronny from calling in. When the men arrived at the Akins house, there was no sign of life even though both cars were still there. They hurried to the front door and knocked hard, but there was no answer.

Doss told the others, "I've got a real uneasy feeling about this."

The day was warm and overcast. The leaden sky threatened rain and made them just that much more apprehensive as they circled the house, checking for anything unusual. The only sound in the secluded neighborhood was the wind moving through the pines. There was no traffic noise and no birdsong.

Abram Watkins saw the men from his window and hurried over to find out what was wrong. He joined them in the backyard, and, when they explained why there were there, stayed to see if he could help. All the doors were locked, but they found one window on the side of the house that was raised a few inches. They didn't even discuss whether or not someone should go in.

Banks and the others hoisted Jenkins up to the sill. J. J. raised the window higher and slipped inside. Moments later, he opened the front door to let the others in. The men made their slow way through the silent house, calling out to anyone who might have been there. No sounds of any kind came to their ears.

One by one, the rooms were checked, but there was no clue as to Ronny Akins's whereabouts. They'd nearly given up finding anything when they reached the end of the hallway and discovered the last door was locked. When knocking brought no response, someone found a small piece of metal that they pushed into the center hole of the doorknob and released the push-button lock.

The door would only open a few inches before stopping against an obstacle. Through the narrow opening, Ronny Akins's body was visible, lying against the door. They alternately pushed and reached through the gap to maneuver the body. Finally, they were able to get into the room. Doss and Jenkins knelt beside Ronny and rolled him over.

"He's still breathing," Jenkins said. "What could have happened to him?"

Ronny's lips were swollen and his cheeks scratched. His nose was caked with blood and he was barely conscious. He looked like he'd been in a fight.

"Ronny!" Doss shook his shoulder. "Ronny!"

The injured man roused enough to look around the room. He mumbled something no one could understand and then slipped out of consciousness again.

Ernest Doss found that the telephone in the bedroom wasn't working, so he followed Abram next door to call Ronny a doctor. Doss knew that Ronny, an airplane pilot, had to have annual exams to maintain his license, and he knew that a recent exam had been conducted by a Dr. Lankford. If anyone was current on the man's health, it should be Lankford. However, Doss couldn't reach him.

"What about his wife? Does she work?"

"No," Abram said. "I wonder if the school knows where the rest of the family is."

A telephone call to Southwest High School revealed that Valerie and Vicki were absent, but when Abram spoke with someone at the middle school, they learned Vanessa had arrived on time. Unfortunately, no one at either place could suggest where Becky Akins might be.

The two men rushed back to check on Ronny's condition. Banks and Jenkins had gotten Ronny onto the bed, but he seemed no better there. However, he wasn't having any trouble breathing.

"He's acting like he's drunk," one of them said.

"That's not like him," Jenkins said.

The four men went outside to discuss what to do next.

While they were standing in line to check out at the convenience store, Becky had told Julie she had a bad feeling.

"I think we'd better stop back by my house."

Julie obligingly drove back to Fulton Drive. When the two women arrived, they found several men gathered in the yard and the front door wide open. Becky recognized Ronny's boss. She jumped out of the car and made straight for him.

"How did you get in the house?" she asked.

He didn't bother answering the question, telling her instead what they'd found.

"Oh, my God," she said dramatically. "He's OD'd again. I was afraid this was going to happen."

J. J. Jenkins heard the statement and was shocked. OD'd *again*? He'd never connected Ronny to any kind of drug use. In fact, the man was almost a teetotaler. In all the time he'd known him, he'd only seen him drink a very few times. Even at the office Christmas celebration, where most everyone would have three or four drinks, Ronny limited himself to one.

"We need to call an ambulance," Becky declared.

She, Doss, and Watkins returned to the bedroom.

"You'll have to plug the phone in," she said.

As Becky hovered over her husband, one of the men plugged the wire into the wall jack and called for an ambulance. The emergency vehicle arrived only a few minutes later. As soon as the attendants appeared in the bedroom, Becky stepped between them and her husband.

"He's overdosed on drugs! And it's not the first time."

After a quick examination, they loaded Ronny onto a stretcher and carried him out of the house. The others followed. As the paramedics were maneuvering the stretcher into the ambulance, Becky again approached Doss.

"He's been drinking again," she told him. "All weekend. I found ten empty whiskey bottles in the trash. He's like a thirty-eight-year-old child."

Doss had a difficult time reconciling what she was saying with the man he'd known for eight years. In all that time, Ernest Doss had seen Ronny Akins take exactly two drinks.

Doss just shook his head. "Do you want me to call any family members for you?"

"No. Ronny's brother and his mother are both real sick. I don't want to bother them."

The ambulance pulled away and Becky and Julie started back for the car. Bea Watkins, who had joined the little group in the front yard, stopped them.

"I can watch the girls while y'all are at the hospital," she offered.

Becky wasted no words. "That's not necessary." Then she climbed back in the car. Moments later, the two women drove away.

Back at the Baldwin house, Becky ordered Vicki and Valerie into the car. She asked Julie to take them all back to Fulton Drive. During the short trip, she offered no explanation to the girls about what was happening. It was only after Julie had let them out and was gone that Becky told them that Ronny had been taken to the hospital.

"Is he going to be okay?" Vicki wanted to know.

Becky didn't answer her; instead, she said, "If anyone asks about your father, you tell them he was drunk and abusive when we left the house. That's all you say, do you understand me?"

The girls nodded that they did. Valerie was as terrified as ever of her mother, but deep inside, she was rejoicing. Her father was alive!

The police had arrived during Becky's absence, and the two officers turned their attention to her and her daughters as they walked up to the front door. Becky hurried the girls past them, sending them up the steps and into the house.

"My daughters are much too upset to talk with you," she said. Then she repeated her story of Ronny's drunkenness and her escape from his abuse the night before. She was convincing enough that they asked very few questions and left in a short while.

Soon afterwards, Becky drove to the hospital, leaving her two oldest daughters in the house alone. She'd been right when she told the police that Vicki and Valerie were upset. They were horrified by what their mother had done, and they were certain that Ronny had almost died. They were also scared of having to lie to the police, but most of all they feared what would happen if they didn't do exactly as their mother said.

Chapter 5

The ambulance delivered Ronny to the emergency room at the Medical Center of Central Georgia in downtown Macon. Since he was nearly comatose, it was Becky who provided the doctor on duty with her husband's medical history and the rest of the information he requested. In her most earnest voice, she told him Ronny had been depressed due to his poor health.

"He used to be a quiet, easygoing man, but he's changed. He's gotten mean and is always ready to fight. He's been drinking vodka and he takes quaaludes to sleep. This time he took Nyquil, Valium, and I don't know what else. This isn't the first time this has happened."

"Was he hospitalized before?" the doctor asked.

"No, I took care of him myself. I'm an LPN."

She seemed so sincere that the doctor had no reason to doubt her when she told him Ronny had tried to kill himself the night before.

Lowering her voice almost to a whisper, she said, "We had to fight him to keep him from killing himself."

After checking in at the office, J. J. Jenkins and Ernest Doss went to the hospital to see about their friend. They found Becky in the emergency room waiting area, behaving as though she was upset, but Jenkins wasn't convinced of her sincerity. She repeated to them the story of fighting Ronny to keep him from killing himself.

"That's how he got the scratches on his face and hands."

Both men noticed that she had no marks whatsoever on her hands or her tanned arms.

"I'm getting Ronny transferred to the psych ward," she told his coworkers. "That's where he needs to be."

That didn't sit well with Ernest Doss. He'd never seen any indication that Ronny Akins had psychiatric problems or issues with drugs or alcohol. With Jenkins beside him, he asked the nurse if they could see Ronny. Minutes later, she took them down the hall to his temporary room. Ronny was still in bad shape and unable to talk with them.

"We'll be back," J. J. told the barely conscious man, but he didn't know if Ronny heard him.

Ronny had first been admitted to an open floor, but the more the staff heard from Becky, the more concerned they became about his mental stability. By late that afternoon, they'd moved him to the psychiatric unit.

As the hours passed, Ronny slowly regained consciousness. While his vital signs had returned to normal, a chest x-ray confirmed what Becky had told the doctors. There was evidence of chronic pulmonary disease and possibly the beginnings of emphysema. He seemed lucid and in control of himself, but the story he told—that his wife and children had tried to kill him—was so fantastic that he wasn't believed.

When the doctors related his tale of attempted murder to Becky, she became tearful, saying he'd blamed her all along for his illness.

"I won't try and see him until the doctors say it's okay," she said. "I don't want to agitate him."

Ronny soon stopped caring whether or not anyone there believed him. All he wanted was out. The nurse suggested he might want to go into the common room and watch TV with the other patients. The third game of the World Series was on. Catfish Hunter and Tom Seaver were the opposing pitchers. With the Mets and Oakland A's tied at one game a piece, tonight's contest was sure to be exciting. But Ronny had no interest in that.

"Why can't I go home?" he asked.

"You really need to wait for the doctor."

He waited for hours, but no doctor arrived that night. Finally, he couldn't stand it any longer. He got out of bed and began shouting.

"I want to see the sheriff. He'll get me out of here! Becky beat me in the face and now you're keeping me here against my will!"

The shift nurse tried to calm him down, but Ronny was beyond reason. She eventually telephoned the doctor and was instructed to administer Thorazine. However, her patient had his own ideas about that. When she returned to his room with a syringe, Ronny refused it.

"Nobody is going to do anything for me here. This floor is for crazy people!"

Around 11:00 P.M., Nurse Betty Pollard came on duty and was making her rounds. Ronny was waiting for her in his room.

"Can I leave or is this a prison?"

"Sir," she said in a voice intended to calm the patient, "I really think you should wait and talk to the doctor in the morning. It's the middle of the night. And there's no one here to take you home."

Ronny realized she was right about that. "Okay," he said with a resigned sigh. "I'll wait."

He didn't make any more demands or do any more shouting, but he did tell the nurse that his wife had tried to kill him while his daughters held his feet. Like the rest of the staff, Betty Pollard didn't believe him. And he didn't bother trying to convince her. He was interested, however, in how he came to be in the psychiatric ward.

"Just how did Becky get me admitted here?"

"You were reported to have overdosed."

He nodded his head wearily. "Yeah, that sounds like one of her stories. It's just like her."

Ronny couldn't sleep that night. Finally, about 3:00 A.M., Pollard offered him a mild sedative.

"It's just to help you rest."

Exhausted, he took it and managed to get a few hours sleep.

The next morning, Nurse Deborah Lee came in when breakfast was over, followed soon after by Dr. T. M. Hall. He examined Ronny and found no physical reason to keep him in the hospital. However, he recommended that he stay for observation.

"Can I leave?" Ronny asked again.

"Yes, but it would be against medical advice."

That was all he needed to hear. "I don't care. I'm leaving."

The nurse and doctor left the room, and Ronny, who was dressed in pajamas and a robe, started searching for his clothes. He called for a nurse and Dorothy Yates came to his room.

"I can't find my clothes. Do you have them?"

When she assured him that she didn't, he nodded. "I guess my wife took them with her." His voice was cold and angry. "Could you call and ask her to bring me some clothes and leave them at the desk? I don't want to see her." He rubbed his hand across his abraded face. "She did this to my face. I need to get out and get a peace warrant for my wife and find me a place to live."

Doss and Jenkins returned to see Ronny that morning. They were relieved that he was up and behaving normally again. He told them what had happened Monday night, and they, at least, seemed to believe his story. They explained how they'd gone to the house and found him.

"I'm sure you glad you did," Ronny said. "Now I just need to get out of here, but somebody—a relative, I think—has to come and check me out."

"Have you called your parents?" Doss asked.

He shook his head. "I don't have any money. I don't have any way to call them."

Doss and Jenkins pooled the money they had on them—about $5—and gave it to Ronny.

Then they waited in his room while he went and found a pay phone and made the long-distance call to his folks.

"They'll be here in a few hours," he said when he returned.

"Is your mother okay to travel?" Doss asked.

"Sure. She's fine. Why do you ask?"

"Becky said she was sick."

Ronny just shook his head.

After his friends left, Ronny sat in the TV room, chain-smoking and waiting to be released. He was discharged to his parents about 1:15 P.M. and returned to Athens with them. They were horrified by the tale he told, but they knew Ronny didn't lie.

The next day, one of his brothers took pictures of his injured face. Then the two men returned to Macon to get some of his belongings from the house. The girls were in school and Becky was gone. He went in, loaded a suitcase, and left.

Ronny and his brother stopped for lunch at the S&S Cafeteria, then they drove to Log Cabin Road, where he rented a furnished apartment before they returned to Athens. He stayed there with his family for a few days, then moved into the new apartment on Sunday. He was back at work, right on time, Monday morning.

Ronny realized he needed a lawyer, but he didn't know any personally. So, he looked in the telephone book and called the local law firm of Westmoreland, Patterson, and Moseley. When he explained that he wanted to file for divorce, the receptionist gave him an appointment and told him he'd be meeting with Emmett Goodman. Goodman was new to the firm, a young associate only a couple of years out of Mercer Law School.

Ronny arrived, dressed in over-the-ankle boots and one of the leisure suits he favored. He was a bit uncomfortable in the quiet, well-furnished offices of the law firm, but he didn't let that bother him. Ronny was used to getting to the point and speaking the truth. After the introductions, he explained his situation to the young lawyer.

"I need a peace warrant on my wife. And I want to get a divorce."

Goodman listened to his new client's story with a healthy dose of skepticism. The tale of the poisoned milkshake and his wife's attempt to suffocate him with a pillow with the help of two of his children was bizarre, to say the least. This was Macon, Georgia, and things like that didn't happen here. Besides, one quick phone call to the sheriff's office revealed that Ronny's wife had taken out a peace warrant on him. Goodman wanted to believe his client. But even though the man sounded truthful and still had scratches on his face, the lawyer couldn't completely accept the story.

However, belief wasn't necessary to do the job. Goodman got the information necessary to prepare the divorce paperwork. They set a follow-up appointment for later in the week.

The two men met several times and Ronny's story never changed. Goodman soon understood that Akins was a straight-arrow kind of a guy, and he came to believe his story. He realized that his client was a genuinely nice man who loved his children and worked hard for them. Ronny wanted nothing more than to raise and care for his daughters.

Goodman hated telling him that there was little chance he'd be awarded custody of the children. Becky had already worked to ensure that wouldn't happen. The first was getting him admitted to the psychiatric ward after his near death. The second was swearing out the peace warrant. She was successfully painting her husband as a violent, unstable man.

The first order of business was the peace warrant. They went to court on it shortly after Ronny's first appointment with Goodman. Rebecca was calm and deliberate in her testimony. She described Ronny as a man out of control and claimed that he'd used drugs and alcohol for quite some time. She said she'd only put sleeping pills in his milkshake to calm him down.

Ronny testified that she had drugged him and, with the help of Valerie and Vicki, tried to smother him. Since he was still scratched and bruised at the time of the hearing and Becky was not, his words had the ring of truth. Goodman's argument that the case came down to one person's word against another was successful. The peace warrant was dismissed.

Soon afterwards, Goodman filed for divorce on Ronny's behalf. Becky found her own attorney and countersued. Ronny called his house over and over again, but Becky refused to let him speak with the girls. He turned to his attorney for help, and Goodman arranged a court date on the matter, but it was scheduled for more than a month away.

While his daughters missed him and wanted to see him,

they were still so intimidated by their mother that they didn't dare question her decisions. After a short time, their lives fell into a routine that didn't include their father.

Autumn is a time of renewal in Middle Georgia. The searing summer heat is replaced by warm days, soft breezes, and cool nights. After months of indulging in as little activity as possible, residents find their energy returning. Football games become the entertainment of choice, but in 1973, Macon's sporting focus shifted a bit. Professional hockey came to town. The Macon Whoopee, the city's cleverly named first hockey team, began its first and only season.

Valerie Akins had another reason for excitement. Her mother had gotten over her anger and was once again allowing her to see Alan Barfield, who was now out of school and had a good job with Diebold, a company that installed, maintained, and monitored alarms and automatic teller machines.

One early November evening, Alan took Val to dinner at the Davis Brothers Cafeteria on Chambers Road. They were sitting in the back room and had just finished their meal when Alan got to his feet, dropped down on one knee before her, and asked Valerie to marry him. Amid applause from their fellow diners, Valerie said yes. The young couple spent the rest of the evening making excited plans for a December 1974 wedding.

Surprisingly, Becky voiced no objection. Soon after the engagement, she approached Alan for help.

"Someone broke in the house and stole my wedding rings," she told him. "I'm terrified. I think the only way I'll ever feel safe again is if I get an alarm system."

Alan was surprised, having heard nothing about such a crime, but he was happy to help. After all, Valerie lived in that house, too, and he wanted her to be safe. He got an alarm system from Diebold at his own expense and installed it in the Akins house. It took the better part of a Saturday, but he didn't mind.

It wasn't until a couple of weeks later, when Becky "miraculously" found her wedding rings in the backyard that Alan began to suspect she'd taken advantage of him. He didn't know why she'd done it, but he knew better than to question her. He didn't want to be separated from Valerie again.

On a cold night a few weeks later, Becky went to Valerie's room and got her out of bed. It was almost midnight.

"Come help me with the ladder."

Valerie had no clue what her mother was talking about, but she did as she was told. She pulled on a coat and slid her feet into slippers, then followed Becky to the backyard, where the big extension ladder was kept. Together, the two clumsily carried it to the rear of the house. They were both slightly out of breath when they finally positioned it under the second-floor window of Becky's bedroom.

Becky gave the ladder a critical look and seemed satisfied. Then she dismissed Valerie by telling her, "You can go back to bed now."

Valerie obeyed, too cold and sleepy to wonder what her mother was doing.

A few hours later, all three girls were awakened by the wail of the security alarm and their mother's screams.

"He tried to kill me! He tried to kill me!"

They found Becky standing beside a broken window in her bedroom.

"Call the police!" she said, and Vicki ran to do just that.

Slowly, Valerie began to understand what had happened and realized the part she had played in the charade. But instead of confronting her mother, she just trailed after her into the living room. They were all gathered there when the police arrived. Becky described how she'd been asleep when she heard breaking glass.

"It was Ronny, trying to come in the window after me. I know he was going to kill me. The alarm scared him away!"

The middle-aged officer took notes as she related the story, then went with her to the bedroom, where he gave the window a quick look.

"Not much glass inside the house," he observed.

Becky acted as if she hadn't heard him. "I want Ronny Akins arrested for attempted murder!" she demanded.

But the officer recognized the incident as a domestic matter.

"You'll have to go down and get a warrant against him yourself," he told her. "We can't help you with that."

No warrant was ever issued.

The next day, Valerie confided in Vicki what had happened with the ladder. The girls agreed they'd never say anything to anyone. They thought it was quite possible that their mother would kill them if they did.

Ronny returned to the house on Fulton Drive one more time. He was accompanied by a deputy sheriff, who was present to prevent any sort of domestic disturbance. It was in the middle of the day. Becky was out, and all the girls were in school. While the lawman stood by, Ronny removed his remaining clothes and personal items from what had once been his home. He was actually glad to be leaving the place for the last time.

After months of the depositions, hearings, and conferences that are the mechanisms of divorce, Ronny and Rebecca Akins finally reached a settlement. The final decree was issued on February 18, 1974. As expected, custody of the three children was given to Rebecca, and Ronny was granted "reasonable visitation." He was also ordered to pay child support in the amount of $900 a month—$300 for each child—and to continue paying for health insurance for the children and to maintain life insurance on himself. The beneficiaries of the life insurance policy were to be his three daughters.

Becky was awarded the household contents while Ronny received field glasses, guns, a camera, a calculator, and all of his tools and electrical equipment. He also asked for and got the family Bible. The Fulton Drive house was to be sold and the proceeds divided between the two. Becky kept the 1970 Ford and 1965 Lincoln Continental. Ronny took his 1965 Chevrolet.

Ronny and Alan Barfield still saw each other occasionally. One afternoon that spring, Ronny called him when he locked his keys in the car. Armed with the tools he used in his work, Alan drove to Log Cabin Drive and met Ronny in the parking lot outside his apartment. While Alan worked on the lock, the two men caught up on what they'd done since last seeing each other. Alan confided that he and Valerie were engaged.

Ronnie grinned. "That's fine. You and Valerie are fine. I don't have a problem with that." Then his expression sobered. "But stay away from Becky."

Although the child support awarded by the court was generous for its day, Rebecca was convinced it wasn't enough. She'd complain to anyone who'd listen just how unfair the settlement had been and how difficult life was for her and the children. Everything from overdue bills to burnt toast was Ronny's fault.

Becky began taking her daughters to services at a small Baptist church near their home. The rural congregation met in a small frame church and had very little in the way of money, but they warmly welcomed the newcomers. Becky was soon telling her fellow churchgoers how hard her life had become. She described Ronny's drinking and abuse and how he'd finally left her. She tearfully declared that often she and her children had no food in the house and no money. Everyone in the congregation felt sorry for them. And one afternoon, the pastor called Becky and told her he and some of the ladies of the church were coming over with food.

"We know how hard things are for you right now and we took up a collection."

Becky got moving.

"Go put on some old clothes," she told the girls.

"But why?" Valerie ventured.

"No, not just old, put on *dirty* clothes. I don't want them to think we have detergent."

Meanwhile, Becky was emptying the cupboards and the refrigerator, hiding their very ample supply of food. Anything of value, like the stereo system, was moved to a closet.

When the church people arrived, Becky took them to the kitchen and showed them the empty cupboards. She said she was embarrassed about the clothes the children "had to wear" and cried at the terrible state of their lives.

As they brought in the food—meat, bread, homemade soups—Becky thanked them, telling them how deeply touched she was by their generosity. One woman had even made a towering coconut cake.

The girls stood by silently watching their mother's performance. Valerie couldn't help thinking they might have been taking food away from people who really needed it. After saying a prayer for them, the little group from the church left. When their car pulled out of the driveway, Becky burst into laughter. She seemed proud of fooling these simple people.

Alan's company provided him with a car, so he sold his old blue '65 Chevrolet to Becky for Valerie to use. Now that she had her own transportation, Valerie got a job at the Ponderosa Steakhouse on Pio Nono Avenue. With her income, she could pay for the gas and insurance. Vicki and her friends often came by to see her when she was working.

In spite of the divorce settlement, Becky refused to allow Ronny to come to the house to see his children. She was so adamant about it that he stopped asking. She forbade the children to see him at all, although they did occasionally talk to him on the phone without her knowing. And one night, Ronny stopped by the Ponderosa. Valerie was working and Vicki was there as well.

It was the first time they'd seen each other since he'd moved out. There were hugs and tears and laughter. They sat at a back booth and talked. One of the first things Ronny did was tell them that he understood what happened the night Becky tried to kill him.

"I know that you had no choice. You don't have to explain it to me. I understand."

With those words, a huge weight of guilt was lifted off his daughters' shoulders.

He also warned them again about their mother. "There's something wrong with her. I know that. I wish I could be there to protect you. Just keep her as happy as possible, and maybe when you're eighteen you can get out of the situation for good."

Chapter 6

Ronny Akins's life was a mess in early 1974. He was living alone in a cramped apartment and working as hard as he ever had. He rarely saw his children, even though a large portion of his income now paid for their support.

There was one bright spot. Without Becky's interference, he was spending more time with his own family. He made regular trips to Athens to see his parents and occasionally drove to the small Georgia mountain town of Calhoun to visit his brother Bill, who was a teacher at the Redbud School in Gordon County. On one such visit, Ronny met Juanita Knight.

Juanita, a graduate of Berry College, was the daughter of a prominent Gordon County family. Her late father, Troy Knight, had been an influential man in agricultural and business circles and was a state legislator for more than ten years. Her mother, Beatrice Knight, was a beloved figure in the educational world. She'd taught in the public school system for years and would eventually go on to become a well-known storyteller and TV and radio personality.

Troy Knight died in 1969, and, after teaching school in Columbus, Georgia, for several years, Juanita returned to Calhoun the next year. She moved back into the family home on Barrett Road with her mother and took a job teaching school in Gordon County.

At twenty-eight, Juanita was a striking young woman—tall, with wide, dark eyes, light brown hair, and an engaging smile. Ronny was immediately smitten, and Juanita soon found herself drawn to the quiet, considerate man from Macon. Even though he was ten years her senior, the two quickly realized they were right for each other. By late spring, Ronny had proposed, and a wedding date was set for August.

Over the next months, Ronny spent as much time as he could in Calhoun, and Juanita visited him on several occasions in Macon. One April evening, Ronny invited Valerie and Alan to meet him for dinner at Shoney's. When they arrived, he introduced them to Juanita. Val thought her father seemed happier than he'd been in a very long time, and she liked the sweet-natured woman he declared he was going to marry.

Not everyone, however, was pleased about the engagement. When Becky learned that Ronny planned to marry again, she was furious. She stormed around the house, screaming that she hated him and that he was a terrible father and had been an awful husband. Her tantrum went on sporadically for days, and she didn't care who heard her ravings.

Alan Barfield was a frequent visitor to the Akins house, and Becky had no qualms about declaring her hatred for her ex-husband in front of him. He was there one evening when Becky announced she was going to have Ronny killed.

"I mean it. I've got friends," she said, "friends who'll take care of him."

She picked up the telephone and dialed a number. As Valerie and Alan listened in shocked silence, she began telling someone she wanted her ex-husband killed.

"I want to arrange a hit on him," she said. Then, as she was really getting into specific details—giving Ronny's name, description, and work address—Alan noticed that she had one finger pressed down hard on the telephone button. He nudged Valerie and nodded toward the phone. She saw it, too. The whole call was a charade.

In the weeks that followed, Becky's threats against Ronny

became routine, so common, in fact, that her daughters stopped paying any attention.

If Ronny knew about Becky's anger, he didn't care. He was anxious for all of his children to meet Juanita. So, in secret, it was arranged that the girls would all leave their house one Saturday afternoon, ostensibly to go shopping. But instead of driving to the department store, the three met Ronny and Juanita at a fast food restaurant.

The visit was a brief but pleasant one. Everyone got along well, and the girls were on their best behavior. Ronny even began to hope that someday soon he might resume regular visits with them.

During the drive home, the older girls warned Vanessa that she must not say a word about seeing their father. But at thirteen, Vanessa didn't really understand the seriousness of the situation. Soon after their return to Fulton Drive, she ran to show Becky the little toy horse Ronny had given her.

Valerie and Vicki started talking fast, trying to convince their mother that they'd run into Ronny by accident, but it was a losing battle. Her anger was terrible. She threw anything she touched and severely beat the two older girls with a belt and her fists.

"You're going to quit your job right now!" she screamed. "And drop out of school. I'll teach you at home and you won't be allowed to go anywhere!"

Hours later, when Becky finally grew calmer, Valerie and Vicki went to her and assured her it would never happen again. If they ever went anywhere and encountered their father, they promised, they would leave immediately. The girls were convincing enough that she eventually believed their story.

But Valerie and Vicki did see Ronny again. He came to the steak house one night, a week later, when both girls were there. His appearance was enough to terrify them. They were afraid to risk even being seen in his company and kept watching the door as they related what had happened after their last visit. He seemed to age before them as he said he wouldn't see them again.

"It's for your own safety," he said sadly. "I love you both very much, but I can't put you in danger anymore."

He gathered his daughters in his arms and held on tight. There were tears in all their eyes as they pulled away from each other, and Ronny hurried out of the restaurant. Vicki and Valerie would never speak to their father again.

Life in Macon wasn't turning out the way Becky hoped it would. Too many people had heard her lies, and now her friends and acquaintances were beginning to discover cracks in the facade she'd crafted. Becky was ready for greener pastures. She told her astonished daughters that they were moving to Miami.

Florida had always been Becky's promised land. Now, she was ready to make her dreams come true.

"There's a great beach," she told the girls, "and nightclubs and racetracks. There are even casinos over in Nassau. And a lot of Italians live there."

The presence of a large Italian population actually made the move more understandable for the girls. For reasons they never knew, their mother was fascinated by all things Italian. In her mind, it was the most glamorous nationality in the world. Becky even did her best to look Italian. She had an olive complexion and dark hair and, every summer, baked for hours under the sun, trying to achieve a look of Mediterranean ancestry.

Becky withdrew her daughters from school two weeks

before the 1974 school year was over. They packed their clothes and some personal possessions but left the furniture in the house. They also left the 1970 Ford behind.

"We'll come back for the rest when the house sells," she told the children.

Early one May morning, they left Macon for Miami. Valerie cried all the way to the state line because she had to leave Alan behind.

Becky, with Vanessa beside her, drove the Lincoln. Vicki and Valerie took turns driving the Chevrolet. Two days later, they checked into the beachfront Aztec Hotel on Collins Boulevard in Sunny Isles, Florida.

Sunny Isles, a small seaside resort area in northeastern Dade County, had been a popular tourist destination for decades. Its most notable claim to fame was the fantastic design of the hotels built along the beach. The Suez sported a huge Sphinx. A twenty-foot, robed Arab and two enormous camels adorned the front of the Sahara. There were also pyramids, Polynesian masks, mermaids, and covered wagons along the strip. Neon signs flashed out the names of the hotels—the Dunes, the Aztec, the Blue Mist, the Mandalay, the Thunderbird, the Tangiers, the Deauville, and Castaways.

Years and years of celebrity visitors had made this strip of beach famous. Burt Lancaster, the Kennedy and Vanderbilt families, Grace Kelly, and Frank Sinatra had all wintered there. Sunny Isles had provided a backdrop for Sinatra's 1959 movie *A Hole in the Head*.

The Beatles even visited there in 1964, staying at the Deauville Hotel and spending most of their time in its famous Peppermint Lounge.

But by the time Becky and her daughters arrived in town, Sunny Isles was a bit past its prime. There were signs of age and wear, and it had lost some of its original shine. But it was still a pretty glamorous location compared to Macon.

As soon as they arrived in Florida, Becky went to a drug store, bought the necessary chemicals, and bleached her dark brown hair blond. She also found time every day to sunbathe. Her tan deepened quickly and contrasted prettily with her newly lightened hair.

The family soon fell into a routine. They'd all sleep late, then Becky would leave for the racetrack around noon. The three sisters were on their own. They spent their days roaming the beachfront, going from one hotel pool to the next, or laying on the sand by the ocean. They bought food with money Becky left each day on the bed.

At night, the bar scene beckoned and Becky answered. Her favorite club was the ShoBar Lounge in the Aztec Hotel, but she frequented several others as well.

Valerie, Vanessa, and Vicki were free for the first time in their lives. Their mother was gone for most of their waking hours. Sometimes several days passed and the girls wouldn't see her. Even when she was with them, the angry outbursts were less and less frequent. With their father hundreds of miles away, the Akins girls began to believe that he and they were safe and they could relax.

On the evening of June 1, Becky met forty-four-year-old John Eldon Smith in the ShoBar Lounge. He was an insurance agent from New Jersey, living it up on the last night of his vacation. Smith was slight of build with a receding hairline and sideburns that spread from his ears across most of his cheeks. A bushy mustache completed the picture. For some reason, he and Becky clicked immediately.

When the bar closed, she went with him to his room and stayed the night. By the next morning, they'd decided they were in love. Eldon, as he was called, was married at the time. In fact, his third divorce wouldn't be final for another two weeks, but that didn't stop him from talking to Becky about marriage. The two were unofficially engaged when Smith said goodbye and left for the airport to return to New Jersey.

Just because she was now committed to Smith didn't mean that Becky was going to change her lifestyle. The next night, she returned to the ShoBar and met two more men. John Maree and his friend Darrell Campbell were spending a few days in town and staying at the Aztec. Maree, a recently divorced father of four, had just sold his vending machine and janitorial business on Florida's west coast. He and Darrell were taking what they described as "an open-ended vacation."

Maree was originally from Pennsylvania and had moved to Florida a couple of years before. He told Becky he'd been a dairy farmer in Pennsylvania, worked with a trucking company in New Jersey, and, more recently, had sold distributorships in a pyramid company called American Be Independent.

He was a good-looking guy with a quick smile and the outgoing personality of a natural-born salesman. When Becky introduced him to her daughters a few days later, Valerie thought he looked a little like television actor Dennis Weaver.

The only money Becky had coming in was the child support Ronny sent right on schedule every month. She also was still using one of his credit cards. But living at the Aztec was growing costly. After a couple of weeks there, they moved two doors down the beach to the less expensive Mandalay, where Becky rented two connecting rooms.

John Maree lived in Fort Myers, 150 miles across the Florida peninsula, but he was spending more and more time now in Miami. When he was in town, he stayed with the

Akinses at the Mandalay. The girls took one room while Becky and Maree shared the other. She made Maree promise to say nothing about that to Eldon Smith. She insisted to her daughters that the relationship was platonic.

Maree loved horse racing as much as Becky did and often accompanied her to the track. She regaled the girls with stories about the racetrack, making it sound like a glamorous place filled with fascinating people. Betting on horses, she said, was a great way to make a living. It was easy to win if you knew what you were doing, and she'd met several people who were happy to teach her all about it.

"They're very important people with connections!"

John Maree quickly became a part of the Akins girls' lives. As far as they could tell, he never worked. In fact, the only thing they ever saw him do was play the horses. He had a system that, according to him, paid off.

"I bet so much money on the first race of the day," he explained. "If it wins, I'm through for the day. But if it loses, I bet a bigger amount on the second race. And if that one loses, I bet even more on the third, and then the fourth. And somewhere along the line, I'll win. I know it sounds crazy, but it works."

The girls weren't sure they quite understood Maree's system, but that didn't matter. He was a likeable guy and seemed to enjoy spending time with them.

Becky had become fascinated with the Mafia. She bragged about meeting several members of that organization at the racetrack. And John Maree wasn't above a bit of swaggering himself. Since Becky seemed so interested in organized crime, he occasionally dropped hints that he might have been involved with it himself in the past. He also let her and the girls believe he'd been arrested before, although he didn't share any details of his crime. The suggestion of a dark past made him seem mysterious and a bit dangerous.

Becky and Eldon Smith exchanged numerous letters and spoke several times a week by telephone. She liked telling him about the people she met at the track who were, as she put it, "in the organization." More than once she hinted that one of these men, people she called lieutenants, was looking for a hit man.

"You can make a lot of money as a hit man," she told Smith. "We could be set for life after only one successful kill."

Smith seemed agreeable to the idea, and the two discussed it at length. Although she never used the word Mafia, there was no doubt about what she meant. And since she and everyone else had seen *The Godfather* and its sequel, they thought they knew what went on inside that shadowy organization.

But Becky saw one big problem in the plan. "You have to have an Italian name," she told Smith. "Otherwise, they won't hire you."

The two of them spent hours on the telephone considering and discarding various names. They finally came up with what they thought was a winner. John Eldon Smith would become Anthony Israldo Machetti. Not only did it sound Italian, the initials spelled AIM. It was the perfect name for a killer.

Valerie, who'd overheard her mother's side of a few of these conversations, considered the whole idea ridiculous, a fantasy that Becky spun for her and Eldon's entertainment. Val was sure Smith had no real intention of becoming a hired killer. He was only going along with the story to keep Becky happy.

Chapter 7

The Fulton Drive house was finally sold, and Becky left her daughters in John Maree's care and flew to Macon for the June 7th closing. After receiving her share of the profit from the house sale Friday afternoon, she checked into a motel for the night. The next day, she picked up the two poodles and, late that evening, flew with them back to Miami. The plane arrived at 2:30 A.M. Sunday morning, and it was nearly dawn before she got back to the Mandalay.

Eldon Smith regularly wrote to Becky from his apartment on Clubhouse Drive in West Deptford, New Jersey. And she answered just as regularly. On Monday, June 10th, she wrote that John Maree had taken her to Calder Racetrack that afternoon.

"I won $52—just about what I spent yesterday and today at the grocery & etc." She was a convert to Maree's system. "I'm going every day. It's closed Sun. & Tues. Lasts from 1:30 to 6:00 then from 7 till 10:30. The dogs run at Flagler. John has a system & so far today it has worked. I will be careful, but John says with careful planning that a person can win $100 a day. You & I could live in style. I could just have loads of exotic robes to wear over my naked body when you are not using it."

As June continued, Becky spent her days at the racetracks and her nights in the clubs. The Mardi Gras Lounge, where a pianist named Art played, was one of her favorites. And she made time to work on her tan at the beach or the hotel pool. In one letter to Eldon, she boasted that she was writing from the pool and, "I'm wearing a gold bikini and all the men are really staring."

Vicki, Valerie, and Vanessa continued doing just about whatever they wanted. Except for walking the two dogs, they had little responsibility. They slept late, ate when they were hungry, and did few chores. Laundry often waited until there were no more clean clothes to be found.

Eldon Smith was back at work, selling insurance and running his branch agency. It was a good job and he didn't like the idea of having to start all over in Miami. In spite of Becky's declaration that she could never live in the North, he hoped he could persuade her to move to New Jersey. On June 12, he sent her a map and the key to his apartment "just in case."

He promised her exotic drinks and delicious food. He was practicing in advance the meals he planned to cook for her. He wanted to show her all of nearby Philadelphia and take her on a day trip to New York City, where they'd see a play. He tried everything he could think of to entice her to come visit him. And she finally agreed.

Eldon bought her a round-trip Miami-to-Philadelphia ticket on Eastern Airlines. Her flight would leave Miami on July 3, and Eldon would meet her and drive her to his apartment. He was so excited by the prospect of her arrival that his letters fairly burst with plans and anticipation. He wrote that he'd bought a Merle Haggard album for her, but after playing it, doubted she would like it. "What a boo-boo," he wrote. "Every song except one is about lovers breaking up. I'll let you hear it when you get here and I bet you we'll end up burning it. I never did really trust Merle Haggard anyway. One song was good, however, 'Too Used to Being With You,' and we'll play it together."

In turn, Becky told Eldon about her life in Miami. And she continued to criticize Ronny Akins. At one point, she wrote of how the girls had been mistreated and neglected by their father. Eldon responded that he was eager to become their father and make up for the past.

Becky's dreams now included a perfect family with Eldon as the father. Even though the girls had never even met Eldon Smith, she insisted that they send him a Father's Day card. They did so, reluctantly. In that matter, as in most others, she got her way.

Most of what Smith wrote in his many-paged correspondence was romantic drivel, suited more to a teenager than a man in his forties. He called her a "pretty Southern belle" and declared, "Love, beautiful as it is, can be tough going at some times." Another time he wrote, "Whew, baby, you have lit my torch and nothing or nobody but you can put a damper on it. Honey, hurry on up here and wrap your damper around my torch."

In his more down-to-earth moments, Eldon tried to explain what he did for a living. He was making, he said, $325 a week. He ran the office and was the boss and he liked his work. However, the business was a small, family-owned operation and he knew his chance for advancement was limited.

"Maybe now you can better understand why I face getting another job with mixed emotions. But I've made that decision with only the slim hope that you'll like it here so much you want to move here. That's all I'm holding out for—just for you to be here, see the country and if you still feel Miami is best, then off we go!

"Let me restate: I don't care about title, geography or job security, just so we can be together. What I must hold out for, tho, is a salary at least equal or greater than now. After all, the male animal has his pride!"

One odd note among the love talk and future plans occurred in Eldon Smith's June 10 letter. "Having, of course, nothing to do with the previous subject, am having my 12-gauge double-barreled shot-gun re-stocked."

No matter how attractive he made New Jersey sound, Eldon was coming to realize that Becky wasn't interested in moving to the Northeast. His future, he knew, was going to be in Miami. In pursuit of that, he asked her to bring a current newspaper when she came up so that he could have a look at the want ads. He also requested that she check the telephone book for insurance agencies and a few employment agencies. He was, he declared, determined to become the breadwinner there in Miami.

The house in Macon sold, and Becky's furniture had to be removed by the end of the month. But first she needed a place to put it. She began searching for a rental house in the area. After a couple of weeks, she located one she believed would suit them. It was a small, white stucco structure at 1191 Northeast 159th Street in North Miami Beach.

She signed the lease. Now all she needed was the furniture. She went to John Maree with a deal. She'd pay him $150 if he would go with them to Macon, help them load the furniture, and drive the rental truck back to Miami. He'd have done it for nothing, but he didn't mind picking up some extra money. He agreed immediately.

So, during the last week of June 1974, Becky, John Maree, and all three girls drove to Macon in Becky's big Lincoln. Once there, they rented a Ryder truck and took it to Fulton Drive and loaded it with her furniture. It was hard work and took most of the day.

Becky had also found someone to buy the 1970 Ford she'd left at the house, but she needed Ronny to sign over the title to her. She called him, and, on the day they were loading the truck, he brought it to her.

Ronny was there only long enough to put his signature on the paper. He'd have liked to have seen his daughters, but Becky said they were too busy. They were at the back of the house with John Maree trying to get the lawn mower started. The girls watched their father arrive and even told Maree who he was, but they stayed where they were, hoping to avoid any trouble with their mother.

It was an all-night drive back to Miami—Becky in the Lincoln and Maree at the wheel of the rental truck. Once there, they unloaded the truck, and Becky and her daughters moved in. There were two bedrooms in the small house. Becky took the largest and gave Vanessa her own room across the hall. Valerie's and Vicki's beds were set up in the large, multi-windowed Florida room at the back of the house. On the occasions that John Maree stayed with them, he shared Becky's room.

Although there was plenty of furniture in the house—Becky had even brought both of the jukeboxes back to Florida—she purchased a black, padded-leather bar from John Maree, paying him $150 for it. The bar was set up in the living room and was always fully stocked.

Becky flew to New Jersey for the July 4 holiday, leaving Vicki, Valerie, and Vanessa with Maree. Rather than stay at the North Miami house, he drove them to Fort Myers and put them up in a Sheraton motel close to where his ex-wife lived. He stayed with his former wife and, during the days, he and his children visited the girls at the motel. The Akins girls got on well with Maree's children. They played in the pool together and ate their meals in fast food restaurants.

Becky's trip to New Jersey was a great success. The couple finally had what they'd been dreaming of—hours and hours together, talking and planning their future. Eldon cooked all the special meals he'd promised to prepare. He showed Becky the very best of his home state and those surrounding it. But in the end, she still wouldn't change her mind. She was determined to live in Miami and Eldon bowed to the inevitable. He agreed to move to Florida as soon as it could be arranged.

Soon after Becky returned home, Eldon flew down for a visit. This was the first time Vicki, Valerie, and Vanessa met the man who would be their stepfather. He was pleasant and went out of his way to include them in the plans he and Becky were making, but he was still little more to them than a stranger. During his visit, Eldon and Becky applied for a marriage license, and she began making plans for what she believed would be the perfect wedding.

Tuesday, July 16, was a typical summer day in Macon—humid, hazy, with temperatures climbing into the 90s by noon. Alan Barfield was working on an ATM machine at the C&S Bank in Macon when he got a page from his service telling him to call Mrs. Akins in Miami. It was an emergency. His mind racing, he rushed to find a telephone. Could something have happened to Valerie? He called the house and Becky answered on the second ring. She sounded upset.

"Somebody tried to break into the house last night," she told him. "I'm scared to death! I want you to buy me a pistol.

Since we just moved here, I can't buy one in Florida."

"Uh, okay," Alan said, trying to make sense of what she was saying. "You want a pistol? What kind?"

"Eldon said to tell you to try and get a Smith and Wesson .32."

Relieved that Valerie was all right, Alan agreed to do what he could.

"We're all driving to New Jersey tomorrow," Becky went on. "Listen, if you can get the gun, call me back tonight. Then we can stop by on the way and get it from you."

Alan was excited about seeing Valerie. Getting Becky a gun was a small price to pay for a visit with his fiancée. He left the bank and walked up the hill to Arvin's Pawn Shop on Poplar Street to see what was available. There were a number of Smith and Wesson models, but they were expensive. He finally settled on a new H&H .32 revolver for which he paid $65. That night, he called Becky back and told her he had the gun.

Becky, Eldon, and the girls left Miami soon after that conversation and headed north, arriving at Alan's apartment in Lakeside Manor off Riceville Road between 4:00 and 5:00 the next morning. The first thing Becky asked about, after their knocking woke Alan, was the gun. He got it and gave it, still in the box, to Eldon.

The older man looked it over, checking to be sure it wasn't loaded and pointing it at a wall. He dry-fired the weapon several times and nodded. "This will do fine."

He took money from his wallet and paid Alan for the gun. Alan, a bit nervous about purchasing a gun for someone else, had him sign a receipt.

His five visitors had been on the road for more than ten hours and were exhausted, so Alan offered them his apartment for a few hours' rest. They all found places to sleep, settling in his bed, on the sofa, and even on the carpeted floor—all of them, that is, except Valerie. She and Alan went outside and sat on the playground swing set, where they watched the sun rise and talked about their upcoming December wedding.

Two hours later, Becky, her girls, and Eldon Smith climbed back in the Lincoln and left Macon. Alan took a shower and went to work.

The Akins girls had never traveled any farther north than Athens, and New Jersey was like a foreign country to them. But they didn't have much time to explore this new world. The day after they arrived, they helped to load most of Eldon's belongings into a rental truck. It was during this time that Vicki saw two shotguns—one single barrel and one double barrel—in a gun rack in his apartment. They didn't leave his place completely bare because he had to return for a while before his permanent move to Miami.

On the weekend of July 20, they drove back to Miami, and Eldon's belongings joined Becky's in the house. Smith spent one night there, then, on Sunday, he flew back to New Jersey.

Eldon spent several days taking care of the last-minute chores in what would soon be his former home. He arranged to have his utilities cut off and had his mail forwarded. And he made good on a promise he'd made to Becky and filed a request for a name change in the Gloucester County Court in Woodbury. In his accompanying affidavit, he stated he was seeking to change his name to Anthony I. Machetti because of the confusion having a common name like Smith created among his associates and clients when they tried to contact him. A more distinctive name, he contended, would remedy the problem.

Once the paperwork was all filed, the clerk informed him

that there was a mandatory waiting period. His request would have to be published for a week in the *Woodbury Times* before the September 13th hearing. The next morning, Eldon left New Jersey for his new life in Miami.

Rebecca Akins and John Eldon Smith were married on Saturday, July 27, 1974. The evening ceremony took place high above Miami, where about thirty guests gathered in the legendary Starlight Room on the roof of the Doral Hotel to watch the couple exchange vows. Becky had sold one of the jukeboxes and the Lincoln Continental to help pay for this party.

John Maree, who had only met Eldon Smith a week before, was best man. John escorted Vicki to the event and his son Michael squired Vanessa. Alan Barfield flew down the day of the wedding to be with Valerie and returned home on Sunday. A few familiar faces from the racetrack were among the guests, as were several other people Becky had met during her two months in Miami. Dinner followed the ceremony. A piano player provided music for dancing.

The newlyweds took only a couple of days in a Miami Beach hotel for their honeymoon. John Maree had recently rented an apartment in Hialeah with his friend Darrell Campbell, but he was once more pressed into service and stayed with the girls in their house while Becky and Eldon were away.

Only a week after the wedding, Eldon returned to New Jersey to wrap up some final details of the job he was leaving. While there, he and Becky continued their phone calls and correspondence. He even wrote to the girls, trying, it seemed, to ingratiate himself to them.

"Hi girls of my life," one letter began. "Told your mother I wouldn't write to you tonite (this morning) because second daddy was drunk. But, that was a couple of hours ago & the sun is coming up. And now, breakfast coffee is waking me up. No sleep at all last night—combination of an extra big day—mom will explain—and inability to sleep because of missing you all.

"Still haven't received a letter from my pea-pickers. Write, damit. Now that I've been up all nite (and no hanky-pank, because I love Becky) for 24 hrs. without sleep, your Don Quixote is going out for a tennis match."

The long-lived national drama that was Watergate climaxed on August 9 with Richard Nixon's resignation and Gerald Ford's assumption of the presidency. But Becky and Eldon were too wrapped up in their new lives to pay much attention to politics. That was Eldon's last day of work in New Jersey. Becky flew up that evening to join him, and the next morning, they packed his last few belongings into his yellow Opel, and Eldon Smith left New Jersey for the last time.

Ronnie Akins and Juanita Knight were married on the same day that Becky and Eldon arrived back in Miami. At 2:30 that afternoon, Juanita walked down the aisle of the Belmont Baptist Church in Calhoun on the arm of her brother, Loy. It was a traditional wedding. The bride was beautiful in a flowing white gown. "Bless This House" and "The Lord's Prayer" were sung during the ceremony. The reception afterwards was held in the church's fellowship hall, and fruit punch and wedding cake were served.

The couple spent their honeymoon in Nashville and the Tennessee mountains. A week later, they set up housekeeping in a duplex apartment at 4247 Napier Avenue in Macon. They rented it from Raymond Wilkes, who, in addition to being their landlord, was the chief deputy in the Bibb County Sheriff's Office.

Even before all their boxes were unpacked, Juanita applied for work at the Bibb County Board of Education. Within a week she was hired to teach at Fort Hawkins Elementary School.

Chapter 8

Becky learned about the marriage soon after she and Eldon got back to Miami. During a telephone conversation, her mother mentioned that the announcement of Ronny and Juanita's wedding had been in the Athens paper.

The news sent Becky into a rage. Her daughters watched, puzzled, as she ranted. Ronny wasn't even part of their lives anymore. Becky had remarried. Why should she care what her ex-husband did? It was as if she hated him for not dying when she'd tried to kill him the year before.

"If I had a gun with a barrel 500 miles long," she said, "I'd shoot him right now."

The girls were accustomed to this kind of outburst. Becky had threatened to kill their father, or have him killed, so often that they no longer paid much attention. It was just her way of letting off steam.

The very next day, Becky began trying to locate Ronny's new address. Her first step was to call his boss at Southern Natural Gas.

"This is Rebecca Akins. I'm calling you long distance. I want to talk to Ronny. It's important."

"He has the week off," Ernest Doss told her.

"How can I get in touch with him?"

"I don't have any idea," he said, although he did. He knew that Ronny had remarried the day before and was on his honeymoon, but he wasn't about to tell Becky that.

When she couldn't get any information out of Doss, Becky tried Alan Barfied. She called him several times, but he repeatedly told her he didn't have any way of getting in touch with her ex-husband.

Next, she called Richard Brown. He'd been their insurance agent when she and Ronny were married and had been friends with Ronny for years. Along with handling the couple's car and homeowners insurance, Brown had been a frequent visitor to the Akins home. Although he knew the couple had divorced, he was surprised to learn she and the girls were living in Florida.

Becky told him she was calling because she wanted him to handle her auto insurance in Florida.

"I'm sorry, Becky, but there are laws regulating and controlling insurance. A Georgia agent can't write coverage outside the state."

"Oh, okay." And with that the conversation turned to other things.

"So what are y'all doing in Miami?" Brown finally asked.

"I'm not working at all!" she said delightedly. "I've gotten connected with a member of the Mafia and he's taught me how to bet on horse racing. I've accumulated a small fortune betting on horses."

"The *Mafia*? Isn't that dangerous?"

"Well," she said, backing off from her original statement. "I've actually broken off my association with this man, but I still do some betting on the horse races." Then, almost as an afterthought, she asked, "Do you know where Ronny is now?"

"No, I don't really know how to contact him. As I understand it, he's moved and remarried."

"I need to talk to him real bad," she said. "If you can find out how to get in touch with him for me and let me know, I'd really appreciate it." She gave him a telephone number and her mailing address. "And if you're ever in Miami, drop by to see me."

Becky struck out with everyone she contacted in Macon, but she wasn't ready to give up. She called a long-distance operator, identified herself as Mrs. Akins, and said it was an emergency that she get in touch with her husband. That call finally got her Ronny's new phone number and address.

Since the change was already in the works, Becky insisted that she and Eldon start using the Machetti name,[1] even though it wouldn't be completely legal until the middle of September. From then on, she never called him anything but Tony and insisted the girls and John Maree do the same.

Because Becky believed that all Italians were Roman Catholics, she decided that the whole family had to attend mass at St. Rose Catholic Church in North Miami Beach. Her new husband had been raised in the Church, but she and her daughters had not. So, she arranged that she and her children would start their religious training in the Catholic Church in the fall. To three Baptist girls from Georgia, holy water, crossing themselves, kneeling, and lighting candles were unfamiliar, exotic things. But Valerie, Vicki, and Vanessa knew better than to complain.

The telephone bill at Becky's house in North Miami Beach had gone unpaid for almost two months and totaled $450 when the phone was disconnected in August. Neither she nor

[1] Note: since Becky and Eldon Smith began referring to themselves as Becky and Tony Machetti at this time, they will be so referenced for the remainder of the book.

Tony had the cash to have the service turned back on, so the family used the pay telephones in the lobby of the Jefferson Department Store. It was only a two-block walk from the house.

Even though Tony didn't much care for it, Becky still went to the racetrack regularly. System or not, she didn't always win. She'd even borrowed money from John Maree to gamble with in July and still owed him $200. One August morning, when she and John were at the track watching the horses run, she asked him a strange question.

"Would you drive a car for me if I paid you $1,000?"

"Sure."

Maree wasn't naïve. He assumed the activity would be illegal, but he liked the money. His best guess was that Becky was planning some sort of robbery, but he was wrong. A week later he learned exactly what she had in mind.

The two were alone at her house when John's curiosity finally pushed him to ask, "What is this driving you want me to do?"

"You'll go to Macon and kill Ronny Akins and anybody else that happens to be in the apartment, " she said matter-of-factly.

"But why?" Maree asked, his voice a bit shaky.

She calmly explained that a friend of hers wanted to "get Tony into the Mafia" and that committing a murder and getting away with it would assure his being admitted into the criminal organization. Maree would later claim that he had refused to commit such a crime but that Becky threatened him and his family if he didn't go along with her plan.

A strong attraction had been growing between Vicki and John Maree all summer. Vicki was a beautiful girl—only seventeen years old—and she was flattered by the attention of an older man. For months they'd flirted and sneaked kisses when they could. Then, while Tony and Becky were on their honeymoon, John and Vicki took their relationship to the sexual level. They were besotted with each other. Any time they were alone, they were in each other's arms. Soon after that, Maree proposed to the young woman. She accepted his proposal, but they never set a date and kept the engagement a secret.

Tony Machetti enjoyed talking with Becky, hour after hour, about becoming a Mafia hit man. It was a pleasant fantasy for them, but it didn't pay the bills or put food on the table. And he'd been sincere when he told Becky he wanted to be the breadwinner. As soon as he moved to Miami, he started looking for work. In only a couple of weeks, he found employment as an agent for the Hull Insurance Agency in Fort Lauderdale.

In spite of Becky's marriage and their impending religious conversions, Vanessa, Valerie, and Vicki believed their lives might actually be getting back to normal. School would be starting soon, bringing order to their days. And even though they knew they'd never think of him as a father, they had no real objection to Tony. He was easygoing in most areas, and Becky was so engrossed in her new husband that she had little time for her children and left them alone.

The first problem arose when Becky decided that the girls should call Tony "Dad." It wasn't something they felt comfortable with, but their mother was adamant. As usual, the three acquiesced to avoid trouble, and when their mother was around, they tried to remember to call their stepfather by that name. But they forgot a lot of the time and that angered Becky.

A second problem surfaced when Becky insisted that her daughters join her in convincing Tony that Ronny Akins had been a terrible man. Her favorite time for this exercise was when the family sat down to dinner.

She would tell the girls, "Tell Tony how your father used to be mean to you. Just tell him how your father used to treat you and how mean he was to me."

The girls tried to do what she asked, making up things that Ronny had done, but it got harder and harder. They knew their father was a good man and that he'd never mistreated any of them. The situation grew more and more tense, and finally the children reached the point that drove them to do the unimaginable—they refused to do Becky's bidding. The resulting blow-ups usually ended with Becky screaming abuse at them and one or more of the girls leaving the table.

All three of the Akins girls were scheduled to attend North Miami Beach Senior High School in September. Just before time for them to register, their mother made a surprising announcement.

"You're all going to have new names!" Becky told them delightedly. "We're all going to have the same name."

She was determined to be part of a big Italian family, so she decided they were all going to take the name Machetti, just as she had. Even worse, from the girls' point of view, she wanted to change their first names as well as their last. Vicki was now Dante. Valerie became Danielle Antonia, to be called Toni. And Vanessa was Brandy Alexandra. It was a bizarre thing to do, even for Becky.

If they called each other by their old names, she warned them, they would be sorry. She didn't say what the punishment might be, but from experience they could guess. When they went to register for school, Becky blithely explained to the woman in the office that the girls were in the process of having their names changed because her husband was adopting them. In order to save confusion, she wanted them to start the school year with their new names. Incredibly, the school went along with her wishes.

John Maree was still a big part of the Machetti family's life. He visited often, and he and Tony became casual friends. Becky had warned him not to let Tony know about their former relationship. It was an unnecessary warning—John had no more interest in Becky, and he sure didn't want anything to upset the arrangement he had with Vicki. They still hid their affair—neither of them wanting to be the object of Becky's wrath—but they looked forward to marrying. As soon as John had saved up some money, they planned to leave Miami together.

Along with Maree, there was another frequent visitor to the house. Becky became acquainted with Dr. Salvatore Genori when she and Vicki had both been his patients earlier in the summer. He'd performed a hysterectomy on Becky in July, and he treated Vicki for kidney problems in August.

It's possible that Becky might have once entertained romantic intentions where Genori was concerned, but then Tony Machetti had stepped in and taken all her attention. Still, she and the doctor were friendly and he dropped by some evenings, often quite late. He'd join the couple, and sometimes Maree, for drinks at the living room bar while the jukebox played oldies from the fifties and sixties.

One night during the last week of August, Tony, Becky, and Maree gathered at the bar in the Machetti house. It was late and the girls were already in bed. Over drinks, Becky told the two men that they were going to kill Ronny Akins the following weekend. She sounded no more excited as she gave them their orders than she would have been explaining what food to buy in a grocery store.

"You have to go to his apartment early in the morning and force your way in," she told them. She left the room and returned a moment later with a glass vial and a syringe. "Knock him out and shoot this stuff in his arm. It'll look like an overdose."

"Where'd you get that?" Maree asked.

She told him she'd stolen the drug from a doctor's office. "This is enough to kill anybody. It'll kill him in two or three minutes. And there's enough there for two or three shots, because there's the possibility you might have to kill two people if his new wife is there."

She handed the vial to Tony. He looked at it without expression and passed it on to Maree. John couldn't believe it was really poison, but whatever it was, it smelled terrible. He was glad to give it back to Becky. Tony fixed them all another round and Becky continued with her tutorial. She explained to Tony how to knock someone out by hitting them on the back of the neck with the butt of a gun. Using her hands, she demonstrated on her own neck exactly where he should strike Ronny. When she was sure he understood, she moved on to demonstrate how to inject drugs into the vein of an arm. She spoke with such assurance that neither man doubted her. Maree figured she knew what she was talking about since she was a nurse.

Then the talk turned to alibis. A fishing trip, they decided, would be the best cover for John's and Tony's absence.

"Since I'm the only one they might associate with Ronny," Becky said, "I'll stay here in Miami." And to strengthen her own alibi, Becky decided to have Alan Barfield come down for a visit.

Valerie and Alan stayed in close touch. They wrote occasional letters and spoke frequently on the phone. Alan had been a visitor to their Florida home only twice since they'd left Macon. He'd made the drive from Macon to Miami in June, bringing some items that Becky had left in storage. And a month later, he flew down for the wedding. He and Valerie were anxious to see each other again.

In August, they began planning for her to visit him in Macon. Becky had surprised them by giving her permission for Valerie to fly up and spend a long weekend with her fiancé. The two young people were excited, talking by phone several times a week, anticipating all they'd do when they were together. However, those plans changed abruptly.

The week before Valerie's scheduled trip to Macon, Alan was attending job training in Atlanta. The one-week school was held at a large motel and conference center. When he finished with classes on Thursday evening, he had a message waiting for him.

"Your mother-in-law wants you to call her," the slip of paper read. A phone number was written across the bottom.

Since he wasn't married and didn't have a mother-in-law, Alan was a bit surprised, but he recognized the telephone number. It was the pay phone that Valerie and her family had been using since their own phone had been disconnected. He made the call from his room and Valerie answered on the first ring. She didn't sound happy. She told him her mother had changed her mind.

"I can't come to Macon this weekend."

Alan was disappointed. "Can I talk to her? Maybe I can

get her to change her mind."

"She's not here right now. But she said you could call her at 9:15 in the morning."

Alan spent a restless night. He'd been so looking forward to seeing Valerie again and now it seemed the trip wasn't going to happen.

He called Florida the next morning and spoke with Becky. Being careful to say nothing that could upset her, he tried to persuade her to let Valerie come to Macon after all. But Becky wasn't inclined to do that.

"No, I want you to come down to Florida this weekend," she said. "I don't think Valerie should come up there by herself. You come here and we can all go to Disney World."

He tried to explain that he couldn't afford the trip. He was in the process of building a house and money was scarce, but she was insistent.

"You really need to come down," she told him. "I don't want you to be in Macon this weekend."

That didn't make any sense, and he honestly didn't have the money to make the trip. He was on the verge of refusing when she said something guaranteed to change his mind.

"I know you and Valerie are in love. And Tony, her new stepfather, wants to talk to you about y'all getting married."

Alan couldn't say no to that. He loved Valerie and wanted nothing more than to make her his wife. Although she'd accepted his proposal, he knew it was really up to Becky. She controlled Valerie the same way she did her other children. And if Becky refused to allow the wedding, it wouldn't matter whether Valerie was seventeen or twenty-five, there'd be no marriage. If he could convince Tony that he and Valerie were right for each other, their future together might be assured. He told Becky he would come.

When his training ended at noon on Friday, Alan drove

back to Macon. It was a hot day. Thunderheads were building in the southwest sky, but he didn't encounter any rain and was in Macon by 2:00.

Like most of his contemporaries, Alan lived from paycheck to paycheck. And his paycheck was mailed to him from the home office, usually arriving in his mailbox on Friday. But on this afternoon, there was no check waiting for him.

He wasn't going to let that stop him. He wasn't going to lose his chance to talk to Becky's new husband just because he was short of money. Since his job involved the repair and maintenance of automatic teller machines and alarms, Alan knew people at most of the local banks. So, that Friday afternoon, he called on the friendships he'd made. At a nearby C&S Bank, he met with a loan officer. In fifteen minutes, he had secured a ninety-day note for enough money for a round-trip ticket to Miami and some spending money while he was there. He'd pay the loan off the following week—just as soon as his paycheck arrived.

On Friday, August 30, John Maree left his apartment in Hialeah and drove to the Machetti house in North Miami. There, he picked up some fishing equipment Tony had left out for him. Then he drove to Hull and Company in Fort Lauderdale and met Tony in the parking lot at 5:30 P.M. Machetti was waiting in a green 1974 AMC Gremlin he'd rented at Avis earlier in the day. Maree parked his car, got into the Gremlin, and the two men started the long drive north to Macon, Georgia.

~~~
~~~

There was excitement at the Machetti house that evening. Alan Barfield was coming, and the girls were looking forward to a fun weekend. Their mother had promised that they were all going to Disney World. But after dinner, Becky called her daughters into the kitchen. She looked very serious when she told them to sit down at the table.

"I'm going to get your father this time. I got him this time. Tony and John have gone to kill your father."

"No, Mama," Vanessa said. "They went fishing." She had no knowledge of the earlier attempt on Ronny's life and was just confused by her mother's words.

"You'll find out soon enough." She calmly explained that the two men were going to break into Ronny's house and give him a shot with enough poison in it to kill him.

"If that doesn't work, Tony has a gun to shoot him."

Valerie remembered seeing the guns when they moved into the house, but she couldn't remember how many or what kind. She did know, however, that they'd been stored in the closet in her mother's and Tony's bedroom. Did Tony have one of those guns with him? She wanted to go and look to see if they were still there, but she didn't dare.

"You can go now," Becky said.

But as they left the kitchen, she had a warning for them. "If you say anything, you're going to wish to God you hadn't. I'm getting rid of him and I can get rid of you. If you ever tell *anyone* what I told you, I'll see to it that you're charged as murderers as well. You'll all be accessories. Do you understand?"

Vanessa started crying, which annoyed her mother. She told her to be quiet several times, but the girl couldn't seem to stop.

"If you don't shut up," she finally said, "I'm going to beat you."

The other girls hurriedly took Vanessa to another room, where they told her they were sure that their mother didn't mean what she said, that she'd made up things like this before. They said it as much to reassure themselves as their sister.

Alan Barfield took the 10:40 flight from Atlanta to Miami. He tried to read a newspaper, where much of the front page was devoted to President Ford's newly announced agenda for the country, including the possibility of amnesty for draft evaders. But Alan found it hard to concentrate. He was nervous about talking with Tony and mentally rehearsed everything he wanted to say to him.

It was nearly midnight when the airplane touched down in Miami. Alan was met at the gate by Becky, Valerie, Vicki, and Vanessa—although Becky confused him immediately by introducing the girls as Toni, Dante, and Brandy Machetti.

Although everyone seemed to be acting normally, he thought Vanessa looked like she might have been crying. He got his single bag at baggage claim, and then they all walked back out to the parking lot. Even at midnight, it was very warm. While the high temperatures in Miami were usually no warmer than those in Macon, the difference was that here the air didn't cool as much at night. Alan could feel dampness on his face as he stowed his bag in the trunk and crowded into a tiny yellow Opel with the others. Becky said the car belonged to Tony.

Tony Machetti wasn't with them, but Alan hardly paid any attention to that fact. He was too happy to see Valerie again to worry about his welcoming committee. But when he learned a few minutes later that Valerie's stepfather wasn't even in Miami, he was confused.

"Tony and his friend John are on a fishing trip," Becky told him.

"When will they be back?"

"I'm not sure. Tomorrow or maybe Sunday," she said, not even acknowledging the fact that she'd asked Alan to come down especially to talk with Tony Machetti.

Back at the house, the two little dogs danced around Alan's feet, deliriously happy to see him again. Becky fixed drinks for herself and her guest, and they all settled down in the living room for a visit. Alan had a hard time adjusting to the girls' new names, and Becky had to correct him several times.

They fixed him a pallet on the floor in the Florida room where Valerie and Vicki slept. But, Becky warned them, they were definitely not allowed to share a bed. They were both too frightened of Becky to even consider disobeying her. Around midnight, Alan went to bed. Becky and Vanessa did, too. Valerie and Vicki stayed up a while, talking about what their mother had told them earlier.

"Why does she do that?" Vicki asked. "She keeps saying stuff like that."

"I don't know," Valerie said. "Just let it go."

Neither of them really believed what their mother had said. She'd made so many baseless threats in the past that they'd lost their impact. But just the suggestion of their father being killed was disturbing.

"They went fishing," Vicki said, putting the matter to rest. "Why else would they take fishing poles and tackle boxes?"

With that, the sisters were able to sleep.

Chapter 9

Sunrise was still a couple of hours away when Tony and John arrived in Macon, but the sky was beginning to lighten a bit as they exited the interstate at Forsyth Road. Using the directions Becky had written out for them, they easily located the Catherine Arms Apartments on Napier Avenue. In the parking lot in front of the duplexes, they checked mailboxes for the right number. Finding Ronny Akins's apartment was no problem.

John stopped the car near the building. Tony pulled on a pair of white cotton gloves and got out of the vehicle, carrying a briefcase that contained the vial of drugs, the syringe, and a .38 revolver. He pushed the car door closed just until the latch caught, making as little noise as possible.

While John turned the car around so that it was facing the street, Tony silently approached the front door of the duplex. He tried the knob, but the door was locked. Next, he made a quick circuit of the building, but the back door was also secure and there weren't any open windows. After a few minutes, he came back to the car.

The two men conversed in low voices, trying to decide exactly what to do. They were considering knocking on the door and then forcing their way in when they were startled by a sudden wash of light across the buildings and another car pulling into the lot. A young man hopped out and began delivering newspapers. He was much too close to their car for them to remain. Hoping to avoid notice, Tony and John left the lot and drove back the way they'd come.

They soon found a quiet neighborhood near Wesleyan College where the houses were set back from the road. John pulled the car to the curb and turned off the engine. They left the windows up because the predawn air was cool and damp.

Tony was as relaxed as if he were in his own living room. He settled down in his seat, leaned his head against the window, and was asleep in a few minutes. John Maree wasn't nearly so complacent. He couldn't sleep. He squirmed around, trying to find a comfortable position. To keep his mind off the coming hours, he watched the neighborhood coming to life around him. Dogs were walked and morning papers fetched. A few early risers were out jogging. Finally, John couldn't sit still any longer. He woke Tony.

"We better find out what we're going to do next," he said.

But no discussion was necessary. Tony had already decided on an alternate plan, one he had discussed with Becky before they left Miami. He had John drive to a convenience store on Forsyth Road and got out to use a pay phone.

The Akinses weren't accustomed to getting telephone calls before 9:00 on Saturday mornings, so Ronny was already a little annoyed when he answered. The man calling wanted to discuss installing a television antenna on the house he was building.

"Could you meet me there this morning?"

"Sorry," Ronny said. "I've already got plans today."

Tony injected polite disappointment into his voice. "Oh. I really hoped we could do this today. Are you sure you're not going to have a little free time? It shouldn't take very long and I'll pay you in cash."

Ronny looked across the kitchen to where Juanita was pouring a second cup of coffee and smiled at her. The extra money would come in handy.

"Tell you what," he finally said, "why don't you call back this afternoon. Maybe I'll have some time then."

Back in the car, Tony told John they needed to find a secluded place to meet Ronny Akins. They drove around the area, cruising through neighborhood after neighborhood. Finally, about 11:00 A.M., they turned into Fairmont North subdivision. It was a new development. Only three houses had been completed, and they were located at the beginning of the street near the intersection with Forsyth Road.

John steered the little green Gremlin along the main street as it gently sloped away from the subdivision entrance and dipped up and down several small hills. Once the few houses had been left behind, the area became heavily wooded. Pines and hardwoods crowded together in dense forest.

After half a mile or so, the road curved to the left. There, a small strip of asphalt, the beginning of a cross street, had been laid to the right. The main road continued, then ended after a couple of hundred feet. That's where John stopped.

He and Tony got out, stretched, and walked around the car, surveying the prospective ambush location. The only sound was birdsong. They were hidden from view by trees and distance from the front of the subdivision.

"This looks like a good place," Tony said. "Yeah, this will do just fine."

Ronny had a treat planned for his new wife that Saturday morning. They drove to an airport on the south side of Macon. At Lowe Aviation, Ronny rented a Piper Cherokee 140. He paid $24, and he and Juanita walked across the tarmac and climbed into the small, single-engine plane.

Once they were both buckled in and ready for take off, Ronny told her, "I want to show you your new home from the air!"

The couple spent the next few hours soaring above Macon. Ronny pointed out landmarks and Juanita laughingly tried to take it all in. It was a happy time for them both.

They were back home in their Napier Avenue apartment by two o'clock when Tony Machetti called again. This time Ronny agreed to meet him at Fairmont North at five that afternoon.

"Just tell me where it is."

Ronny wrote the directions on a piece of paper that he folded and slipped it into his shirt pocket with his cigarettes and lighter.

John and Tony had several hours to fill before five o'clock. They took Interstate 475 north twenty-five or thirty miles until they found a place to eat. After their late lunch, they returned to the same north Macon neighborhood where they'd rested that morning. All they could do then was wait.

~~~

Alan Barfield was an early riser. When he woke just after sunrise on Saturday morning, he was the only person stirring in the Machetti household. Trying to be as quiet as he could, he waited in the living room, watching TV and playing with the dogs, until about 10:00, when Becky got up and made coffee. One by one, the girls joined them, and, by 11:00, everyone was awake and ready to start the day. The girls were excited about the prospect of going to Disney World, but Becky suggested that the next day would be a better time, that they had a lot to do this afternoon.

Since Tony had taken the blue Chevrolet when he left Friday morning and Becky declared she needed the Opel to run errands, Alan decided to rent a car. Becky dropped him
~~~

and Valerie off at a nearby agency, and he rented a little red compact, a Vega, for two days. The car was a good idea for another reason—it gave the young couple the freedom to spend time alone together.

It was a hot day. Alan and Valerie drove around North Miami Beach, seeing the sights. They even found time to take Shannon, the poodle, for a ride and buy him a roast beef sandwich at Arby's. Late in the afternoon, they and the rest of the family went swimming in the pool at the Aztec Motel.

Juanita Akins had planned an early supper. A loaf of bread lay on the kitchen counter for sandwich making, and she'd just emptied a can of soup into a saucepan and put it on the stove when Ronny reminded her he had to go out and meet a man about installing a television antenna.

"Oh, I forgot. Will it take long?"

"Just a few minutes, I think. Why don't you come with me?"

Juanita turned off the stove and followed him out to his company car, a white Ford. Once inside, she slid over, cuddled up next to Ronny, and gave his arm a squeeze.

John and Tony got back to Fairmont North shortly after 4:30. They drove straight to the cul-de-sac at the back of the subdivision and were both standing outside the car when Ronny and his wife arrived. Tony once again held the briefcase. John knew that, along with the revolver in the case, there was a shotgun in the back seat of the Gremlin, hidden under a coat.

Ronny pulled his vehicle into the little turn off, parked, and got out. He voiced some sort of greeting, but Maree, who was standing several feet away, couldn't hear what he said.

Tony motioned for Juanita to get out, too, and she slipped under the wheel and got out on the driver's side. As soon as she was standing beside her husband, Tony slipped a hand inside the briefcase and came out with the gun.

"Put your hands on top of the car!" he shouted.

"What are you doing?" Ronny asked, even as he and Juanita were obeying the order. Juanita was crying. He moved close to his wife and slipped his hand under hers, so that their arms were entwined.

"Please don't hurt us," she begged.

Ronny asked, "Is this a robbery?"

"No."

He pulled his hands off the car to half face Machetti. "Is this a robbery?"

"No, it's not."

"If it is, you can have all I've got, you can have everything I've got. I have $22 in my pocket." He reached for the cash. "Here, you can have everything I have."

"Get your hands back on the car! Now!"

As Ronny turned back toward the car, Tony took two steps forward and struck him hard on the back of the head with the gun barrel. This was the blow Becky had assured him would produce immediate unconsciousness, but she was wrong. Even though Ronny slumped against the car and blood sprang from his scalp, he remained conscious, trying to get back on his feet.

"Oh, my God! Oh, my God!" Juanita screamed.

"Can't you shut her up?" Tony asked John.

To Maree, the whole experience had taken on an air of unreality. Tony's voice seemed to come from a great distance away. He looked around in a dazed way for a weapon and spotted a surveyor's stake in the ground nearby. He yanked the short piece of wood out of the dirt and struck Juanita ineffectually on the head a few times. She didn't seem to notice. She dove back into the car, reaching for the company radio. John watched, but was rooted in place.

"Tony, she's trying to use the radio!"

Tony ran back to the Gremlin and grabbed the shotgun. John turned away, not wanting to see what was going to happen. He noticed the revolver on the ground where Tony had dropped it and, with some vague idea of being helpful, picked it up and put it back into the briefcase. That's when the first shotgun blast sounded and Juanita's crying was silenced.

John had to look. He turned in time to see smoke coming from the end of the barrel and Tony removing the spent shell and reloading another. He didn't look at the woman who'd been shot and quickly turned away again. There were two more shots in quick succession.

Heart pounding, Maree turned around to confront the scene. This time he couldn't avoid seeing the carnage. Ronny Akins lay on the asphalt beside the car, a wash of blood spreading away from his body. Juanita's feet, absolutely still, dangled out of the driver's side of the car. Tony again broke the gun open, unloaded the spent shells, and put them in his pocket.

"Let's go," he said.

Maree followed him to the car. They climbed back into the Gremlin, John once more behind the wheel, and made their way slowly out of the subdivision. Maree took care to come to a complete stop at Forsyth Road. That was when he noticed a couple standing in front of a house to his left. He hurriedly put his hand up to hide his face.

"There are two people standing right over there," he said worriedly.

"Just pull out," Tony told him impatiently. "Just move off."

It was 5:20. John turned right on Forsyth Road, and, a few minutes later, they were southbound on Interstate 475. Twenty minutes later, they merged back onto Interstate 75 and left Macon behind them.

For a while, neither man spoke. John concentrated on maintaining a constant sixty miles per hour and had a hard time keeping his eyes off the rearview mirror. He didn't want to chance attracting the attention of the state patrol. About thirty miles south of Macon, they ran into a rain shower. John switched on the wipers and Tony finally broke the silence.

"I better get rid of these," he said, fishing the slips of paper Becky had given him from his pocket. He tore the papers with Ronny's address and phone number, and the directions to his apartment, into tiny pieces and then let them go, one by one, out the window.

Next, he pulled the clothes he'd worn to work on Friday from the back seat and awkwardly changed into them. He tossed those he'd just taken off into the back seat.

"It looked like a pretty professional job, didn't it?" Machetti asked.

Maree swallowed hard and agreed that it had.

"I'm going to burn those clothes," Machetti said. "And I'll bury the drugs and the briefcase. And the guns, too. You know, that's my father's shotgun. I don't want to lose it if I can help it. If I bury it where I can find it again, I can go dig it back up later on."

Maree had no comments to make. There didn't seem to be anything else to say.

Ronny Akins wasn't the only person who rented an airplane in Macon that day. Quinton Cotton had grown up in Middle Georgia. A Pan American airline pilot, he was based in Miami but still considered Macon his home and visited often. His parents still lived there, as did his fiancée, Ruth Senseman.

Late that Saturday afternoon, Quinton, Ruth, and her sisters, Rebecca and Rachel, climbed aboard a Cessna 172 at Herbert Smart Airport, east of the city. With only four seats in the small plane, every passenger that day had a window seat.

Quinton's destination was north Macon, where his brother and sister-in-law were building a new home just off Bass Road. The little group had decided it would be fun to fly out and locate the house. They were especially interested in seeing the swimming pool that was being installed.

Once they were in the air, Quinton picked up the railroad tracks in downtown Macon and followed them out of the city. Between 6:00 and 7:00, he located his brother's place. He circled around it several times, flying low so that everyone got a good look at the pool site.

Then they spotted an open pasture where several deer grazed in the waning sun. Quinton dropped to treetop level to chase the deer. The animals ran toward the shelter of the tree line, and he pulled up fast and turned sharply to avoid the trees. That's when he saw the bloody scene in the cul-de-sac below.

"We've got to go back!" he shouted to the others.

It was noisy inside the little plane. "What?" one of the girls yelled back.

"We've gotta go back! There's a guy back there with his head blown off!"

The others hadn't noticed anything out of the ordinary, but Quinton knew what he'd seen. He turned the plane around and made several passes over the area, but couldn't locate the scene again. There were few if any landmarks in that rural area. Finally, he backtracked to the railroad tracks to regain his bearings.

Once more he flew over his brother's house, dropped down as if to chase the now absent deer, and made the same banked turn over the cul-de-sac. They were flying at about 300 feet, and this time everyone in the plane witnessed the gruesome sight below.

"It's awful! It's awful!" Fifteen-year-old Rebecca kept repeating.

Quinton made one more pass, but worried that whoever shot the man might still be present. He was careful not to get too low in case someone turned the weapon on them. That last look was enough. He climbed back up and headed south.

By radio, he notified the airport of what they'd seen and asked them to call the police. He was able to provide a fairly accurate location of the murder scene since he'd recognized the intersection of Bass Road and Forsyth Road.

"Tell them it's the first street off of Forsyth Road going north from Bass."

When they landed, Quinton and the girls piled into his car and headed for north Macon. They were sure the police would want to talk to them.

Chapter 10

About that same time, seventeen-year-old Sammy Cox and his girlfriend, Candy Kelly, were out riding around. They'd been together for several hours, visiting friends and enjoying the summer day. It was 7:25 when Sammy drove into Fairmont North subdivision. One of their high school counselors, Bobby McElroy, had just moved there, and Sammy wanted to show his girlfriend Mr. McElroy's new house. As they passed the first house on the right—a tan brick set off by a circular driveway—Sammy pointed to it.

"That's it. That's where Mr. McElroy lives now."

The teenagers drove on. Sammy planned to turn around at the end of the road. As they approached the back of the subdivision, he and Candy saw a white car and a body on the ground beside it.

Sammy couldn't believe it was real. Maybe it was just someone playing a prank. He drove on past and turned around at the dead end. As he came abreast of the vehicle again, he slowed nearly to a stop and looked at the scene before them. He knew now that it wasn't a prank. The man on the pavement wasn't moving and there seemed to be blood everywhere. A pair of legs protruded from the car itself.

Sammy drove back up to the McElroy house as fast as he could. He jumped out of his car and ran to pound on the front door. When no one answered, he raced across the street to a brick ranch perched up on a hill. Homeowner Gary Johnson answered his frantic knocking.

"It looks like some people have been shot down the

road!" Sammy was breathless from excitement and exertion. "We need to get the sheriff out here!"

Johnson made the call. Then he and his family went outside and waited with the two teenagers for the police to arrive.

~~~

Lt. Billy Guy and Dep. Jerry Butterworth were partners working the four-to-midnight shift in the uniform patrol division of the Bibb County Sheriff's Department. Saturday afternoons were usually slow and this one hadn't been any different. They stopped for dinner at 7:30.

They ordinarily ate in fast food restaurants when they were on duty, but on weekends one of their wives often fixed them a meal. They got just such a treat that Saturday evening.

The two officers were having a home-cooked dinner in Jerry Butterworth's apartment on Columbus Road when the telephone rang. They'd had taken only a few bites of the meal but knew the odds were that the call would be for them. Jerry reluctantly went to answer it.

"Somebody says they found a body," he told his partner when he hung up the phone.

The half-finished meal was left on the table and the two men headed for Fairmont North. Theirs was the first car on the scene, arriving at 7:51. They stopped first at the Johnson house, where Sammy Cox told them what he'd seen, then drove on into the cul-de-sac.

It was a bad scene. In the diminishing daylight, a man lay sprawled on the asphalt beside a white Ford sedan. He was on his stomach, his face turned away from the car. A long smear of blood trailed away down a slight incline.

As the two officers stood over the body, they thought they could make out two gunshot wounds—one to his head and one on to his back near the left shoulder blade. A pair of
~~~

sunglasses lay beside his face. One of the lenses had popped out and lay separate from the frames.

But that wasn't the worst. The driver's door was open, and a woman's body was sprawled across the front seat, her legs extending out of the door. Her face was an unrecognizable mass of bone, blood, and tissue. Both her wrists had been shattered, as if she'd instinctively put up her hands to ward off the gunshot. A small wooden stake was oddly out of place beside her head. As they stood there taking in the scene, a scratchy transmission came from the two-way radio on the Ford's dash.

They automatically checked to see if either of the two were alive, but both men knew their actions were futile. It was obvious the victims were dead. The officers' first quick look around revealed no weapons. Except for the driver's, all the car doors and windows were closed and locked. Touching the hood with the back of a hand, Butterworth found the engine was still warm.

Guy keyed his radio mike and requested assistance. Soon the investigators on call, the sheriff, the coroner, and the photographer were en route to the scene. The lieutenant stayed with the bodies and sent Butterworth back up to Johnson's house to talk to the witnesses.

Sammy and Candy felt like they'd been waiting for hours, although it had actually been less than thirty minutes since they'd discovered the bodies. It was a relief when Butterworth took them aside to get their story. He then took statements from the Johnsons. It was during that interview that Quinton Cotton and the Senseman girls arrived. Minutes later, they, too, gave their information to the officer.

Robbie Johnson was the detective on call that weekend. When he was notified of the deaths, he called his partner's house. Bill Freeman wasn't home, but Johnson left word for him to meet him at the scene.

When Johnson arrived on Fairmont Drive around 8:15 it wasn't yet dark. The sun had set only a few minutes before. This time of year, twilight could stretch past nine. He got out, spoke briefly with Guy, and then slowly walked around the car.

"Looks like she was reaching for the radio," he observed. "Both of them got a shotgun blast."

Bill Freeman was only a few minutes behind his partner and joined Johnson at the scene. Using flashlights, they examined the car's exterior surface. It appeared there were palm and fingerprints on the top of the driver's side above the rear door.

By 8:30, Coroner A. R. King was there, along with police photographer Carl Barker, who immediately began photographing the scene. When he was done, Coroner King carefully extracted a wallet from the dead man's back pocket and laid it on the trunk of one of the police vehicles. The wallet contained a driver's license that identified the man as Joseph Ronald Akins, $22 in bills, and a woman's picture. Looking at the image, the happy smile, Johnson thought the photo might be one of the other victim, but he couldn't be sure.

Ray Wilkes began working for the Bibb County Sheriff's Office in 1952. In the twenty-two years since then, he'd risen through the ranks to the position of chief deputy. While Freeman and Johnson were examining the murder scene, Wilkes was pushing a lawn mower across the front yard of his

Sprucewood Drive home. Even that late in the evening there was plenty of light for the job at hand and it was still very hot. He'd already cut the backyard and was looking forward to finishing the front and rewarding himself with a big glass of iced tea.

But before he could finish, his fifteen-year-old son, Ray Jr., came outside to tell him he had a phone call. He knew they only called him for something serious.

"I'm on my way," Wilkes told the dispatcher. He hurried to shower and change clothes. He was almost out the door when Ray Jr. stopped him.

"Daddy, can I go with you?" Over the years, Wilkes had been called out to many crime scenes and had occasionally allowed his son to accompany him. However, from what he'd heard on the phone, he feared this might be a bad one.

"No, not this time. I may be out too late," he told the boy, "and I won't have time to bring you back."

Later, he'd be glad Ray Jr. hadn't come with him.

When Wilkes turned into Fairmont North, he met Johnson and Freeman leaving. The two cars stopped side by side.

"What have we got?" Wilkes asked.

Johnson told him, "We've got one on the ground and one in the car. There's no notes and no weapons. Female's in the car. The man on the ground, we've got him identified. His name is Akins. And the woman in the car, we don't know who she is. Maybe his wife or girlfriend. He had a picture of her in his wallet." Johnson pulled the photo from his shirt pocket. "We're going now to try and identify her."

"Let me see it."

Johnson held the snapshot up.

Wilkes sighed. "Turn around and come on back. I know who she is. Her name is Juanita Akins. She and her husband rent an apartment from me."

The two detectives accompanied their boss back to the scene, where the uniform officers had secured the area and waited as he, like the others before him, walked around the cul-de-sac. Wilkes found it hard to reconcile his two tenants—who'd been so happily starting a new life together—with these two lifeless bodies.

Johnson had already called Kitchen's Garage for a wrecker, and one arrived about 9:15, driven by Terry Fred Busbee. Busbee did paint and body work for the garage during the day and, if he was needed, pulled cars at night. He was ready to go as soon as he got there, but he had to wait nearly forty-five minutes until the ambulance arrived and removed the bodies from the scene. Then Busbee hooked up his wrecker cable to the front of the car, taking care to touch only those surfaces that he had to in order to accomplish the job.

"Can you knock it for me?" he asked a group of officers, meaning to put it in neutral.

One of the men did so, and a minute later Busbee was on his way.

Once the Ford was removed, the investigators took a close look at the space it had occupied. Johnson found fragments of hair and a single buckshot on the pavement.

Ronny Akins's car was towed to Kitchen's Garage on Jeffersonville Road, where Busbee maneuvered it into a building. He left it there. The only door to the building was then locked. Only Busbee and Mr. Kitchens had keys. A deputy in a uniform car was stationed there to make sure no one touched the car until technicians from the Georgia State Crime Lab could process it.

While Maree and Machetti were driving south on I-75 and the Bibb County Sheriff's Department was beginning to investigate Ronny and Juanita Akins's murders, Becky Machetti was heading out to dinner in North Miami Beach with her daughters and Alan Barfield. She chose a steak house called the Black Angus. Only four blocks from their house, it was located very close to Jefferson's Department Store and the pay phone the family often used.

They arrived about 7:30, and as soon as they were seated, Becky declared they would split the check. Alan wasn't given any say in the matter. He would pay for his, Valerie's, and Vanessa's dinner. Becky would pay for hers and Vicki's. Although he wasn't expecting it, the young man did some quick math and figured he could handle his part of the bill with no problem.

The food was good and they had a pleasant meal. However, when the check arrived, Becky looked in her purse and reacted with less-than-genuine surprise.

"I don't have any money with me! I really thought I did." She turned to Alan. "Can you take care of it? I can give you a check later tonight."

Trapped in the circumstance, all Alan could do was agree.

"Well, then," Becky said, standing up, "Vicki and I are going to walk over to Jefferson's. Tony's going to call at nine."

After they left, Alan, Valerie, and Vanessa lingered for a while at the table. They got a to-go box to take the steak scraps to the dogs, then the three young people walked to the front counter, where Alan paid the bill. However, he'd been so busy trying to figure out how much money he'd have after tonight that he'd forgotten to leave a tip.

As soon as they were outside, Vanessa realized she'd forgotten her purse. She ran back to fetch it, only to encounter an angry waitress.

"I thought I took care of you real good tonight, but you

didn't even leave me a tip."

Vanessa didn't know how to respond. She just nodded and hurried out the front door. The waitress wasn't going to be put off that easily. She followed the embarrassed young girl out the front door where the others waited, still complaining about the lack of a tip. Alan hurriedly gave her all the change in his pockets. While she wasn't entirely mollified, it was enough to send the woman back into the steak house.

Alan and the two girls walked across the street to Jefferson's. Becky was still at the pay phones, waiting for her call, so the others went inside to look around.

Maree and Machetti had driven south through intermittent rain. They were low on fuel but didn't want to stop while they were still in Georgia. About 8:30, they crossed over into Florida and left the interstate at the first exit, which was Jennings. There, they found a PaceCar service station. They filled the tank with gas and walked around a bit. Then they used the restroom and got some food and drinks out of the vending machines.

Tony was waiting for 9:00. That was the time Becky had told him to call her at the pay phone at Jefferson's. She'd written both telephone numbers on a piece of paper. He was to call at nine, on the hour. If he was delayed for some reason, he was to call at 10:00 or, if necessary, at 11:00.

At exactly 9:00, Tony put a coin in the box and made a person-to-person call, asking the operator to make sure the person on the other end was named Becky.

The conversation was brief.

"Everything's okay," he told her. "We bagged two fish."

"Where are you now?"

"In northern Florida—over the line. Hoorah!"

~~~

It was after 10:00 when Becky, the girls, and Alan returned to the house. A short time later, Dr. Genori stopped by. He and Becky had a drink and talked quietly in the living room for about half an hour before he took his leave.

When the young people were getting ready for bed, Becky announced a change in their plans. She told Alan that he and Valerie, whom she called Toni, would be the only ones going to Disney World the next day.

"So the two of you will have to get up early. Tony and I are going to 7:00 mass," she said.

That brought a puzzled look to Alan's face. As far as he knew, the family had always been Baptist. He glanced at Valerie for an explanation, but she just shook her head.
~~~

Chapter 11

Several officers remained at Fairmont North as the night wore on, either processing the area or talking with neighbors. Guy and Butterworth stayed until the end of their shift. Then they were replaced by Bob Boren, a deputy on the midnight watch. His less-than-exciting assignment was to sit in his car and guard the scene all night. It was very quiet in the cul-de-sac. When the clouds broke occasionally, a full moon lit the scene brightly enough to cast shadows, but the young officer had nothing to do for eight long hours. Coincidentally, nearly a decade later, he'd have much more significant involvement in this same case.

While the deputies had talked at length with the Johnson family, the McElroy house across the street had remained empty all night. Then, around 11:00, the three McElroy teen-aged daughters and their dates arrived home within minutes of each other. They were surprised to find a sheriff's office checkpoint at the entrance to the subdivision. The three young couples were allowed to pass. Having learned what had happened, they hurried into the McElroy house and locked the doors behind them in case the killer was still in the area.

The girls' parents, Bobby and Ann McElroy, had been out to dinner and a party, and it was after midnight when they arrived back at Fairmont North. The sight of the sheriff's cars parked near their house filled them with fear that something had happened to their children, but the deputy who approached their car recognized Bobby and immediately reassured him.

"It's okay, Mr. McElroy. There's nothing wrong with your family." He briefly explained the circumstances, then allowed the relieved parents to go to their house.

When Det. Robbie Johnson came to talk with them a few minutes later, he discovered that Ann and Bobby McElroy were two of the best witnesses he'd ever met.

Bobby obligingly recounted how he'd spent the day. Saturday had been hot, humid, and overcast, and he and the family had stayed inside their air conditioned home most of the time. But as the afternoon progressed, the sun broke through the clouds a bit, and Bobby took the opportunity to wash his car.

"It was about 4:45, I guess," McElroy told Johnson. "I backed the car out of the garage into the driveway to wash it."

That was what he was doing about 5:00 when he noticed a 1974 Gremlin enter the subdivision and drive down the road toward the end of Fairmont Drive.

"It was a two-door Gremlin," he recalled, "green with a gold stripe down the side. I especially noticed it because I owned a Gremlin myself."

"Can you describe the driver?"

McElroy shook his head. "The sun was glaring off the windshield, I couldn't see anything except that there were two people in the car."

McElroy remembered that a few minutes after the Gremlin passed, a white Ford LTD turned off of Forsyth Road and followed the same route. But this time, he'd seen more.

"There was a couple in that car. The woman smiled and waved at me when they passed the house." A picture of Juanita Akins's body flashed through Johnson's mind. She'd never smile or wave again.

"Anything else?"

A short time later, McElroy said, he'd heard several gunshots from the direction of the cul-de-sac. "It sounded to me like a shotgun."

"Did you go check on it or call the police?"

"No, it didn't worry me. People go back there all the time to shoot. I've done it myself."

Johnson then turned his attention to Ann McElroy. She told him she'd joined her husband outside and was sweeping the driveway when the Gremlin left the neighborhood. That time both McElroys were able to see that there were two men in the green car.

"And it had a Florida tag," Ann contributed.

It wasn't surprising that the couple paid attention to strange cars in their subdivision. Since they'd moved there, they and the Johnsons had been victims of thefts from their houses. As the Gremlin had passed, both Ann and Bobby got a good look at the driver.

"He put a hand up to cover his face," Bobby told the detective, "but not before I saw him."

They described the driver as a white male with dark, bushy hair. Neither of them were able to tell much about the passenger except that he, too, was white.

It was just after 1:30 A.M. when the Bibb County Sheriff's Office issued a lookout for two white males in a green AMC Gremlin with Florida tags, but by then Machetti and Maree were already deep into Florida.

Ray Wilkes left Fairmont North and drove downtown to Hart's Mortuary. A number of law enforcement people were already there—Sheriff Jimmie Bloodworth, Robbie Johnson, Bill Freeman, Tommie Everidge, and Ray Stewart. Investigator Harry Harris had been called out and arrived close to the same time Wilkes did.

The victims' bodies had been brought to Hart's because the county had no morgue. Bibb County medical examiner Leonard Campbell would perform the autopsies there.

He began his work and Coroner A. R. King took photos of the procedures. Not surprisingly, Campbell concluded that both deaths were due to shotgun blasts. Ronny had been shot once in the chest, just above the heart, and once in the head. Both shots had been delivered from close up. He couldn't say which shot was fired first, but thought it was the one to the chest. Juanita had been shot only once and at a greater distance.

While the autopsies were being conducted, the officers began gathering bits and pieces of the story. Wilkes knew from his previous contact with Ronny Akins that he worked for Southern Natural Gas and that Ernest Doss was his immediate supervisor. He called Doss, woke him up, and, after breaking the news of the murders, asked if he could meet him at Hart's Mortuary.

"I guess so," Doss said, "but I don't know what help I can be."

"We'd just like to talk to you, find out more about Mr. Akins and his wife."

"Okay. I'll be there in about an hour."

Wilkes and two of his investigators interviewed Ernest Doss in one of the mortuary offices. Less than an hour later, they had the story of the bizarre attempt on Ronny Akins's life the previous October. Doss also related the conversation he'd had with Becky two weeks before when she'd called trying to get Ronny's new address.

At that moment, Rebecca Akins became their prime suspect, and they immediately began trying to locate her in Miami. Doing that wasn't as easy as they'd expected. The Miami area consisted of numerous municipalities, none of which seemed to communicate with the others. Wilkes realized they weren't going to find their suspect as quickly as they'd hoped.

Maree and Machetti arrived back in the North Miami area around 5:00 A.M. After dropping off the rental car, Tony transferred the clothing, briefcase, and guns to his Chevrolet. He drove Maree back to his vehicle, and then the two drove to the Machetti house.

They let themselves in the front door and turned on a light. No one was up, but Becky must have been awake. She emerged from the bedroom only a few seconds after they entered.

"Is everything all right?" she asked, going to Machetti for a quick embrace.

"Well, we're here," Maree told her.

He went to sit in an easy chair and Machetti dropped onto the sofa. Becky curled up on the floor beside him, her head on his knee.

By seven, the rest of the household was stirring. Becky and Tony had planned to go to 7:00 A.M. mass, but didn't make it. When Alan Barfield got up and went to the bathroom, he was surprised to see Tony Machetti, dressed in a white shirt and slacks, sitting on the sofa in the living room. He looked more like a businessman than someone who'd just returned from a fishing trip. Becky sat at his feet, looking up into his face, her arms propped on his knees. It was a strange tableau for seven in the morning.

The girls all were up and dressed within the next hour or so. Becky made coffee and they gathered in the kitchen. At one point, Tony told Alan, "I want to thank you for taking my family out to dinner last night."

All Alan could do was say, "You're welcome." After that, he knew that he couldn't ask Becky for a check.

The temperature was already over 80 degrees when Valerie and Alan left for Disney World minutes later. Soon after their departure, Becky and Tony walked out the door, headed to church.

"We're meeting with a Mafia lieutenant there," Becky told Maree. He didn't know whether to believe her or not.

Chapter 12

Most information gathered in murder investigations is the result of routine police work. By telephoning people who had known her, the Bibb County investigators learned that Becky's mother, Sara Zuber, lived in Athens. Ray Wilkes called her. He explained that Ronny and his new wife had been killed but gave no indication that her daughter was a suspect. During the conversation, he learned that Becky was now Mrs. John Eldon Smith. Mrs. Zuber also provided him with her address.

Wilkes phoned the North Miami Police Department and spoke with Lt. Albert Wooters. As it turned out, the address Wilkes had for Becky wasn't actually in the North Miami Beach jurisdiction, but when Lieutenant Wooters learned why Wilkes was calling, he agreed to go out to the house the next day to verify that Becky and her new husband lived there.

"It'd be real helpful to know where they were Saturday evening," Wilkes said.

"I'll ask," Wooters told him.

Meanwhile, Sara was growing concerned about Becky and the girls. She believed they had a right to know what had happened. And since she knew their home phone had been disconnected, Sara, too, called the North Miami Police Department. She told the man who answered that there'd been a death in the family and asked if they could have an officer go out to the house to deliver a message.

Only Maree, Vicki, and Vanessa were home. One of the girls noticed a police car in the driveway, and as the officer walked up to the house, Maree suddenly retreated into a bedroom. He stayed there as the officer told the girls that there had been a death in the family and their mother should call her mother in Athens.

"Who's dead?" Vanessa asked.

The officer didn't know.

"It's probably just some elderly relative," Vicki reassured her. "Probably someone we don't even know."

But when John and Vicki were alone again, he set the record straight.

"Your mother is going to give me $1,000. We can take that and get married."

"Why would she do that?" Vicki asked.

"Because Tony and I are the ones that knocked off your father."

She just stared at him, unable to make sense of what she was hearing. She hadn't taken Becky seriously the night before and now decided that John was must be playing a part in one of her mother's sick fantasies.

When Becky and Tony returned from church, Vicki told her mother about the visit from the police, so, shortly after noon, Becky, Tony, and John drove to Jefferson's Department Store to use the pay phone. Vicki and Vanessa stayed at home.

When the three adults returned, Maree announced he had things to do and drove back to his Hialeah apartment. He'd already decided to move and, after a short nap, began cleaning the place and packing up his things.

~~~
~~~

Becky's voice was calm and unemotional when she told Vanessa and Vicki that their father was dead. Vicki's mind whirled in shock. The make-believe game she'd thought her mother was playing was suddenly real. And John, she now knew, had told her the truth. Tony left the room without a word, but Becky had more to say. She warned them to keep quiet about what she'd said the night before.

"Don't act like you know anything about it. Tony doesn't know you know. Act like you're upset."

The last part was unnecessary. They *were* upset. They didn't have to pretend and their tears were real. And they had only each other to turn to for comfort.

Driving up to Disney World was exhilarating. Valerie and Alan were delighted to be off by themselves. During the three-hour trip, Alan worked hard to convince Valerie to go back to Georgia with him.

"We could get married as soon as we get there."

But she refused. She wouldn't even consider defying her mother.

Alan had been carefully watching his money since he'd been in Florida, wanting to be sure he had enough for Valerie's plane ticket in the event she'd agreed to go back to Macon with him. Now her refusal meant he had some extra funds for their day out. They did just about everything there was to do at the amusement park.

It was a nearly perfect day. When the young couple left Disney World around 9:00 that night, they drove home under clear skies and a full moon. It was a little after midnight when they arrived back at the Machetti house. As soon as they walked in the door, they knew something was wrong.

Vicki was with Vanessa in her little front bedroom. The

television was on, but they seemed to be paying little attention to it. The girls were subdued and their eyes were red and swollen. Val and Alan had an armful of souvenirs for them—Mickey Mouse hats, cups, and the like. They were anxious to give the girls their gifts, but Becky called them from the living room.

"Y'all get yourselves in here! Right now! Didn't you hear me calling you?"

They dropped the souvenirs on the bed and hurried into the living room where Becky sat alone. Since the door to the other bedroom was closed, they assumed that Tony had already gone to bed.

"Sit down," Becky ordered. She dabbed at her eyes with a tissue. But Alan, who'd witnessed this sort of performance before, didn't know if she was crying or only pretending to.

Valerie sat on the sofa but Alan continued to stand.

"Ronny is dead," Becky said, then told them what she'd been told by her mother.

Valerie cried, but, like Vicki, she had a hard time accepting Ronny's death as fact. Becky had lied so many times in the past. This time, however, her sisters were upset and her mother's voice had the ring of truth. With a chill, she realized that Becky must have been telling the truth Friday night.

Along with grief and anger at her mother, Valerie was overwhelmed by guilt. If her father had been killed, were she and her sisters responsible, too? She now thought that she should have called to warn him—but she hadn't known how to get in touch with him. And she'd had no way of knowing that this threat had been serious when so many others in the past had just been Becky's stories.

~~~
~~~

The murders of Ronny and Juanita Akins were front-page news in the *Macon Telegraph* Sunday morning, but few details were known and it was a small article well below the fold. The arrest of a highway sniper in California and the Macon mayor's race got more space.

At 11:00 that morning, Kelly Fite, microanalyst from the Georgia State Crime Laboratory, drove down from Atlanta. At Kitchens Garage on Jeffersonville Road, Terry Busbee was waiting. He unlocked the building, hooked his wrecker up to the Ford, and pulled it outside.

As the wrecker driver watched, Fite carefully examined the car in which Juanita Akins had been killed. He retrieved blood from the front seat and the left rear door and shotgun wadding from the floorboard on the driver's side. He also lifted latent prints from the interior and exterior of the car, finding four palm prints over the driver's door and one on the door itself above the handle. When Fite was finished, Busbee pulled the car back into the garage and once again locked the door.

Fite then drove across the river and into downtown Macon. It was a hot day and he'd been working in the sun for more than an hour. It was a relief to enter the cool interior of Hart's Mortuary. The staff greeted him cordially and led him to one of the embalming rooms where the victims were laid out on metal tables. Fite rolled the palms and prints of both Ronny and Juanita Akins and took scrapings from under their nails.

When he was done, he met with Ray Wilkes, who turned over all the evidence that had been gathered at the scene: a wooden stake, a pair of broken sunglasses, a cigarette butt, and an empty sixteen-ounce Schlitz beer can. Fite packed it all up and took it back to Atlanta that afternoon. Two days later, he delivered the latent prints to Louis H. Cuendet III, an expert in that field.

Ray Wilkes went to the Ronny and Juanita's apartment on Napier Avenue late Sunday afternoon. A hanging basket with a flourishing fern adorned the front porch. The apartment itself was clean and rather sparsely furnished. Only two items had been hung on the walls—a deer's head and a pendulum clock—and there were partially unpacked boxes in the bedroom.

It appeared that the residents had been about to eat when they left the house. Canned soup still waited in a pot on the stove and a loaf of bread sat on a kitchen counter. Ronny and Juanita had left home expecting to return quickly.

The mood in the Machetti house was subdued Monday morning. The girls just seemed to want to be alone with their thoughts. Even Alan couldn't keep Valerie engaged in conversation very long.

John Maree came over early, still concerned about the guns. While the young people were occupied in the kitchen, he, Becky, and Tony stood around the black bar in the living room and talked in low voices. Tony tried to reassure him, and, minutes later, the two men went outside. Tony opened the trunk of the Chevrolet and quickly moved the guns and briefcase to the trunk of the Opel.

"I'll take care of them today," he promised. "You don't have anything to worry about."

Maree was feeling a little better when they rejoined Becky in the living room. They were discussing how best to dispose of the guns when Alan Barfield walked into the room.

Fearful he might have heard the word "shotgun," Becky said, "We're talking about this drink they call a shotgun. Have you ever heard of it?"

Barfield was just young and inexperienced enough to not want to admit ignorance in this area. So he said, "Oh, sure. I've heard of the shotgun drink."

The other three exchanged looks and chuckled.

Tony left in the Opel a few minutes later. Soon afterwards, Alan and Valerie went to return the rental car. Becky had some errands to run with Vanessa and told them she'd pick them up later at the rental agency.

That left John alone again with Vicki. She was uneasy about Maree. Although, she didn't doubt now that her father was dead, she couldn't believe John had actually killed him. It was much more likely that Tony had done the killing and John had just been along for the ride. Besides, he was still her best bet for getting away from her mother.

When Lt. Albert Wooters arrived at 1191 Northeast 159th Street late Monday morning, the driveway was empty and no one answered his knock, so he went to several neighboring houses. He didn't find anyone who knew Becky or her family, but he did locate one woman who knew their landlord, a Marie Kenney. When Wooters contacted her by telephone, she verified that she rented the property to Mr. and Mrs. Smith.

Becky and Vanessa went to Jefferson's Department Store before picking up Valerie and Alan. Becky used the lobby phone. She called her mother first, but Sara had no new information except that the Bibb County authorities wanted to talk to her. Becky was never happy waiting for someone else to act, so she called the Bibb County Sheriff's Office herself. In short order, she was put in touch with Ray Wilkes.

The words poured out of her mouth as if a floodgate had opened. "First off, I called Athens. I am upset with...not you in particular...but everything in general. Last evening I talked to my mother on the telephone. I found my ex-husband was dead. But then I found my ex-husband had been shot dead in a field; that the body was in a funeral home in Calhoun, Georgia. I told my children, and this information was enough to satisfy me. But then my mother was saying that rumors were flying thick and fast that I was involved in the incident...you know the people around were talking and all."

"Now, just slow down, Mrs. Smith. I know you're upset and all," Wilkes interrupted, "but I need to get this information down. We're checking into this homicide. I understand you've remarried. When were you remarried?"

"I became Mrs. Rebecca Ann Smith on July 27, 1974. I would rather not even talk about what my name was before. I married John Eldon Smith. But...but let me ask you this...why are you asking me about my life?"

"When anyone is involved in and comes out of a distasteful divorce, where there is a lot of emotion, there is concern when robbery is not the motive in a death of this sort."

There was a tiny hesitation, then she asked, "Can I tell you what I think the motive is?"

"Let me just get some more information about you," Wilkes said, "then you can tell me about the motive. How old is John Smith?"

"He was born...he'll be forty-four. He's an executive with an insurance company in West Deptford, New Jersey."

"Is he still working there?"

"No, he left that firm and went to a company in Fort Lauderdale, Florida, and now is affiliated with Lloyds of

London."

Wilkes asked for her phone number and Becky said she was calling from a pay phone.

"When were you last in Macon?"

"Probably late in June. I came up and brought my furniture back. I moved my things myself in a Ryder truck.

"Let me tell you this, Alan Luther Barfield is going with my middle daughter. He lives in Macon. He flew down...my daughter Valerie and he are engaged. My three children are with me. And my children and Alan and I have been together since Friday night."

Becky then described the weekend they'd spent.

"Was your husband there?" Wilkes asked.

"No, he was not there."

Wilkes asked her to contact Lieutenant Wooters and provided his phone number. She said she would.

"About my mother," Becky said. "She is very sick. She was so upset she started hemorrhaging and everything. You understand she doesn't need to be...."

"I understand. Can you tell me what you think happened to Ronny?"

"Oh, yes. Being married to that man was the most awful thing...the worst years I have ever spent. He began to take drugs.... The last eighteen months he began to bring drugs in from Atlanta. He was bringing a kilo or half of drugs...an undetermined quantity of heroin. He told me he'd emptied them on a roadside once during a road check. He had been told to do this...they told him to do it like this. He told me then that they didn't believe him and that he owed them $8,000."

Wilkes pointed out that that quantity of heroin would be worth many times that amount of money, but Becky didn't even acknowledge his words, so eager was she to get her own story out.

"It was a nightmare," she continued, "one I didn't think I'd wake up from. I'd been sick since April when he came by last. I told him he'd better not fall behind on his payments. When I married him he dealt in drugs. I know you're sitting there wondering why I didn't go to the police. At this point I didn't care anymore about anything. He brought heroin and cocaine. The only name I can give you that he said was Darrow.

"Ronny overdosed four times the past summer when I was there. I called an ambulance. They took him to T-7. Dr. Tom Hall was his doctor. He told me Ronny was paranoid and schizophrenic and so on. Chlorol hydrates, Seconal, and Nembutol, I think he called them."

She sounded strangely unsure about the names of the drugs for a woman who'd studied nursing. "Well," Wilkes said, "chloral hydrates are knock-out pills."

"Yes, well, that's what he was taking."

Wilkes next asked if she knew anything about a Gremlin.

"No, Ronny only talked about this green car. He used to say 'green for go.' No, wait forget that...forget about the green buggy. I'm remembering this as I go along. He said Darrow had bought a new car. It was a white Volkswagon.

"He had other contacts. One was a one-armed painter named K. P. Carroll. He was homosexual, too. You probably know about him. He dealt with him."

"Mrs. Smith, that's a serious statement. Do you have any proof of this relationship Carroll and your husband had?"

"Why, yes, I came home one day and found them in bed together. You can't get much better proof than...and he dealt drugs with him, too."

Wilkes had heard nothing like that from all the other people he and his staff had interviewed. He doubted that, along with everything else this woman was telling him.

He finally ended the conversation by telling her he would have Lieutenant Wooters come to her house to take a written statement.

Later on in the afternoon, Maree and Vicki left the 159th Street house, bound for Hialeah, where they would finish cleaning his apartment. As they were getting into his car, another vehicle pulled into the drive. The American-made sedan with no chrome or decoration was immediately identifiable as an unmarked police vehicle. Two men got out. One of them was Albert Wooters of the North Miami Police Department, back again at Wilkes's request to interview Rebecca and John Eldon Smith about their whereabouts on August 31.

Eldon wasn't home, and Becky told the detectives he was working at his office, which seemed curious since it was Labor Day. Becky invited them in, and, at Wooters's prompting, told them how she'd spent the weekend. Her account of Saturday afternoon and evening was especially detailed.

At 12:15, she said, they left the house, got gas, and took Valerie and Alan—whom she described as her "son-in-law"—to pick up a rental car on Collins Avenue. They ate lunch at McDonald's at 2:00 and then went shopping. At 4:00 P.M. she and Vicki were at Judy Lynn's Bridal Shop, where they returned two evening bags that had been used in Becky's wedding. Becky even remembered the names of the clerks they'd dealt with. They returned home, changed clothes, and went swimming with Alan, Valerie, and Vanessa in the pool at the Aztec Motel.

Finally, she described their dinner at the Black Angus and the resulting altercation with the waitress. Wooters reflected that Becky and her party would certainly be remembered at the restaurant.

Becky explained they'd gotten home from dinner at 9:30, talked, and listened to the stereo. At 11:00, Dr. Salvatore Genori came to see Vicki and brought her a prescription. Her daughter, she told the detectives, had recently been hospitalized. The doctor stayed for an hour.

"Where was your husband?"

"He was on a fishing trip. He got home at five after one that morning."

Chapter 13

Luther and Betty Barfield had read the newspaper accounts of Ronny and Juanita Akins's murders and had seen the story on the television news. They knew their son occasionally spent time with Ronny and immediately called him, but there was no answer at Alan's apartment. At first they weren't concerned, but after calling for two days, they began to worry.

Phone calls to his friends didn't help. No one seemed to know where Alan was. They went to his apartment but found no sign of him there. Even though it was a farfetched idea and there'd been no mention of a third victim, the couple couldn't dismiss the nagging fear that Alan might have been with the murdered couple and come to harm himself.

When Alan called them from Florida Monday afternoon, they were very relieved. He assured them he was fine and would see them the next day.

Alan's flight was scheduled for the middle of the night. He and Valerie stayed at the house that afternoon and evening, just passing time until they would leave for the airport. By sunset, John Maree had joined them. No one was really relaxed. Becky couldn't sit still. She paced around the house, looking outside every few minutes, evidently worried about Tony. He'd left that morning and she expected him home by dark.

At one point, Vicki followed her mother into the kitchen.

"Where's Tony?"

"He's been to the Everglades to get rid of the guns."

Vicki felt suddenly sick but knew better than to say anything to Becky. She absorbed the information in silence. More than ever now, she knew she had to get away from her mother. She just wasn't sure how she was going to do it.

Valerie tried to stay awake, but just before 11:00 she gave in to sleep and went on to bed. A little later, there was a rattling at the front door.

"Who do you think that could be?" Becky asked. The nervousness in her voice made them all jittery as the rattling came again.

Alan waited a moment, looking at the others, then went to open the door. He stepped outside and flipped on the porch light just as Tony Machetti came around the corner of the house.

"Couldn't find my key," he explained to them. "I was looking for another way in."

Alan, Tony, Becky, John, and Vicki stayed up, waiting as the minutes passed. Alan tried to nap on the couch but wasn't able to fall asleep. Finally, around 2:00 A.M., it was time to go.

Vicki and John drove Alan to the airport, dropping him outside the terminal. His flight was on time and the plane took off from Miami just before 3:00.

Alan was in Atlanta before the sun rose on Tuesday morning, but it was after seven when he got back to Macon. He went straight to his parents' house. The Barfields were just getting up when he arrived.

Over coffee, he told them what had happened in Miami, and they related what they'd heard on the radio about the murders, including the fact that the police were looking for a green Gremlin with Florida tags.

"Ray Wilkes down at the sheriff's office wants to talk to you," his dad said.

Alan went to the phone that minute and called Wilkes.

"Can you come down to the courthouse now and talk to us?" the chief deputy asked him.

"Yes, sir. I'm on my way."

Alan called his employer and explained why he'd be late to work then drove downtown to Mulberry Street. There were lines of people waiting to vote when he got there, and he remembered that Tuesday was primary day.

At that time, the Republican Party had almost no presence in Georgia. Although they put up candidates for some state offices, they never won. So whichever Democratic candidates won the primary elections, they were assured of victory in the November general election. In 1974, Lester Maddox was waging a bitter campaign against George Busbee for the Democratic nomination for governor. There was also a hotly contested race in Macon for mayor, with incumbent Ronnie Thompson pitted against Harold Dye. Thompson, who'd been mayor since 1967, had gained national attention with his hard stance against crime and the unrest due to simmering race relations. He'd issued submachine guns to the police, along with "shoot to kill" orders. He'd even driven a tank into a playground and promised a vacation trip to any officer who shot and killed an armed robber.

Alan made his way through the crowd to the sheriff's office on the first floor of the courthouse. There, he met with investigators Robbie Johnson and Bill Freeman, who guided him through an account of his weekend with Becky Machetti and her family.

During the telling of the story, Barfield mentioned a man named John. The detectives were immediately interested.

"Describe him," Johnson said. "What does he look like?"

"Oh, John's about five foot nine or ten, I guess. He's got a moustache, and his hair is dark and about the same length as mine."

"How old would he be?"

"He's older than I am, I know that. He must be about twenty-eight or something like that. He's just kind of a friend of the family. They met him when they moved down there. He helped find this house they are living in now."

"What kind of car does he have?"

Barfield, as interested in cars as most young men, didn't hesitate. "He's got a Charger—about a '68 or '69 Dodge Charger. Blue with a black top. He lives in Fort Myers, I believe. He just comes over there every once in a while. Him and Vicki were the ones who took me to the airport."

"But you don't know his last name?"

"I'm trying to think what his last name is. I have it written down at the house in one of Valerie's letters. I'll call you when I find it. Seems like it's John Burry or something. I'm not sure."

As he was leaving, Freeman asked Alan, "So Tony wasn't there hardly any the whole weekend?"

"No, Tony wasn't there hardly at all, like I say." Alan thought he knew what the detectives were thinking. "But I don't think Tony, I don't know...I don't think Tony would have come up here and done it and gone back. He just don't hit me as the kind of guy...I don't know much about him. He's just small, he's not as tall as I am. He's baldheaded for the most part. He's got a little hair on him. Got a moustache and he's just kind of a small-framed guy, just kind of quiet."

After signing his statement, Alan went on to work. Then a couple of hours later, he called Investigator Johnson.

"It just came to me," he said. "I think the guy's name is John Marll or either Marle." He also provided the telephone number of the pay phone at Jefferson's Department Store.

~~~

Tuesday was a hot day in Macon, with the temperature soaring into the 90s by noon. Two of Wilkes's investigators spoke further with the people at Southern Natural Gas, and Ernest Doss repeated what he'd told Wilkes about his phone conversation with Becky. By checking his records, he was able to tell them that the conversation in which Becky had tried to learn Ronny's new address had taken place on August 12.

Other odd details about Ronny and Becky's marriage surfaced. A few days before Ronny's "overdose," he'd come to work with scratches on his face. When asked about it, he said a limb in the yard did it, but they'd all suspected his wife had been responsible. The detectives also learned that Becky had once told pipeline supervisor Herman Swindle that Ronny had lung cancer.

During interviews with his fellow workers, the officers learned nothing to discredit Ronny Akins. By all accounts he was a friendly, hard-working man who did a good job for Southern Natural Gas. On his own time he installed television antennae for Pinkerton Television.

Lieutenant Wooters had said he'd be back to see Tony. Becky was surprised by the attention they were getting from the police. She'd believed that, with her solid alibi for Saturday afternoon and evening, she and Tony would be in the clear. But now she felt she needed to make some preparations for the officer's return.

Becky told Valerie and Vicki that they had better not say anything about what she'd told them. She also ordered them to say, if asked, that Tony and John got back around 1:05 in the morning. They told her they would. They were nervous
~~~

about upsetting her in any way. If she could get away with killing their father, they reasoned, she could get rid of them as well.

Detective Wooters finally managed to interview Tony, or John Eldon Smith, as the investigator insisted on calling him, on Tuesday. Tony tried to explain that his name change to Anthony Machetti would be final on October 14 and that it was being handled in Gloucester County, New Jersey, but Wooters didn't seem to care.

The questions Detective Wooters asked were as predictable as Tony's answers, at least to a point. No, he didn't have a criminal record, and he worked for the Hull Insurance Agency in Fort Lauderdale.

Tony, Maree, and Becky had agreed what their story would be weeks before. But for some reason, when Wooters asked about his whereabouts the previous weekend, Tony abandoned the story of the fishing trip. Instead, he told the officer that he and Maree had just started doing some after-hours work for a New Jersey firm called Hessian Construction.

"They specialize in building additions," Tony said. "So Friday we left for Naples about 7:00."

"What did you do there?"

Tony shrugged. "Looked around. Then we went on to Fort Myers and looked around some more. It was mostly for orientation and locating sales for the new business venture."

Tony said they'd done the same thing in Tampa, Pensacola, and Tallahassee, then returned home.

"We got here about one o'clock Sunday morning."

Maree went home, Tony told the lieutenant, and he went to bed.

He said that he and Becky had learned about her ex-husband's death Sunday afternoon when they called her mother.

"Then we went back home and hung around till about 1:00 P.M."

After that, he said, he, Becky, Vicki, and Vanessa rode down to the Keys and got back around 9:00 that night.

"So you stayed home after that?"

"No, the news about the girls' father being killed kind of put a damper on the family, so I went for a ride."

"What time did you get back?"

"Don't know."

Wooters next asked, "Where were you yesterday? On Monday?"

"Why?" Tony asked with an edge to his voice. "Was anyone killed on Monday?"

"Not that I know of."

"Then it isn't necessary for you to know what I did on Monday."

Wooters chose not to push that, trying instead to find some way to verify Tony's story of the business trip.

"Did you see anyone you knew when you were out of town?"

"Only John."

"Where did you stay? Did you pay for gas or anything with a credit card?"

"No, we paid cash for everything. And we slept in the car. We just grabbed a quick sandwich for lunch."

After a while, Wooters gave up trying to get more details. Back at his office, the lieutenant called Ray Wilkes and related what he'd gotten from Machetti.

Wilkes thanked him, hung up the phone, and sat back to consider what Wooters had told him. Then he pulled out some maps and plotted a course that would have taken the men from Miami to Naples to Fort Myers, Tampa, Pensacola, and Tallahassee, and then back to Miami. He then compared that mileage against the mileage for a round trip from Miami to Macon. The distances were very close to the same.

Chapter 14

Overnight, a cold front moved through Georgia, and the state's citizens woke Wednesday morning to showers, cloudy skies, and temperatures in the low 80s—and a new governor. George Busbee had won by a landslide. The race for mayor of Macon, however, was still too close to call. It wouldn't be until the next day that Ronnie Thompson was declared the winner by a scant 305 votes.

At 3:00 that afternoon, a double funeral service was held at the Johnson Street Baptist Church in Athens. Immediately after the service, the bodies of Ronny and Juanita Akins were transported by Thomas Funeral Home to Juanita's hometown of Calhoun. The following day, a second service was held at Belmont Baptist Church, conducted by the Rev. John Allen and the Rev. Dewey Braden. Gordon County teachers and educators who had worked closely with Juanita were the honorary escort.

Ronny's daughters had not attended either service. Soon after learning about their father's death, the girls had asked if they could go to his funeral, but Becky wouldn't even consider it. The subject wasn't raised again.

On Thursday, Ray Wilkes drove to the Georgia mountain town of Calhoun, some 150 miles northwest of Macon, and met with some of Juanita Akins's family and friends. He found nothing that could have possibly been a reason for murder.

But the next day, he did discover a motive—a financial one—when he spoke by phone with Cecil R. McInnis, the assistant vice president of personnel for Southern Natural Gas in Birmingham. McInnis explained that the face value of Ronny Akins's group life insurance was $53,000, $29,000 of which would go to his parents, Raymond and Thelma Akins. The rest would be dispersed to his children.

"Ronny changed beneficiaries in February," McInnis said. "Before that, the beneficiary was his wife, Rebecca." Wilkes heard a rustle of papers, then the other man continued. "And there was also a group accidental death policy for $500. Hmm, he must have forgotten about that one because Rebecca Akins was still the beneficiary."

"Would that have covered murder?"

"I am told the insurance company considers it an accidental death."

As Wilkes digested that information, McInnis asked, "Are you interested in stock and the stock purchase plan?"

"Yes, sir."

"Okay. At the end of July 1974, he had fifty shares of Southern Natural Resources stock in the employee stock purchase plan. Southern Natural Gas is a subsidiary of Southern Natural Resources. Rebecca A. Akins is the main beneficiary as of 8/6/69."

"What is the value of that?" Wilkes asked.

"Well, the market value, I think it's somewhere around $30 a share. It's on the New York Stock Exchange."

"About $1,500?"

"Yeah, I guess so, depending on what the market does."

Wilkes learned there would also be a Social Security survivor benefit to be paid to the children—$113 a piece each month—until they were eighteen or, if full-time students, twenty-three.

"Mr. McInnis, has anyone else called you about the insurance?"

"No, not yet."

"Let me ask you this. How long can we hold up on payment of this?"

"Well, these are insurance matters. The procedure is that we would send claim forms based on instructions from the insurance company, and they would come back through here and then be presented to the insurance company. As far as I know, no claim forms have been sent out to anybody. My guess is that the insurance company is not going to hasten to pay any claim."

Wilkes thought he saw an advantage here. "We would appreciate any delay. We have strong suspicions in this thing, and I would like to see them hold as much as they can to keep this thing back. Do you know what I mean?"

"Right."

That afternoon, Wilkes met with his investigators and shared the insurance information with them. He also told them about his trip to Calhoun to learn what he could about Juanita Knight Akins.

"She had a spotless character," he reported. "She came from a good family and only had one boyfriend before Akins."

The chief deputy had recorded his telephone conversation with Becky Machetti, and he now passed copies of the transcript around the table. Freeman and Johnson shared the details of Alan Barfield's weekend in Florida. Finally, they discussed whether or not they had enough to charge anyone, but everyone knew they didn't. The possibility of putting a wiretap on the pay phone nearest the Machetti residence was suggested, but no decision was made.

The expected insurance money didn't come as quickly as Becky had hoped, and their financial situation worsened. She found a job as a receptionist in a doctor's office, and Tony took a second job as a security guard.

In the week after the murders, Becky and Tony spoke occasionally about the crime, sometimes in the presence of one or more of the girls. She urged Tony to figure out a way to change his fingerprints "just in case you made a mistake." Becky thought they wouldn't be able to take fingerprints if his hands were cut and bandaged, so at her direction, Tony cut up his fingers and hands on an underwater reef. He wore bandages for over a week, and Becky seemed satisfied that he'd accomplished their goal.

John and Vicki saw each other a few times that week. And in the beginning he seemed to want to talk about the crime, but his swagger the day after the murders had been replaced by a combination of guilt and anger.

"I thought I was only supposed to go up there to drive," he said one evening. "I didn't know I had to do the actual work. Tony chickened out." He told her how Ronny had had his hands on the car and how the woman had gone for the radio. "I had to haul off and hit her on the head because she started talking on that radio."

But he never gave Vicki any details of the actual shootings.

At the end of the week, John moved back into his ex-wife's house in Fort Myers. Although Becky still hadn't paid him the money she'd promised, he remained on good terms with the Machettis.

A week after he and Tony killed Ronny and Juanita Akins, Maree and his thirteen-year-old son drove to the Machetti home in North Miami. Their visit lasted several hours, but Becky never brought up the money he was owed, and John was disappointed. He could have used some extra cash to take his boy shopping for school clothes.

That weekend, Hurricane Carmen was churning in the Gulf of Mexico. No one knew exactly where it might make landfall, and people in all the coastal states were on alert, nervously checking the news broadcasts for indications of danger. When it finally turned inland in southern Louisiana, the Machettis joined their fellow Floridians in a big sigh of relief.

Sometimes, when they were sure they were alone, Valerie and Vicki talked about the killings. In addition to grieving for their father, they were growing more and more afraid of their mother. They now knew she was capable of making good on any threat. If she threatened to kill them, as she had in the past, she just might do it. They tried to do exactly as she wished, working hard to give her no reason to get upset with them.

The police followed one lead after another. On Monday, September 9, Louis Cuendet compared the palm prints Kelly Fite had taken from Ronny Akins's car with those of the victims. Four of the prints matched Ronny's and Juanita's hands, but the one from the driver's door matched neither.

When the Bibb County investigators received the report from the crime lab later that day, they finally had something concrete—a piece of real physical evidence. Now all they needed was a suspect's print to compare with what they had.

As expected, the court in New Jersey issued a final judgment on September 13 and advised John Eldon Smith by mail that he would be authorized to legally use the name Anthony

Machetti after the 14th of October. Since he was already calling himself that, the legal notification meant little to Tony.

The following Sunday, John Maree wrote Becky a letter demanding payment. It read:

> "Dear Becky,
>
> "Hi! How is every little thing going with you and yours? Things here are moving along. I had to take another test for life insurance agent. Also got another job to help things along. All these jobs or positions (whatever you want to call them) don't leave me with much time for myself.
>
> "I will be visiting you on Saturday, September 21, and I will expect to receive payment for the recent bit of work for your friend. I really do need this money. During all my previous experiences with these people, work was paid for in <u>advance</u>! Don't let me down on this request for I will hold you <u>responsible</u>!"
>
> "Yours truly, John Maree."

Becky wrote a letter that week as well. Hers was sent to A. R. King, the Bibb County coroner, and stated that she had twice requested her husband's death certificate, which was necessary for filing any insurance claim:

"I am now demanding it! I am the mother of his only three children who not only need clothes for school but other essentials also."

Maree was as good as his word. On the 21st of September, he drove to North Miami to see Vicki and Becky. Holding a bouquet of flowers, he rang the bell. Perhaps he expected to be welcomed at the house, but Becky was angry when she opened the door. She had, she told him, already planned an outing for her and the girls that day.

"So you'll just have to go."

Before she could close the door, Vicki joined Maree on the porch.

"I'd rather spend the day with John," she told her mother.

That sent Becky into a rage. Although she must have known of the romantic involvement between Vicki and John, she now acted as if she hadn't. She ordered Maree to leave and told him he wasn't allowed to see her daughter anymore.

But John wasn't leaving without a fight. "I want my money. I wrote you a letter," he shouted, as if that explained everything. "I want my money or I'm going to tell 'em!"

Becky's response was a burst of profanity. She jerked Vicki back inside the house and slammed the door in Maree's face. After pounding his fist on the door for several minutes to no avail, he left.

The blowup between Becky and Maree happened on a Saturday afternoon. The following Tuesday, Vicki wrote to Alan Barfield and complained about her mother's treatment of her. "I am going to see John whether she knows it or not. I told her that if she hurt him in any way, she was going to regret it. I told her that I would come stay with you unless she cooled off. I'm telling you, Alan, she's not going to ruin my life."

Becky was growing more and more concerned about the situation with the insurance. She'd called Ronny's employers several times without getting a satisfactory reply. On September 22, she wrote to the Protective Life Insurance Company, asking when she would receive payment.

"As the guardian and mother of the late Joseph Ronald Akins' [*sic*] children I would like to inquire into his life insurance. Each of my children desire to learn of the beneficiaries of said policy and what your company is doing in reference to the dispensation of the policy. I am in possession of legal documents which state how some of the money must go."

Bibb County chief investigator Harry Harris contacted Special Agent Robert Bates of the Florida Department of Criminal Law Enforcement on the last day of September. He gave a brief explanation of the Akins case and requested help. Primarily, he told Bates, they wanted to determine Becky and Tony Machetti's activities on August 30, 31, and September 1.

"And we really need their prints."

Bates agreed to do what he could.

When Robert Bates and his partner, Larry Bieltz, drove out to the Machetti house later that day, only the girls were home. The two officers left word with them, asking that Tony and Becky come in to make a statement concerning the weekend of August 31st.

Becky wasn't a happy woman right then. Nothing seemed to be going as she'd planned. No insurance money had come in and the bills kept mounting up. Tony had just been fired, and they received an eviction notice for failure to pay their rent. Now she had to go in and talk to the police again.

Late that afternoon, Becky arrived alone at the Department of Criminal Law Enforcement Miami field office to meet with Bates and Bieltz. She showed no sign of nervousness as she took a seat in the office and calmly met the eyes of both men.

"We'd hoped to interview you and your husband," Bates said.

"Tony had to work," she explained, "but I can tell you whatever you need to know."

Bieltz asked if she knew of anyone who might want to see her ex-husband dead. In answering, Becky took the opportunity to describe Ronny Akins as an alcoholic, drug-using homosexual.

"He was involved with drug dealers and people like that. I'm not surprised one of them killed him."

Then, to further vilify the man, she added that Ronny had once attempted to rape her daughter Valerie.

"Did you report that to the police?" Bates asked.

"No. I was too ashamed to let anyone know."

The officers chose not to follow up on that statement. Instead, they asked how she'd spent her time during the Labor Day weekend, and Becky gave a detailed account of those three days. She was, however, less specific about her husband. She said Tony had left for work on Friday and she hadn't seen him again until very early Sunday morning.

"Did you know your husband was planning a trip?"

"He mentioned going on a fishing trip with John Maree. He's a friend who lives in Fort Myers."

She didn't give him an exact time her husband came home late Saturday night, but did add another detail. "His clothes had a fishy smell to them."

"Does your husband own a 12-gauge shotgun?" was the last question Bates asked her.

"Not to my knowledge."

Listed from top to bottom, Victoria Akins, Valerie Akins, and Vanessa Akins, 1963.

Courtesy Valerie Akins

Ronald Akins with Victoria, Valerie, and Vanessa Akins, 1964.

Courtesy Valerie Akins

York Place house.
Courtesy Valerie Akins

Rental house on Hartley Bridge Road, Macon, Georgia.
Courtesy Valerie Akins

Valerie Akins, 1972.

Courtesy Valerie Akins

Fulton Drive house, Macon, Georgia.

Courtesy Valerie Akins

Valerie, Victoria, and Vanessa Akins, 1974.

Courtesy Valerie Akins

Ronald Akins, 1974.

Courtesy Valerie Akins

Juanita Knight, 1974.

Courtesy Valerie Akins

1973 Gremlin rented by Machetti and Maree.

Courtesy Bibb County District Attorney's Office

Ronald Akins's car recovered from the crime scene.

Courtesy Bibb County District Attorney's Office

PaceCar service station, Jennings, Florida.

Courtesy Bibb County District Attorney's Office

John Maree, 1974.

Courtesy Bibb County District Attorney's Office

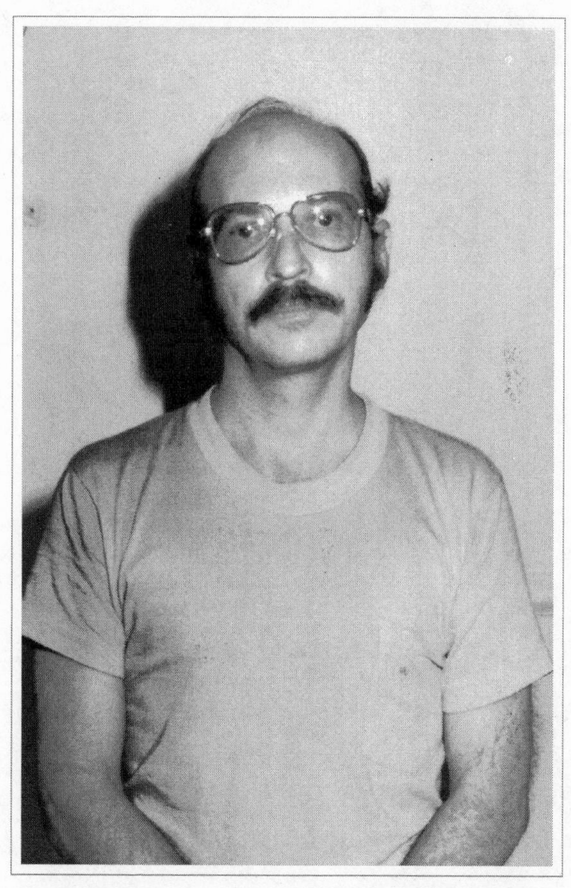

John Eldon Smith (aka Anthony Machetti), 1974.

Courtesy Bibb County District Attorney's Office

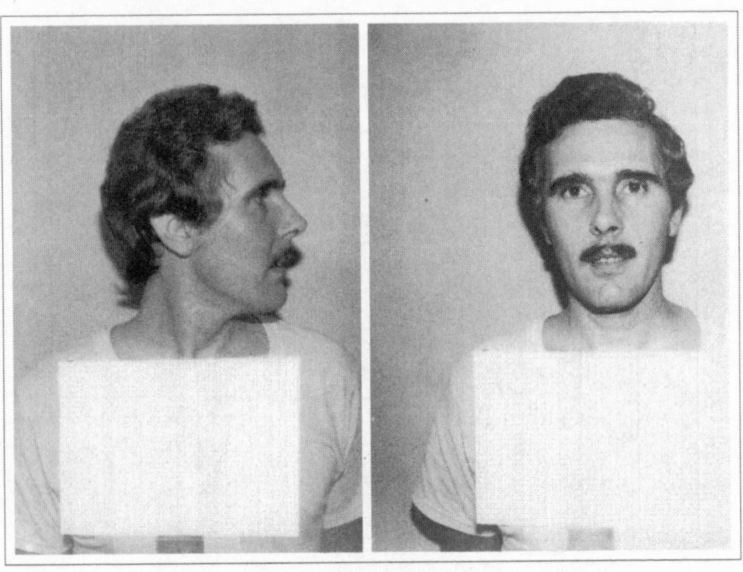

John Maree arrest photo, 1974.

Courtesy Bibb County District Attorney's Office

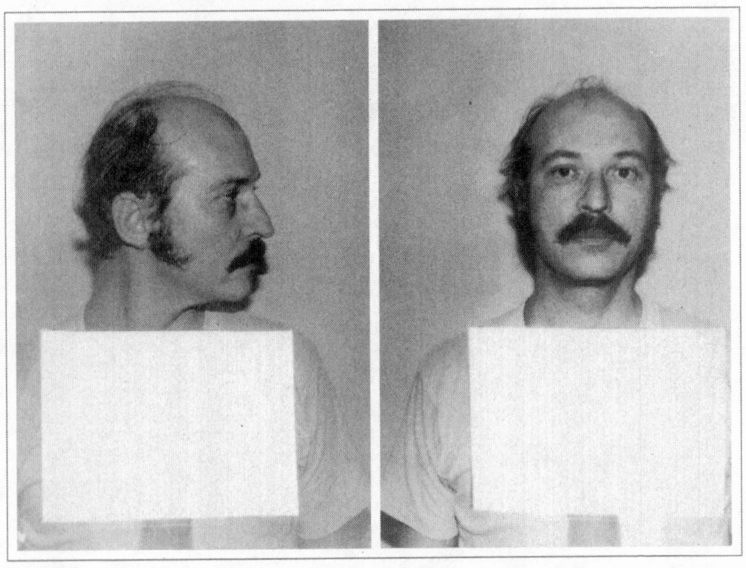

John Eldon Smith (aka Anthony Machetti) arrest photo, 1974.

Courtesy Bibb County District Attorney's Office

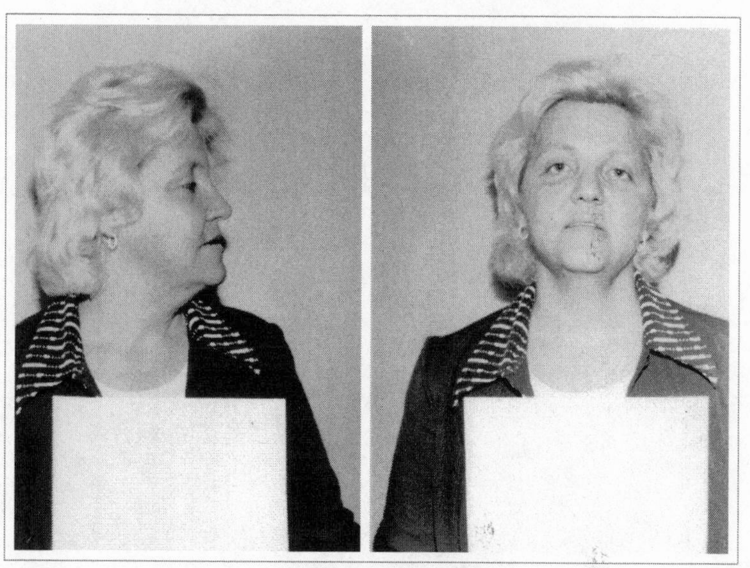

Rebecca Akins Smith (aka Rebecca Machetti) arrest photo, 1974.

Courtesy Bibb County District Attorney's Office

Valerie Akins, 1976.
Courtesy Valerie Akins

Vanessa Akins, 1976.
Courtesy Valerie Akins

Victoria Akins, 1978.

Courtesy Valerie Akins

Rebecca Akins Smith (aka Rebecca Machetti), photo taken while in custody, circa 1980.

Courtesy Valerie Akins

Rebecca Akins Smith (aka Rebecca Machetti) during the trial.

Source unknown

Chapter 15

Tony Machetti had avoided talking to the police as long as he could. Finally, on October 1, he went to the DCLE office and met with the same men who'd interviewed Becky the day before. In response to their questions, he described his and Maree's trip as a combination fishing and business trip.

In this version, Machetti said he'd met Maree on Friday afternoon at Hull Insurance Company in Fort Lauderdale. Then, they went back to the Machetti home, where he changed clothes and picked up fishing equipment.

"We went to Naples first, I think. Or maybe it was Fort Myers—I'm not exactly sure which cities we traveled through. I'm not all that familiar with Florida."

"Where did you fish?" Bieltz asked.

"We never really did any fishing—just didn't get around to it."

As Lieutenant Wooters had several days before, Bates asked if they'd used credit cards during the trip.

"No. We paid cash for food and gas."

"Where did you spend Friday night?"

Tony shrugged. "We didn't stop at a motel, just didn't feel like it. We slept in the car when we were tired. But most of the time we drove around looking for location sites. I did most of the driving."

"How did you look at those sites when it was dark?" Bates asked.

Machetti didn't make a response.

Bieltz asked if he'd ever been to Georgia.

"No, never."

"Do you own a shotgun?"

"Not now. I used to have several guns, but I sold them two years ago when I gave up hunting."

Then Bieltz got to the real reason they'd wanted Tony to come into the office. "Would you be willing to let us take your fingerprints?"

"Absolutely not. I don't feel I have to do any more than I've already done. I'm tired of being harassed by the police." Tony got to his feet and started toward the door. But he stopped before leaving, turned back to face the two agents, and asked a question. "Do you know how to get death certificates from Georgia?"

Bates and Bieltz exchanged a glance.

"Maybe you should contact the medical examiner's office up there."

Bibb County chief investigator Harry Harris and Assistant District Attorney Walker Johnson arrived in Miami on Wednesday, October 2. The next morning, they met with Bieltz and Bates, who brought them up-to-date on the Machetti interviews. While the others listened, Larry Bieltz called the number they had for John Maree in Fort Myers.

Bieltz identified himself to the woman who answered and asked for John.

"He's not here right now," the woman said. "I'm Wendy Maree, John's wife."

"His wife? I thought he was divorced."

"We've been separated, but we're trying to work things out."

Bieltz left his number, and about noon Maree called him back. When he heard they wanted to talk to him, Maree volunteered to see them that afternoon, but Bieltz scheduled a meeting with him on Friday at the Sheraton Motor Inn in Fort Myers. The investigators had a more pressing problem to deal with before they investigated John Maree.

The next morning, the two Florida special agents, Harris and Johnson, met with Assistant State's Attorney Ira Dubitsky and explained that Tony Machetti had refused to allow them to print or photograph him. Dubitsky listened to their story and, in less than an hour, obtained a witness subpoena.

The subpoena was served on Machetti that afternoon. Promptly at 9:30 the next morning, Tony appeared at the State's Attorney's Office. Ira Dubitsky welcomed him and invited him to have a seat. The office was a bit crowded with Bates, Bieltz, Johnson, and Harris all present, along with a court reporter who'd been brought in to record the proceedings.

"Mr. Smith," Dubitsky began, "I subpoenaed you here. I am assisting these other individuals in an investigation arising from an incident in Georgia. I have subpoenaed you not to speak to you, but because I want to take a sample of your finger and palm prints. I am not going to be speaking to you, to have you give any testimony. Naturally, in my own mind that satisfies me that you're not entitled to an attorney since I have the absolute right to take your finger and palm prints.

"If you wish to, you may telephone an attorney and question an attorney on this. I am more than willing to do so if you wish to. And if you don't wish to give me a set of fingerprints, I will be glad to go downstairs to where the judges are and let you make inquiry of them pertaining to what your rights are. I don't know what your desires are in this particular situation, but that would be what the situation is."

"Let's save a lot of time and take the prints," Tony said, his voice free of emotion.

"Well, I don't want you to do so unless you're satisfied that..."

He sighed impatiently. "I am satisfied on your word that it is legal."

Dubitsky got to his feet. "All right, sir. What we'll do, then, is go across the street to the Public Safety Department where the fingerprinting facilities are. It will take all of five minutes, then you can go away out of here."

"Fine. Thank you."

On Friday, Bates and Bieltz drove Harry Harris and Walker Johnson to Fort Myers, where the four men met with John Maree in the lobby of the Sheraton Motor Inn. John seemed nervous, but he smiled a lot and shook everyone's hand. Then the lawmen asked about the trip he'd taken with Tony Machetti.

"Well, we'd originally planned to go to Lake Okeechobee to go fishing."

"Is that what you did?" Johnson asked.

"No, we decided to make it a business and fishing trip." As he elaborated on the events of that Labor Day weekend, Maree grew a bit critical of his companion. "We never did any fishing. Tony's about as much a fisherman as the man in the moon."

Maree contradicted Machetti, saying that *he* drove most of the time. "Tony took along four or five six-packs and a couple of bottles of wine. He did a lot of drinking during the trip—he's got a capacity for the stuff."

Harris delved a bit deeper into the Machettis' lives, and Maree told him he didn't think Tony was happy with his marriage.

"How do you know that?"

"Well, he doesn't seem to be, and he told me, 'Boy, I really got myself into one this time.'"

"Did you see anyone you knew during this trip? Where did you spend the night?" Bates asked.

"No, we didn't see anybody. We ate in the car because Tony was too drunk to be seen in public." His voice took on a bragging note. "And I never slept on the trip. I enjoy driving. I never sleep on a trip."

Finally, they asked if he had any objection to having his prints taken.

"None at all."

They went immediately to the Lee County jail, where Maree's palm and fingerprints were taken. While they were there, he also agreed to be photographed.

The trip to Florida had produced prints and photos of the two men who were closest to Becky Machetti and were therefore suspects in the eyes of Bibb County law enforcement. Now that the officers had something to work with, they wasted no time getting their news to the DA's office.

Only a few days later, Ann and Bobby McElroy were called into the District Attorney's Office to meet with Don Thompson and Fred Hasty. The husband and wife were taken to separate rooms, where each was shown a fifteen-photo lineup. The pictures were handed to Ann in one stack. She took her time examining each one and finally set three of them aside. She stared at those for another long minute, and then chose one and handed it to Don Thompson.

"That's him."

It was the photo of John Maree.

"And how do you know him?" Thompson asked.

"He's the man I saw driving the Gremlin out of the area

below our house the night those people were shot."

A few minutes later, Bobby McElroy identified the same picture as the man who'd driven the green Gremlin.

Although the Georgia investigators had returned home, the Florida Department of Law Enforcement agents were still working on the case. On October 10, Larry Bieltz went to the Hull Insurance Company, where he interviewed the owner, Richard Hull, and the personnel manager, Leonard R. Layton.

The two men told him that Tony Machetti, whom they still knew as Eldon Smith, contacted them around the first of August. After a couple of lunch meetings and a check of his background, Hull hired him on August 19. However, he worked for the company only six weeks before he was fired. His last day of employment was September 30.

"He couldn't cut it," Layton told Bieltz. "He was unproductive, kept to himself, and didn't associate with anyone around the office. We also caught him in a couple of lies."

Chapter 16

The suspects' palm prints were sent off to the Georgia State Crime Lab. There, print expert Louis Cuendet compared them to the unidentified print that had been found on Ronny Akins's car door. On October 11, he telephoned Harry Harris.

"I made a positive on your prints."

"Who?" Harris asked.

"John Maree."

In Washington, the trial of Watergate conspirators was underway. But at the Bibb County Sheriff's Office, the big news was the fingerprint match.

Briefings on the case were held, and investigators compared statements, zeroed in on contradictions, and considered the case as it now stood. It didn't take them long to conclude they had enough. They presented their evidence to a judge and obtained arrest warrants for John Maree, John Eldon Smith, aka Anthony Machetti, and Rebecca Smith, aka Rebecca Machetti, for conspiracy to commit murder. Harris called Special Agent Bates in Florida.

"We're on our way back to Miami—with warrants."

Four men flew to Miami on Tuesday, October 15. Ray Wilkes and Harry Harris were accompanied by two assistant district attorneys—Don Thompson and Walker Johnson. Wilkes couldn't remember another case where investigators had taken lawyers along on an arrest. But he approved of it in this case. Everyone concerned was determined to do everything right on this one. Each move was discussed and considered. If there was any question of legality or procedure, the officers had the people right there to give them an immediate answer.

Robert Bates met Harry Harris and Walker Johnson at the airport and drove them to Fort Myers. The drive took a bit longer than usual, as occasional hard rain showers blew in from the west. It was after 2:00 that afternoon when the three men arrived at 8906 Andover Street, where John Maree was now living with his wife.

Maree seemed genuinely surprised when he was served with the arrest warrant. He barely spoke during the short ride to the Lee County Jail. There, he was taken to an interview room.

"Sit down," Harris told him.

The others also found chairs and Bates advised their prisoner of his rights.

Maree signed a rights waiver, then said, "I don't know why I'm here. I didn't do anything."

"That's not the way we see it," Johnson said.

Harris then confronted Maree with the lab report indicating that his palm print matched the one from the murder scene.

"That's crazy!" he said, but his voice didn't sound as confident as his words. "I don't even know those people. I've never been to Georgia in my life."

The others weren't impressed by his denial.

"Then how do you explain how your palm print was identified to be the same as the latent print found on their car?" Johnson asked.

"I don't know. A friend of mine once told me that trickery could be used to transpose a print from one object to another object."

The interview went on for another hour, but no headway was made.

Finally, Maree said, "Look, you can keep me here all night, but I can't admit to something when I haven't done anything."

That effectively ended the questioning. A few minutes later, the three lawmen gathered up their papers, thanked the Lee County deputies, and took John Maree back to Miami with them.

While their colleagues were arresting John Maree, Ray Wilkes and Don Thompson had been meeting with officers at the North Miami Beach Police Department. They laid out their case and showed the Florida officers photos of the crime scene.

"We'd really appreciate it if you could send a couple of guys with us to serve the warrants," Wilkes said.

However, the North Miami lieutenant was disturbed by the photos and concerned about the suspects' potential for violence. He insisted on sending six officers to help with the arrests.

"That's really not necessary," Wilkes said. "We don't expect any trouble."

But the lieutenant wasn't swayed. "We don't want a bloodbath."

So, late that afternoon, Wilkes, Thompson, and six North Miami detectives went to the Machetti house on 159th Street. Adrenaline pumped as they took positions around the house and the two men from Georgia approached the front door and knocked. But no one was home. The men returned to their cars to wait.

That fall, the three Akins girls had enrolled in North Miami Beach High School. Overcrowding forced the school into split sessions, and Vicki, Valerie, and Vanessa all attended the noon to 5:00 P.M. shift. During that afternoon, the girls had learned that the neighborhood theater was showing a movie marathon. For five dollars, they'd be able to hang out with their friends and watch movies until midnight. Vicki stayed at the theater with her friends while Valerie and Vanessa hurried home to ask permission.

As they approached their block, they noticed several police cars parked around the area.

"One of the cars is following us!" Vanessa said.

"Don't be silly," Valerie said. "Why would they follow *us*?"

But when the sisters turned the corner and started across their backyard, several men suddenly ran up to them.

"Are you the Akins girls?" one asked.

"Are you Rebecca Machetti?" a Florida detective asked.

Ray Wilkes spoke in a calm voice. "It's okay. No one is going to hurt you. We're the police. We just want to see your parents. Are they here?"

"No," Valerie said in a shaky voice, "but they'll be home any minute."

"We can all wait inside."

"No!" She was sure her mother wouldn't like that. "No one's supposed to go in."

About then, there was a shout from one of the detectives out on the street. "He's here!"

There was a rush to the front of the house. Although Valerie and Vanessa followed more slowly, they arrived in time to see Tony Machetti pull into the drive. Several officers advanced on him, guns drawn. One of them jerked the driver's door open and pulled Tony out. Two of the North Miami officers hustled him out to the street, pushed him into one of their cars, and drove away.

Seeing her stepfather arrested drained Valerie of all resistance. When Wilkes again suggested that they go inside, she voiced no objections.

"Sit down on the couch while we're waiting for your mother," he told them.

The girls sat side by side, scared and almost sick with apprehension about what would happen next. Vanessa started sobbing and Valerie felt tears gathering in her eyes, too. She wished Vicki were there with them. Meanwhile, the police started searching the house. Valerie was horrified to see them emptying drawers and going through closets. No one explained anything to the sisters, but Valerie knew. The police had found out who killed her father.

Minutes later, there was the sound of a car in the driveway, and the sisters went to stand by the front window. It was Becky. One of the police cars pulled into the driveway behind her. As her daughters watched, two officers quickly got her out of the car and brought her inside the house where Ray Wilkes waited to confront her.

"John Maree and John Eldon Smith have already been arrested," Wilkes told her, "for the murder of Joseph Ronald Akins and Juanita Akins. You're being arrested as well, Mrs. Smith."

"I didn't kill anyone. I have proof I was in Miami when Ronny was killed."

"Well, John Maree has implicated you," Wilkes said, hoping to shock an admission from her.

"He's a liar! I was here in Miami the whole time!"

He didn't devote any more time to questioning her right then. Instead, he had her sit in a chair as the search continued.

"I need to see a search warrant," she told them in a measured voice.

They showed it to her without explanation, and she didn't say another word.

Meanwhile, one of the officers asked where Vicki was, and someone went to the theater and brought her back to the house. She joined her sisters on the couch.

By the time the search of the Machetti house was complete, the police had boxed up a wide assortment of items—bills and receipts, a whistle and chain, photos of Becky and Tony, newspaper clippings, a letter to Becky from Tony, a letter from John Maree to Becky demanding payment of $1,000, a blue steel .32 revolver, and four wigs—two blonde and two brunette.

The police loaded the boxes into their cars. Then they brought Rebecca and her daughters outside. They put Becky in one car and the girls in another. Valerie was terrified that she and her sisters would be arrested, too. After all, Becky had told them they would be.

The caravan of vehicles first drove to the North Miami Beach Police Station, where Becky was photographed and fingerprinted. Next, everyone got back in the cars and rode for another half hour before arriving at the jail in downtown Miami. There, as the girls watched, Becky was printed and photographed once again.

Assistant DA Don Thompson approached the three tearful girls and introduced himself.

"Your mother is under arrest for killing your father," he told them. Behind him they could see Becky being led down a hall by a matron. "What can you tell me about the weekend your dad was killed?"

"Tony and John went fishing," Vicki said, sticking to the story Becky had given them. "They got home at five after one in the morning."

"That's right," Valerie agreed.

"Where was your mother?"

"With us," Vicki said. "The whole time."

It was well past dark when the three girls were taken to a juvenile holding facility, where they'd stay the rest of the night.

Of everything that happened that day, being held in that strange, frightening place might have been the worst. The girls had to surrender their clothes and shower in open stalls with their caretakers looking on. Next, they were subjected to body-cavity searches "for drugs." Finally, they were allowed to dress again and were shepherded into a dining hall. They were given food, but none of them could eat. They could only cry.

In a large dormitory filled with other girls, Valerie, Vanessa, and Vicki huddled miserably together all night on a single twin bed. Between bouts of sobbing, they talked in whispers, trying to figure out what was going to happen to them. First they'd lost their father, and now their mother had been taken away. They had no idea where they could turn for help.

As Becky was being booked into the female lockup, she suddenly slumped against the wall as if she were going to collapse.

"Are you okay?" the matron asked.

Becky shook her head weakly. "No, I'm having my period and I'm hemorrhaging."

When the matron reported that to her supervisor, he refused to admit Becky to the jail. Instead, she was transported to a local hospital for treatment. Doctors examined her, but she was found to have no medical problems whatsoever. The next morning she was returned to the jail with a clean bill of health.

Around the same time their mother was being locked in a cell, the Akins girls were in the back seat of a patrol car. Two officers had picked them up at the juvenile facility early that morning.

"We're going back to your house," the younger officer told them. "When we get there, you can each pack one suitcase."

"Suitcase?" Vanessa asked.

"Where...where are we going?" Valerie asked.

"To your grandmother's house in Athens, Georgia."

At the house on 159th Street, one of the officers unlocked the door and the girls were allowed to go in alone.

"We'll wait for you in the car."

The dogs greeted them with shrill barks. The little animals hadn't been outside since the previous afternoon, and evidence of that fact could be seen in several places on the floor. The girls cleaned up the mess and fed the dogs, all the while trying to decide what to do.

"I don't want to go to Athens," Valerie said.

"Me, either," Vicki agreed.

They discussed running away but had no idea where they would go. Finally, they just grabbed some clothes and keepsakes and shoved them into suitcases, resigned to their immediate fate. The family's telephone had recently been reconnected, and Vicki took the opportunity to make a quick call. While her sisters kept watch at the front windows, she dialed Alan Barfield's number.

Alan was getting ready for work and answered on the

first ring. In an emotional rush, Vicki blurted out that her mom and Tony had been arrested and that she and her sisters were being sent to Athens. He was sympathetic and promised to keep in touch. Although the girls knew there was nothing Alan could do to help them right then, they all felt somewhat better just knowing someone else was aware of what was happening to them.

The police officers hadn't counted on the girls returning to the car with two poodles, but it was clear that they were not leaving without their pets. So, they drove the girls and their little dogs to the airport.

The dogs turned out to be something of a problem. The airline couldn't accommodate them on the first plane to Atlanta. Since their grandmother was meeting the flight, it was decided that Valerie would take that one alone. Her sisters waited a few hours and boarded another plane with the dogs.

Valerie's flight arrived on time in Atlanta, and Sara Zuber was there to meet her. Since they didn't know when her sisters would be arriving, Sara drove Valerie to Athens to await word, but the police in Miami never called.

When Vicki and Vanessa finally arrived in Atlanta about 10:00 P.M., no one was there to meet them. They waited almost an hour, but no one came, and they had no idea how to get in touch with their grandmother. They were stranded in a huge airport with their bags and two toy poodles. Vicki called the only person she could think of who might help them.

Alan Barfield didn't know exactly what time it was when he answered the telephone, only that it seemed like the middle of the night. He'd been sound asleep when the phone rang. But as soon as Vicki tearfully explained their situation, he got up, dressed, and drove to Atlanta.

It was midnight when Alan arrived at the Atlanta airport. The lights in the huge terminal seemed unusually bright. Alan made his way to the baggage claim area where Vicki had said they'd be waiting. Vanessa spotted him before he saw her. She shouted his name, ran to meet him, and jumped into his arms. Vicki wasn't quite so demonstrative, but she was equally glad to see him.

Minutes later, Alan got the girls, the dogs, and the luggage into his station wagon and they headed for Athens. It was chilly in Georgia. For three girls who had spent the past several months in the subtropics and were dressed for that warm weather, the 45 degrees they met leaving the airport might as well have been zero.

It was after 2:00 AM when they arrived at the Zuber house, and nearly 5:00 by the time Alan said his goodbyes and left the girls at their grandmother's house. Back home in Macon, he had just enough time to shower and eat a quick breakfast before going to work.

Chapter 17

The house at 300 Camelot Drive was a brick and frame split-level on a pine-covered lot in a quiet Athens subdivision. The Akins girls hadn't seen much of their grandmother since she'd married John Zuber. The couple had a twelve-year-old son named Jody, who they were surprised to realize was their uncle.

Valerie, Vicki, and Vanessa settled in as well as they could with three people who were essentially strangers to them. Sara and John tried their best to make the girls feel welcome, but the arrangement was as far from normal as possible. Becky—Sara's daughter and the girls' mother—was in jail charged with murder. And that knowledge was never far from the minds of anyone in the house.

A couple of days after her granddaughters came to live with her, Sara Zuber gave an interview to Christopher Bonner, a *Macon Telegraph* staff writer. In the article that appeared on Friday, October 18, she defended her daughter, saying she could never have committed the crimes. She referred to her as a devout Baptist and a registered nurse.

On the same day that the Akins girls had left Miami, John Maree and Tony and Rebecca Machetti made a much shorter trip. The three were removed from their cells and taken before Judge John Tangsley, in Courtroom 3, of the Dade County Courthouse for arraignment. The Machettis had arranged for representation by attorneys Stanley Goldstein and Max

Cogan, but Maree didn't have a lawyer.

It was a brief proceeding. As the Florida and Georgia lawmen watched, the defendants refused to waive extradition, and the court continued the case until November 15 at 4:00 P.M. The three prisoners were to be held without bond until then.

It was no surprise. The police hadn't expected anything else, and the men from Bibb County were already planning a return visit to Miami in the middle of November. However, as they were leaving the courthouse, a female deputy approached Wilkes with an offer of help.

"I'll have the woman moved to the Dade County Jail," she said. "A few days there and she'll be ready to come back to Georgia."

Wilkes didn't know why that should be, but he thanked her. Anything that would speed up Becky's return to Macon was just fine with him. The following day, he and the others went home.

Bibb County District Attorney Fred Hasty had begun the extradition process the same day he was notified of the arrests in Miami. By October 18, the paperwork had been completed and mailed to Governor Jimmy Carter's office. After approving the application, Carter forwarded the request, known as a governor's warrant, to Florida governor Ruben Askew. When Askew approved the application, as everyone anticipated he would, he would then issue the order for Dade County to hold an extradition hearing.

From his cell in the Dade County Jail, John Maree wrote to Vicki. "Georgia's crew was sure caught short for evidence," he told her. He also complained about what he perceived as an unfair situation. "Tony and Becky had two good lawyers. I didn't have one, but their lawyers helped me. These lawyers are good and I wish there was some way to get them to represent me also. No money in this situation hurts."

He was still planning a future with Vicki. "Keep up your Spainish [*sic*] and get a passport if you can. After this mess is over, I will leave the US for good. All this false evidence they say they have makes me feel sick toward any police." Then he cautioned, "They act like this is Russia. They read <u>all</u> letters in and out, so don't write anything you don't want the world to know." He signed it, "Loving and missing you, John." Then an inch to the right of his signature, printed on a slant in tiny letters, was the word "innocent."

Vicki Akins had little time to settle into life in Athens. Less than a week after her arrival there, her grandmother took her downtown, where the two boarded a Greyhound bus for Miami. They arrived in South Florida some twenty hours later.

After visiting Becky in jail, they took a cab out to the 159th Street house. The neighbor who had volunteered to take their belongings into his house had done so, but that's where his generosity ended. Their cars were on blocks in his yard with the tires missing, and he refused to give them any of their things without first being paid a storage fee. Vicki grew increasingly upset. She begged to just be allowed to take the family photographs, but the man was adamant.

Since neither Sara nor Vicki had any extra money, they couldn't pay what he asked and eventually left with nothing. They stayed overnight in a motel and visited with Becky once more the next day.

She complained about the way she was being treated.

"And the food is awful!"

She was so pitiful that Vicki felt she had to do something. She found a vending machine down the hall and used what little cash she had with her to buy her mother several candy bars. But the treats did little to appease Becky. She continued to complain about her treatment.

"They're terrible to me," she claimed. "The deputies make me get on the floor and beg just to use the phone."

Vicki was reduced to tears by her mother's complaints. She was still crying when Becky left the visiting area. But she regained her composure after a few minutes and took the opportunity to meet with John Maree for half an hour. He was still full of plans for their future, but Vicki couldn't share his optimism. The future didn't seem all that bright to her.

Vicki would have visited with Tony as well, but he hadn't put her name on his visitors list and she wasn't allowed to see him.

Returning to Athens was the last thing Vicki wanted to do. While they were still in Miami, she wrote to a friend in Macon:

"I really don't want to go back, but I will if I have to. If this thing drags along for a few months, by that time I will be 18, then I am coming back. I cannot stand the thought of me being up there and Mom, my stepfather and my good friend being down here."

She was also concerned about what her friends thought. "I don't know how your family is taking all of this, but I hope they understand that they are innocent and it is just a matter of time until they are proven so!" She might not have believed that, but she wanted it to be true.

In spite of Vicki's reluctance to do so, she got on a bus with Sara that afternoon and they returned to Athens.

~~~
~~~

Ray Wilkes never knew what the conditions were in the women's section of the Dade County Jail, but he knew they must have been bad. Only nine days after her arrest, Becky Machetti chose to waive extradition and return to Macon.

The Florida authorities notified Bibb County of her decision, and, on October 23, Wilkes and his wife, Pearl, flew to Miami. The next morning, with Larry Bieltz's assistance, Becky was out-processed from the jail and released into Chief Deputy Wilkes's custody.

The three Georgians left Miami on a 1:45 P.M. flight to Atlanta. Wilkes sat beside Becky with Pearl a few rows behind them. He had arranged the seating that way. His instincts told him that Becky Machetti was a poisonous personality. Rationally, he knew she couldn't hurt his wife in that situation, but he just didn't want Pearl to be exposed to Becky any more than was necessary.

That evening, Becky was booked into the Bibb County Jail in downtown Macon. It wasn't until several days later that Wilkes interviewed her there. Although he spent several hours with her, she stuck to her story.

Wilkes hated to give up. He knew he was good at interviewing suspects, and he always felt more secure with a case when he had a confession, so he met with her several more times in early November. Becky never changed her story, but he noticed that whenever she was backed into a corner by the facts, she became overly emotional. While she buried her face in her hands and sounded as if she was crying, he wasn't fooled. Finally, Wilkes lost patience.

"You might as well stop that," he said. "You're not impressing me one bit. The one thing I've seen over and over in these outbursts is the absence of tears."

Becky still didn't tell him what he wanted to know, but at least that put an end to the counterfeit crying.

~~~

John Maree wrote Vicki again during the first week of November. This time he asked for help in hiring an attorney. He gave her the name and Miami phone number of an attorney that he'd heard was good man and a good lawyer. "You might pass this information to your mother. We will need some kind of lawyer for this hearing on November 15. Maybe you and your grandmother could try to find out what kind of evidence the Bibb County fuzz are using as basis for these warrants they are holding us on."

Time passes slowly behind bars, and neither Maree nor Machetti made it to the November 15th hearing. A week before their scheduled court appearances, they both waived extradition. As soon as word reached Bibb County that John Maree and Tony Machetti would soon be brought back from Florida, Becky was moved to the Houston County Jail in nearby Warner Robins. No one wanted to take a chance that she might find a way to communicate with the men during the time investigators were interviewing them.

Ray Wilkes and Deputy Raymond Purvis were chosen to bring the two prisoners back from Miami. Purvis's current assignment was prisoner transportation and he was good at his job. They drove to Miami on Monday, November 4, arriving that evening. The two men checked into a motel and got a few hours' sleep, then picked up their prisoners Tuesday morning. They had planned the trip in two stages. They'd drive to Kissimmee the first day, then finish the trip to Macon on Wednesday.
~~~

They drove in a steady rain most of Tuesday. Wilkes and Purvis didn't speak much because the deputy had to concentrate on driving, but the two prisoners in the back seat grew bored and began conversing in low voices. As the hours passed and the lawmen continued to ignore them, Machetti and Maree grew louder and bolder, complaining to each other that they'd been falsely accused.

"Everybody knows you can't get justice in Georgia," Machetti finally declared. "We're going to be treated like dirt."

"Yeah," Maree agreed. "They're trying to hang this on somebody and we're the best they could find."

When neither Wilkes nor Purvis responded, they continued in the same vein. After exhausting the topic, Machetti announced that he needed a restroom stop.

Purvis steered the car up the next exit and into a service station. One at a time, in leg-irons and waist chains, the prisoners were removed from the car. Purvis escorted each of them as they hobbled across the parking lot and into the restroom at the side of the station. Wilkes remained with the other prisoner, standing beside the car. Machetti went first, then Maree.

When Purvis brought Maree back to the car, the prisoner seemed edgy. His eyes darted around the area, and he glanced several times at the gun on the chief deputy's hip. Wilkes felt sure that the man was considering an escape. He moved forward so that his face was only inches from Maree's.

"I know what you're thinking," he told the prisoner in a voice that was barely louder than a whisper, "and it will be the biggest mistake you ever made in your life. Now get in the car."

Maree complied without a word. But once they were underway again, he became belligerent, telling the deputies that they'd never be convicted in a state as backward as Georgia.

Machetti joined in and the two seemed to be enjoying themselves. That's when Ray Wilkes decided he wasn't going to listen to that all the way back to Macon.

"Pull over," he told Purvis.

When the deputy had stopped the car on the side of the road, Wilkes turned around in the seat so he could see the prisoners face-to-face.

"First of all, I've heard all the crap I want to hear out of you. And I'm telling you, this won't be a hard case to get a conviction on. We've got good evidence. I'm going to tell you how it's going to be.

"Now, you're going to have a day in court. You'll have a lawyer. And when it's over, the jury is going to find you guilty, and they're going to recommend the death penalty. And you'll get it. Then we'll start the appeals process.

"I'll pick you up at the jail. Then I'm going to carry you to Reidsville. On the fifth floor there is the death house. That's where I'll leave you."

Neither Machetti nor Maree had anything to say to that, but their faces had grown suddenly serious.

Wilkes continued, "Your appeal process will go up and come back. It'll go up and come back, and finally it's going to be exhausted. And the day the last appeal is exhausted, the state is going to ask for a resentencing and a new date of execution. And the judge is going to come back and set it.

"After that, you'll be housed in a row of cells that face another row of cells. You'll get to know everybody there. You'll get to know their thinking because you'll all be in the same boat—waiting to die.

"Then one day they'll come for you." Both prisoners leaned forward when he said that. "After you've had a nice meal. Then they're going to slit your britches legs and clip your hair so the electrodes will make good contact. When everything is ready, they're going to start walking you down. The chaplain will be with you. He'll try to give you some comfort.

"You'll walk down a narrow hallway, saying goodbye to the people that's left behind in those other cells. At the end of that hall, you'll turn left. And when you do, I want you to look up. Because there's a bar area there where you can see the sky. And that'll be the last time you'll ever see it on this earth.

"When you make the next turn you'll be in the death house. The chair sets in the middle of the room. The audience will be on your left."

Purvis shifted uneasily in his seat. He didn't like his prisoners to be upset. It only complicated the job. But Wilkes didn't seem to care.

"They are going to set you down in that chair," Wilkes was saying, "and to ensure that you won't have a lot of convulsions, they'll lean you forward and shove a wedge down between your back and the chair to make it tight. The execution will take about three or four minutes. Then it's over.

"From there you're going into the morgue. Of course, you won't know it. They'll put a tag on your big toe, pull out the drawer, and slip you in. That's where you'll stay till somebody comes to claim your body. If they don't, the state will bury you on the prison property."

Wilkes turned back around and nodded for Purvis to continue driving. No one spoke a word until they arrived in Kissimmee an hour later. Deputy Purvis had relatives there, where he and Wilkes would spend the night. But first they dropped their prisoners off at the local jail.

Purvis took care of the paperwork, then joined Wilkes back in the car. The deputy had held his tongue until they were alone, but he was angry and now he was going to tell Wilkes just how he felt.

"Why'd you have to upset them like that? Prisoner

transport is my job and I know how to do it right. I try to keep the comfort level in the car to where everybody's on an even keel. It makes everything easier."

Wilkes wasn't concerned about the prisoners' attitudes. "I'm not here for fun in the sun. I'm here to arrest people and put them in the electric chair. The sooner they know where they stand and where I do, the better."

Chapter 18

There was little conversation during the next day's drive back to Macon. The prisoners were quiet and so were Purvis and Wilkes. It was nearly 5:00 P.M. when Maree and Machetti were booked in the Bibb County Jail. Each man was isolated in his own cell. Wilkes didn't know which of the two would break, but he was fairly confident one of them would. He decided not to interview either man that day. Instead, he went home and got some rest.

Wilkes intentionally stayed away from the jail the next morning. He wanted the prisoners to have time to think. When he arrived at his courthouse office after lunch, he learned that John Maree had asked several times to see him. He went upstairs to the jail, where he met with Maree in a bare interrogation room furnished only with a table and two chairs.

"Where have you been?" Maree asked as soon as Wilkes entered the room. "I've called for you. I told them to tell you to come up here."

Wilkes shrugged. "I've been busy."

"I need to talk to you."

"Okay. We'll talk—in just a minute."

They took seats on opposite sides of the heavy metal table. Wilkes went over a rights form and Maree impatiently signed it, waiving his right to an attorney. Then Wilkes turned on a tape recorder and set it on the table.

"Now, what do you want to talk about?"

"I've been thinking about what you said, in the car, you

know?" Maree took a deep breath. "And I want to talk. I mean, what do you want to know?"

"Oh, I don't know," Wilkes said nonchalantly. "Why don't you tell me something I don't already know?"

"Like what?"

"Where'd y'all rent the car at?"

"Fort Lauderdale," Maree said eagerly. "From Avis. At least that's where we took the car back to. I don't know for sure 'cause Tony rented it."

Wilkes only nodded, careful to display no emotion. "Why don't you just tell me about it?"

"I really don't know where to start."

Wilkes had him start at the beginning, gently guiding him through a history of his acquaintance with Becky and the time he'd spent with her and the girls in Florida.

"I met Tony Machetti about a week before the wedding."

According to Maree, there had been some tension between the two men at first until he'd finally convinced the other man that there'd never been anything between him and Becky.

"Was that true?"

Maree shrugged. "Well, I'm involved with Vicki now."

Wilkes changed the subject. "Did you ever know Ronny Akins?"

"Not really. I saw him once from quite a distance. It was back in the summer, and Becky paid me $150 to drive a Ryder truck from Miami to Macon and back. She needed to move her furniture from here to Florida."

"And that was the only time you saw Ronny Akins?"

"Yeah, I mean, I didn't really see him. When we brought the truck up here, there was a car that drove up. I was behind the house trying to get the old lawnmower out, and after the car had left, they said it was Mr. Akins."

"What kind of car was he in?"

"It was a white Ford."

Wilkes's pulse quickened a bit. He knew he had to proceed carefully here. "You didn't go to the car? You didn't talk to him or have any exchange?"

"No."

Wilkes felt his body relax. If Maree had said he'd been close to the white Ford—the vehicle Akins was driving at the time of the murder—then he and his attorney might have been able to argue that Maree's handprint had gotten on the car at that time, rather than when Ronny and Juanita were killed.

John Maree now leaned back in his chair, finding, perhaps, that talking to the police was easier than he'd expected it to be. Under Wilkes's prodding, Maree explained that he'd been approached to "drive a car" for Becky and Tony. It wasn't until later that he learned about the planned murder.

"Now, I didn't want any part of that," he declared. "I said no. But she—Becky—she said she'll kill my family if I didn't do just what she told me to do."

Wilkes digested that self-serving bit of information without comment. "And what was it she wanted you to do?"

"She wanted her ex-husband dead. She told us to hit Ronny in the back of the neck, then inject him with these drugs she'd stolen from somewhere."

Then, in a chillingly calm voice, John Maree related what had happened the day he and Tony Machetti came to Macon. He laid it all out—the calls to Akins and selecting Fairmont North as the location for their meeting. The only time he faltered in his narrative was when he described what had happened to Ronny and Juanita.

Wilkes knew how to get him past that. "Look, John, I don't think you understand the program. You don't realize what's going on here. Tony and Becky are together in this thing. They're married. They're looking out for each other.

"And their fingerprints weren't on that car. Yours were. They're going to say it was you, maybe that you and Vicki conspired to kill Ronny Akins. You're going with her, aren't you? There's the insurance that she'll get. They're going to say the *two of you* will gain from Ronny's death."

That was enough to spur the other man on. He described the set up and related how Ronny and Juanita had arrived at Fairmont North. With no emotion, Maree told how Tony had repeatedly hit Ronny on the back of the head. He even admitted that he himself had struck Juanita at the base of her neck with the surveyor's stake. But his memory failed him at that point.

"I just don't remember. Well, I'm not really sure after seeing some of the pictures that were taken at the scene. I'm not sure in my mind exactly what did happen...how the stake that I had in my hand ended up being in the car. That part of it I just don't remember at all."

He did, however, remember hearing Tony fire the shotgun behind him. "I was walking toward the Gremlin, and there was a shot and another shot—very quickly—and then there was a slight pause and then there was a third shot—all while I was walking to the car."

"Why'd you walk away?"

For the first time, a crack appeared in Maree's calm veneer. He dropped his eyes to the tabletop and said, in a voice that was little more than a whisper, "Cause I really couldn't stand the sight of anybody being killed."

"You mean you purposely turned away when they were shot?"

"Yes, sir. I did."

Maree couldn't tell Wilkes in what order Ronny and

Juanita had been shot.

"But you do know he used a double-barrel shotgun?"

"Yeah, I'm certain it was. I'd seen the gun and Tony and me had discussed it."

"If it was a double-barrel shotgun," Wilkes said, "it means that the gun would have had to be reloaded to fire the third shot."

"That's right."

"All right. Did Tony prearrange and have shells in his pocket?"

"I believe he did—now that's pure conjecture. I don't know whether he had them just in his pocket and ready to go. I don't know. I think that he just picked them up out of the car with the gun."

After Maree had told the story of the killings and the trip back to Florida, Wilkes pressed for more information.

"Have you ever committed a crime like this before?"

"I've never committed any crime—never been arrested for anything."

"Had Tony ever talked about committing a crime like this before?"

"No, sir, he hadn't."

Wilkes began stacking up the papers he'd spread out on the table. "So, what do you think Rebecca's real motive was? What seemed to motivate her or drive her toward this—was it money or was it vengeance or...?"

"Well, it seemed to be a strange type of thing—she—this is her talk—I really don't know exactly if it was true because I never met anybody that she talked to. She said that she wanted to get Tony into the Mafia and that this would be a good way. This would be his initiation to get into the Mafia by doing this close to home—meaning people that were real close. If he could get away with something like this, he could name his price to be anything he wanted if he became a hit man."

Wilkes stared at him for a moment. That was the craziest motive for murder he'd ever heard. "Tell me that again."

Maree did so.

Wilkes just shook his head. Then he asked if the girls knew anything about the murders.

"They didn't seem like they knew anything until the very last moment. They were real upset."

As they were wrapping up, Wilkes said, "We'll get your statement typed up and then you can sign it. Is there anything else you want to say?"

Maree's voice grew hoarse and sincere. "It's just not in me to be this way. I couldn't hold it on my conscience and I definitely was afraid for the safety of my family. I think now I do feel a lot better that I got it off my chest, and I just hope that whatever transpires in my trial—I just hope that it is a lesson to everybody here."

Wilkes left the interview not knowing how much to believe about John Maree's part in the killings. It wasn't uncommon for a person to present himself as more innocent than he really was. But he now believed that he knew what happened that afternoon in Fairmont North, and that Rebecca Machetti was the compelling force behind the killings.

He was also pleased with the amount of information he'd managed to get from the prisoner. Although they'd assumed all along that Maree and Machetti had rented a car, in a time when worldwide computer networks were simply dreams for the future, the task of finding the right rental agency had seemed monumental. Now, however, they knew exactly where to look.

Wilkes once more called upon the Florida investigators for help. In less than twenty-four hours, they verified that a 1973 green Gremlin had been rented from Avis Rent-A-Car in Fort Lauderdale on August 30 to a J. Smith with a New Jersey driver's license. The information was teletyped to Chief Deputy Ray Wilkes at 4:15 P.M. on Friday afternoon.

But Florida Department of Criminal Law Enforcement agents Bates and Bieltz weren't done. The following Tuesday, they interviewed Joe Suarez, manager of the Fort Lauderdale Avis Rent-A-Car, at his office on North Federal Highway. He provided them with a copy of the rental contract.

The two officers examined it with a combination of excitement and satisfaction.

"I believe this will do," Bieltz said.

"Yep. Looks like they got him," Bates agreed.

The document showed that J. Eldon Smith, who'd used a driver's license with the address of 3401 Clubhouse Drive, West Deptford, New Jersey, had rented a green two-door AMC Gremlin hardtop on August 30. The vehicle had been returned to the agency on September 1 with a total of 1,467 miles driven. The charge for the rental was $34.32, and Smith had paid for it with his American Express card.

There were two disappointments, however. None of the clerks at the agency could provide them with a description of Smith, and the car itself wasn't at the rental lot.

"It's been retired from service," Suarez told them.

The next day, Special Agent J. Korte went to the Lakeland Auto Auction, where the Gremlin was being stored until it could be sold. He thoroughly photographed and processed the car, inside and out, but no clothing, shotgun shells, or any other evidence was found.

Chapter 19

The investigation was now in high gear. On Friday, November 8, Wilkes reinterviewed Maree. This time, ADA Don Thompson was present, and the questions centered on the stop Maree and Machetti had made just over the Florida line on the night of the murders. When Maree had told them everything he could remember about the place, Wilkes called the sheriff in Jennings, Florida. He gave him Maree's description of the gas station where the two men had stopped.

"He says they used a pay phone there."

"I think I know where you're talking about," the sheriff said, "but I'll run out there and have a look just to be sure."

Within the hour, the sheriff called Wilkes back. "Yep, it's just like your man said. Everything fits."

He provided Wilkes with the number for the pay phone at the service station. Wilkes then turned to Dennis Barber at Southern Bell for help. Armed with the pay phone number and the date and time the call to Becky Machetti was supposed to have been made, Barber contacted the North Florida Telephone Company and asked for assistance. Two days later, Wilkes had the information he'd hoped to find. A telephone call had been made at approximately 9:00 P.M. from the pay phone at the PaceCar Oil Company, located at Interstate 75 and State Route 143 in Jennings, to another pay telephone and lasted one minute and 51 seconds. The receiving phone was in the foyer of the Jefferson Department Store in North Miami Beach, just where Alan Barfield told them Becky took a call from Tony Saturday night. And just that quickly, they verified that part of John Maree's statement.

The three Akins girls found life in Athens quite a contrast to their time in Florida. Sara and John Zuber were much stricter than Becky had been. Even though the girls were all enrolled in Clarke Central High School, their grandmother kept them close to home much of the time. The freedom they'd grown used to in Miami was a thing of the past.

Becky telephoned them regularly. It was, in fact, during her first call to her daughters in Athens that she took pains to reinforce her earlier warnings.

"Remember what I told you," she warned each girl in turn. "The only things you tell the police better be things that will get me out of jail."

It was an unwelcome reminder that the lying and fear weren't over for them yet.

In a desperate attempt to find an adult ally, Vicki and Valerie told Mama Sara what had happened in Florida, including what Becky had said about their father's murder. But the revelation didn't produce the comfort and understanding they'd hoped for. Sara became furious, called them liars, and threatened to turn them over to the police. In some ways, it was like being back with their mother.

Mama Sara might have kept a close eye on the girls, but she couldn't control everything. Without her knowledge, Vicki continued corresponding with John Maree. On November 9, she wrote, "I would like you to know that you are still my <u>best friend</u> no matter what. Remember that friends don't forget each other."

Maree's letter to Vicki on November 12 bemoaned his lack of mail. "Have my letters been reaching you or are you afraid to write? I realize your situation is a little precarious.

Please write often as things here are very lonesome. I hope you will send that photo I asked you for. The Court appointed lawyers for us today. I hear your mother has her own lawyer. Sounds a little strange to me. Why can't Tony use the same lawyer."

In mid November, Vicki wrote, saying that she loved him. That declaration and, perhaps, exposure to jailhouse religion seemed to have lifted his spirits. "When you come here to see me," he told her in a return letter, "you will see a slight change in my mental attitude—for the better. I hope you get to see your mother Sunday. Even though we had our differences, I wish her no ill will. The Good Lord has seen fit to forgive her. Try to keep your thoughts and prayers positive!"

He also delivered an almost fatherly lecture about the importance of an education. "Please change your attitude toward this very important part of your life. Those 2 1/2 hours in the library should be spent studying something of interest."

And he mentioned that he'd seen Tony a few days before, and her stepfather had received the package she sent him. "I got mine, too, and I thank you." His observation of Tony was that he "seems to be taking this very well. Even getting fat!" Maree was determined to avoid that fate. "I am doing exercises in my cell and have lost weight! When I get out of here I want to be in good mental and physical shape."

By the first of December, the Bibb County investigators concluded they'd gathered all the information they were likely to receive from Maree. Tony Machetti was still not talking, and, after this much time had passed, no one really expected him to. So, there was no further need to hold Becky at another location. She was returned to Macon and the Bibb County Jail on December 4.

Becky's return made little difference to John Maree. He was growing increasingly uneasy by the day. He'd talked more or less freely to the investigators, but he hadn't received any ironclad promises as to what his fate was going to be. On December 5, he again wrote to Vicki. "Well things here are grinding along very slow. Lawyers had arraignments postponed until Dec. 31, 1974. Trial to start on Jan. 27, 1975. At least this is the word I got from my lawyer."

Vicki hadn't written him in ten days, and Maree was worried that she might be angry that he was going to testify against her mother and Tony. "Sure would like to know why I haven't heard from you! Whatever happens now will not alter my feelings for you. I still love you and need you." He also made reference to how he believed Vicki's family regarded him. "Can't really figure out why your mother and grandmother seem to risent [*sic*] me so much. I haven't done anything to them. I hope they will realize that it is much wiser to cultivate friends than to create enemies."

Maree was right on target about how he was regarded in the Zuber household. Sara was convinced he was framing her daughter for murder and wouldn't allow his name to even be mentioned. The only time Vicki actually received his letters was when she managed to be the first one to the mailbox. More often than not, she missed the mail delivery.

Sara didn't want her daughter represented by a court-appointed attorney, so she hired Vane G. Hawkins for the job. A distinguished Athens attorney, Hawkins had been born in New York but had lived in Athens since 1928. He was over seventy years old and had been a member of the Georgia bar since 1933.

As soon as he was on record as Becky's attorney, Hawkins filed two motions. The first was a request for a continuance of the trial, which was scheduled for early December.

The second was a request to have his client's trial severed from those of the other two defendants. Both motions were granted.

Neither John Maree nor Tony Machetti had family that was either willing or able to hire defense counsel for them, so two Macon attorneys were tapped to represent them—Floyd Buford for Tony and Willis B. Sparks III for Maree.

In November, Valerie called Alan Barfield with disturbing news. Her grandmother had decided they could no longer care for the two poodles. As usual, Alan did what he could to help. The next weekend, he drove to Athens, picked up Bridget and Shannon, and brought them home with him. It wasn't an ideal arrangement. He was gone much of the time and his apartment complex didn't allow pets. However, the owners of the complex knew and liked Alan, so, after he explained the situation, they waived the rules for him. Not wanting to give them any reason to regret that decision, he kept the dogs in their own pen when he was gone during the day and worked hard to keep the place scrupulously clean.

But as much as he cared about the dogs, Alan soon came to realize that the arrangement could only be temporary. The little female, Bridget, was pregnant, and Alan was worried he'd be at work and not available to help when the time came for her to deliver. So, after a couple of weeks, he regretfully took the dogs back to Athens.

Soon afterwards, Bridget had her puppies. Two adult dogs and a litter of puppies was more than the Zuber household could handle at that point. They arranged homes for the puppies and Valerie again turned to Alan. This time she asked that he come and get only Shannon. Once again, he drove to Athens and took the dog back home with him. Shannon became his constant companion from then on. The little poodle lived to be eighteen years old. After his death, he was buried in Alan's backyard.

While Alan and the dog were to remain great friends, his relationship with Valerie was doomed. As soon as Mama Sara learned that Alan had been interviewed by the police and would be testifying for the prosecution, she cut off all contact between him and her granddaughters.

In December of 1974, District Attorney Fred Hasty returned to the Bibb County Grand Jury. Investigators Robbie Johnson and Bill Freeman testified, as did Kelly Fite from the state crime lab. Valerie and Vicki Akins were also subpoenaed. Still terrified of their mother, they both lied, declaring they knew nothing of the murders, maintaining that John Maree and Tony Machetti had gone fishing and returned to the North Miami Beach house at 1:00 A.M. on September 1.

The first indictments, which had charged them all only with conspiracy to commit murdered, were dismissed. Then, at the DA's request, the grand jury returned true bills, reindicting all three defendants on two counts of murder.

Chapter 20

Anthony Machetti's trial was scheduled for Monday, January 27, 1975. The Tuesday before that, District Attorney Hasty filed notice to defendant John Smith (the state refused to use the Machetti name, even though it was apparently his legal name by then) that the prosecution would be seeking the death penalty. As proscribed by law, the notice contained justifications for that course of action. They were that: 1) Juanita Akins was murdered during the commission of a felony—to wit, the murder of Ronald Akins, 2) the murder of Joseph Ronald Akins was committed for the purpose of receiving money, 3) the murders were committed while an agent of another, and 4) the murders involved torture, depravity of mind, and aggravated battery to the victims.

John Maree had more to worry about than his relationship with Vicki Akins. Just before Tony's trial, Maree sent a note to Assistant DA Don Thompson, asking for advice about his forthcoming testimony. "Do you think I should elaborate more on your questions about my background? I am proud of my past history and perhaps more details would be in order. You will no doubt ask me again about my relationship with Vicki. Would you think that a few more detailed answers might save some embarrassment on cross examination?"

The DA's office still wouldn't make a formal deal with him in exchange for his testimony, and Maree's anger and fear were mounting. "Since you can't tell me what you have in mind in my own case, I have to assume the worst. Getting a telephone call to a lawyer at a given time is almost impossible. I realize all jails are about the same in this respect. Therefore I would like you to call Mr. Sparks sometime before Monday because I want him to be at this trial from beginning to end. The only thing I have to say about my part in this affair is I will <u>not</u> plead guilty to those charges you have made against me. You will have to have another trial if this is what you expect."

Tony's trial began on an unseasonably warm Monday, January 27, 1975, in Bibb County Superior Court. Judge C. Cloud Morgan presided. Fred Hasty and Don Thompson were present for the prosecution. At the defense table, Floyd Buford, a former United States Attorney, was joined by Atlanta attorney and former lieutenant governor Garland Byrd.

The case moved quickly. The all-male jury had been chosen by early afternoon and was sworn in at 2:50 P.M. Minutes later, Fred Hasty rose to make his opening statement. He described the murders of Ronny and Juanita Akins in graphic detail. He told the jury that John Smith had committed these dreadful crimes because he wanted to become a Mafia hit man. Hasty declared the defendant had even changed his name because his wife, also charged in the murders, wanted them to have an Italian name, one more appropriate to the Mafia.

Reporters scribbled furiously in their notebooks, anxious to get down every word. Rumors had abounded about an organized crime connection with the case for months. It had been whispered that some of the witnesses had actually asked for police protection because of that, but nothing had been confirmed. Now, here was the district attorney himself talking about Mafia hit men.

When the prosecution's statement was done, Smith's attorneys went to work. In the defense opening, they declared the prosecution had completely misrepresented the facts. They denied all the charges and promised to prove that John Maree had committed the murders.

Generally, by the time a case goes to trial, the investigation is complete, but Fred Hasty and the investigation team were determined to have the answers to every possible question that might arise. So that afternoon, twenty minutes after court adjourned for the day, Ray Wilkes left Fairmont North subdivision in a county car, retracing Tony's and John Maree's route south. Three hours and eighteen minutes later, he pulled into the PaceCar service station in Jennings, Florida. The odometer showed he'd driven 179.3 miles. Confident that the timetable fit the facts of the case and the time the telephone call was made to Becky in Miami, Wilkes gassed up and headed back to Macon.

The courtroom was packed when the trial resumed Tuesday morning. One police officer after another, from Georgia and Florida, testified for the state. Alan Barfield also took the stand, as did Bobby and Ann McElroy.

Bobby McElroy was caught off guard when, after giving his testimony, Hasty put a pointer into his hand and asked him to go over to a big map that was displayed in front of the jury. Once McElroy was in place, the DA instructed him to point out various features of the terrain around his neighborhood. He also asked him about the weather conditions on the evening of the murders. All of this came as a surprise to McElroy since it had never been mentioned during his preparation for testimony.

When he'd finished and the court was in recess, McElroy approached Hasty, "What did you do that for?" he asked. "The map and the pointer. I didn't know that was coming."

Hasty just laughed. "I knew after you'd taught school so many years it wasn't going to particularly bother you."

"Yeah, but that wasn't in front of a courtroom packed full and a jury."

Hasty smiled again. "You did just fine."

John Maree was the last witness of the day. Both sides knew their cases would hinge on this nervous man's testimony. He glanced once at Tony, but kept his eyes on Hasty most of the time. He'd barely started his testimony when the judge adjourned for the day.

Maree went back to his cell vaguely disappointed. When he'd learned that today was the day he'd take the witness stand, he'd been apprehensive but somewhat reassured by the knowledge that it would all be over by the end of the day. Except it wasn't. Now, he'd have to start all over again in the morning. It was a long, sleepless night for him.

Maree was back on the stand first thing Wednesday. His testimony lasted most of the morning. In a clear, controlled voice, he told the court the same things he'd told Ray Wilkes. His cross-examination was rigorous, but the defense couldn't shake his story of the murders. He was followed by several other witnesses, and the prosecution concluded its case at 5:30 that afternoon.

Judge Morgan was determined that the trial wouldn't drag out longer than necessary and told the defense to begin its presentation. Floyd Buford stood and addressed the court. He explained that his client, Tony, wanted to testify, but that he was opposed to such an idea. He asked that the judge inform him of his rights. Cloud Morgan fully explained Tony's right not to incriminate himself and his right to remain silent, but Machetti wasn't discouraged. "But I still want to testify."

Buford shook his head as his client took the stand, then guided him through his testimony. Tony Machetti tried to explain away the evidence that had been presented against him. With his Northern accent sounding foreign in the big courtroom, he did exactly as Wilkes had predicted he would and blamed the killings on John Maree.

The plans for the Labor Day weekend had been set, he testified, when he and Maree had gone for a walk after dinner on August 15. At that time, Maree had asked him to be his alibi for the holiday weekend. He said Maree told him it wasn't illegal, it was a business pursuit, but that he needed him to cover for him.

"Did you use your American Express card to rent a Gremlin automobile that weekend?" Buford asked.

"No. I lent my card and my driver's license to John Maree. He must have rented it."

"Why would you do that?" Buford asked.

Machetti explained that Becky had borrowed $200 from Maree at the racetrack some weeks before and, to pay back that loan, he let Maree use his credit card. "He promised not to charge more than $150 and it would wipe out the debt."

Buford showed him the rental car agreement that the prosecution had already entered into evidence. "Is that your signature?"

"No. John Maree must have forged my name."

As his testimony continued, Tony suggested that Maree's motive for killing the Akinses might have been so that he and Vicki could collect her father's insurance.

"Do you believe John Maree acted alone?"

Machetti shook his head. "He later let slip that he was conducting this business with someone named Darrell. And he begged me not to tell Becky."

"Did he say anything else about the weekend?"

"Yeah, he said if anyone came around asking, to say we'd gone fishing."

"And had you gone fishing?"

"No." Machetti's story was that while he had left his home on Friday afternoon with Maree, they'd soon parted company. "Then I drove to Hollywood, Florida, and spent all day Saturday on the beach." That night, he said, he'd driven back to Fort Lauderdale and met up with Maree as planned. "We got back to my house about 1:00 A.M."

As for having his name changed, he claimed he'd done so because his wife told him he looked "like a Tony."

"Why did you choose the name Machetti?"

Tony shrugged. "I don't know. I guess because it sounded like 'machete' and there's a lot of jungle in Florida. I thought it would help me in my business—the insurance business. Machetti is sure a more memorable name than Smith. And it sounded like an Italian name. I'd thought about getting a job as a bartender in Miami. I could make $400 a week. But it's hard to get in. Without an Italian name, it just wouldn't be possible."

From their expressions, it seemed that many people in the courtroom found Tony's testimony less than believable. He didn't fare any better on cross-examination.

Thursday was reserved for closing arguments.

"If we believe in capital punishment, these are the circumstances that merit it," Hasty told the jury. Although it had been mentioned throughout the trial, he didn't spend much time on the defendant's Mafia aspirations. These murders, he told the jury, were all about money. In addition to the insurance benefits, Ronny Akins's daughters would also receive a $550 a month Social Security survivor benefit. And Tony and his wife would have controlled that money.

In his closing argument, defense attorney Garland Byrd insisted that the state hadn't made its case and had not presented sufficient evidence for a conviction. They hadn't produced the murder weapon or any witnesses to corroborate Maree's testimony. The jury, he maintained, had to acquit his client.

The twelve men deliberated only twenty-five minutes. When they returned to the courtroom, their foreman announced that they'd found John Smith, or Tony Machetti, guilty on both counts. After more testimony and argument, the jury again left the courtroom to consider sentencing. This time, two and a half hours passed before they came back.

Tony Machetti and his attorneys stood silently as the foreman announced that the jury recommended he be punished by death. Minutes later, that was the sentence passed by the court.

Chapter 21

While Tony's attorneys began working on appeals, Becky's trial was fast approaching. Vicki and Valerie were acutely aware of that fact. They met several times with Vane Hawkins to discuss their possible testimony. These meetings were serious sessions. Each time, the attorney emphasized that if they failed her, their mother could spend the rest of her life in prison. As the oldest, Vicki would definitely have to take the stand, and Valerie might have to as well. Hawkins cautioned the girls over and over that they must be careful not to say *anything* that could incriminate their mother. Becky had already told him that Ronny had mistreated her for years, and Hawkins explained that he expected them to confirm that.

The sisters were terrified. They knew that you were supposed to tell the truth in court, but if they were truthful about the events of that Labor Day weekend, there was no way they could do anything but incriminate their mother. They also knew you went to prison for lying in court.

Whenever they were alone, the two talked about their situation, looking for some way out. They reasoned that it might not be too bad for Valerie if she lied on the witness stand since she was still a juvenile. But Vicki was an adult in the eyes of the law. If she committed perjury, she could go to jail. It was that knowledge that finally decided things for Vicki.

"I can't do it," she tearfully told Valerie as the two talked in their bedroom late one night. "I'm going to leave. Just get away."

"But where will you go?"

"I don't know. Away from here. Maybe back to Miami."

Valerie wanted to go, too, but Vicki convinced her that wouldn't work. It would be easier for one person to hide than two, besides Vicki would turn eighteen in a few weeks. She'd be a legal adult then, and they both believed that, after the trial, it would be a simple matter for her to come back and get custody of her two sisters.

So they agreed. Vicki would return to Miami, somehow get their belongings from the neighbor, and sell them. When she was settled, she'd send for Vanessa and Valerie. It seemed straightforward enough, although there were a few things to work out. They turned to a school friend named Diana. She had a car, a job, and had saved a little money.

The girls put their plan into action in the early-morning hours of the Sunday before Becky's trial was to begin. Diana drove to the Zubers' neighborhood, parked in front of their house, and turned off her lights. Vicki raised her bedroom window, pushed off the screen, and climbed out as quietly as she could. Valerie handed her suitcase out the window, and Vicki ran to the waiting car. Diana drove to the bus station in downtown Athens, where she bought Vicki a ticket to Miami. By sunrise, Vicki was on her way.

Valerie lay awake after her sister had gone, dreading the upset she knew morning would bring. When Mama Sara came in to wake them at 7:30, she discovered Vicki's bed was empty.

"Where's Vicki?"

"I don't know," Valerie told her. "In the bathroom?"

But, of course, Vicki wasn't in the bathroom. Sara began a search of the house, growing more frantic by the minute.

"She ran away!" she told her husband. "But the police will bring her back. That's for sure."

However, her call to the police was disappointing. The officer she spoke with explained that, at seventeen, Vicki was considered an adult.

"She can go anywhere she wants, ma'am. She's not breaking any laws."

Frustrated, Sara's next call was to Vane Hawkins. After a brief conversation, she hung up and turned to Valerie.

"He said you'll just have to testify instead."

Valerie felt like the floor had just dropped out from under her feet. She'd known it was possible that she'd have to testify, but the idea had been an abstraction. Today, in the face of her sister's absence, it was fact. It was real.

On Sunday afternoon, strong storms rolled across Georgia, and tornadoes touched down all over the Southeast. Sara Zuber drove her two granddaughters through the bad weather to Macon, where they checked into a hotel near the courthouse. By morning, the thunder and lightening had passed, but the rain lingered.

Rebecca Machetti's trial began at 9:00 A.M., February 24, 1975. Becky knew that she would be fighting for her life. District Attorney Fred Hasty had filed notice with the court two weeks before that the state would be seeking the death penalty. Nevertheless, Becky's demeanor as she was led into the courtroom was calm and unemotional. Her blonde hair was gone, replaced with a modest short, brown style.

But just because she appeared unruffled didn't mean the defendant was above trying to cause trouble. Just before court was called to order, Vane Hawkins approached Ray Wilkes. His face was stern. "Mr. Sheriff, we've got a problem."

"What is it?"

"My client is three months pregnant. Since she's been in

your jail longer than that, there's a problem."

Wilkes just shook his head. "Have you seen Becky's medical records?"

"No, I have not."

"So, you don't know that she's had a complete hysterectomy?"

Judge Cloud Morgan took the bench once more and the trial began. Jury selection took up the entire morning. During the questioning of the prospective jurors, Becky sat quietly at the defense table. She occasionally read from a small book of prayers. Eventually, eleven men and one woman were selected.

During opening statements Monday afternoon, the difference between the opposing attorneys quickly became apparent. Hasty was all business, neatly and logically laying out the pieces of the case he expected to make. Hawkins, on the other hand, seemed to delight in portraying himself as a bumbler. Dressed in a somewhat ill-fitting suit, he referred to himself several times as a "country lawyer." He tried to paint his client with the same rural brush, alternately calling Becky a "country girl" or a "child." He played down his successful career, wanting the jury to see him as an underdog, and declared that his opponent, Mr. Hasty, was "a giant of the bar association."

From his first statements to the jury, Hawkins singled out John Maree as the villain of the case. Maree, he told them, was scheming to marry Vicki Akins and had committed the murders so that she would inherit her father's insurance benefits. The Mafia connections and aspirations, Hawkins contended, were Maree's, not Becky's. And he claimed that Maree hated Becky Machetti because he'd proposed to her and been turned down.

Valerie and Vanessa heard none of the opening arguments or any of the prosecution's case. Sequestered as possible witnesses, they waited in the corridor outside the courtroom for five days, not knowing when or if they'd be called to testify.

Without her older sister, Valerie felt terribly alone. With each passing day, she grew angrier and more afraid. People she'd known all her life walked right by her without a word. They'd stare at the two girls, then move on, speaking in whispers. Valerie just wanted it to be over. If she was going to have to testify, she decided, then she was going to tell the truth. It couldn't be any worse than the way she was feeling right then.

Alan Barfield was one of the very few people who stopped to speak. "Hey, how are y'all doing?" he asked.

Valerie longed to respond. She missed Alan and wanted nothing more than to be held in his arms and comforted. But because he was testifying against her mother, Mama Sara despised him. Val was certain that even talking to Alan would cause more trouble for her and Vanessa. So she just shook her head and motioned for him to move on.

When Alan was called to the stand, he testified at length about the Labor Day weekend he'd spent in North Miami Beach. Becky just glared at him. So hate-filled was her stare that he only glanced her way a couple of times. He hated what he was having to do and knew that his part in the trial would probably end forever any hope he had of getting back together with Valerie.

Ronny Akins's parents approached him after he left the witness stand. During the first couple of days of the trial, they'd been a bit standoffish. Alan didn't blame them, since they hadn't known what he was going to say on the stand. Now, however, they were friendly and invited him to join them for dinner that evening. Drained by his testimony and depressed by the prospect of not seeing Valerie again, he tried to beg off, but Ronny's mother persisted.

"No, come on and go with us. Please."

In the end, he agreed and was glad he had. Ronny's family were nice folks and the dinner actually made him feel a bit better.

In addition to Alan, a number of law enforcement and scientific witnesses appeared for the prosecution. And Ronny's coworkers testified to Becky's attempt on his life in October of 1973.

On Wednesday, the state put up their star witness, John Maree. Wearing a garish plaid sport coat and a nervous smile, he took the stand. He gave Becky one defiant glance before beginning his damning testimony. When the time came for cross-examination, the defense was again unable to get him to change his story.

The state rested on Thursday, and the defense was expected to begin its case first thing Friday morning. But when court was called to order, Vane Hawkins made an unusual announcement.

"Your honor, our key witness, Victoria Akins, mysteriously disappeared from her grandmother's home over the weekend. We've attempted to locate her with no success."

If he'd hoped for help from the bench, Hawkins was disappointed.

"Was she under subpoena, Mr. Hawkins?"

"No, sir. We didn't feel that was necessary."

"Then I don't believe that this court can do anything to compel her to appear."

Hawkins had no choice but to proceed without Vicki, and, in the end, he decided not to call Valerie Akins to testify. She never knew why she was spared, but thought it might have been that the attorney feared what she would say. So, the defense's entire case was limited to one witness—Rebecca Machetti.

Since they were no longer considered witnesses, Valerie and Vanessa were allowed to join their grandmother in the courtroom. They watched as Becky took the stand, got settled, and smiled calmly at her attorney. Hawkins's first request to his client was that she name her children who were in court at the time. She did so, giving Valerie's and Vanessa's names and ages.

"And where is your oldest child?"

"I don't know. She's missing."

He wanted to follow up this line, but Hasty objected on the basis of relevance and the court put an end to it.

Under her attorney's guidance, Becky told the jury that Ronny had been a drug and alcohol addict and had physically and emotionally abused her. She declared that, on the night she was supposed to have tried to smother him with a pillow, she was actually just trying to hold him on the bed to prevent him from injuring himself while in a drug-induced frenzy.

She described in great detail how her friend Julie Baldwin had come to the house and taken her and her daughters away the next morning. She had confided in her friend about the abuse she suffered, and Julie, she assured the court, had seen Ronny under the influence many times.

Her bitterest words were for John Maree. She had pointed a gun at the man, she declared. Not only had he seduced her daughter, Vicki, but he'd brought his friend Darrell Campbell to her house to have sex with Valerie. Finally, she said, Maree had raped her youngest daughter Vanessa!

As their mother's testimony unfolded, Valerie and Vanessa couldn't help shaking their heads. None of that had ever happened, of course. Valerie tried to tell her grandmother that it wasn't true, but Mama Sara shushed her. "Just be quiet now."

All this had happened back in August of the previous year, Becky told the court. Those incidents, especially the last, were why she threatened Maree with a gun. And after that, he'd threatened her.

"He told me at my door that I would live to regret that I had ever aimed at him, that he had enough power, his word was power, that he could ruin me and my husband. And he did not want my daughter Vanessa. He wanted Vicki and her money." Becky took a deep breath. "Mr. Hawkins, at this time Vicki had no money and I told John this. And John told me that day, the 22nd of August, that Vicki would be coming into some money."

And in case the jury wasn't able to leap to the obvious conclusion, Becky added that Maree had later confessed to killing Ronny and Juanita Akins. "John stated to me he and another man named Darrell Campbell had come to Macon and murdered my husband. This was the knowledge given to me on September 22nd. At that time, Mr. Hawkins, I went to my bedroom. I took a gun and went back to the door. I pointed the gun at Mr. Maree. I told him to get away from me.

"When my husband came home from work, I related this to him, and he told me to keep quiet about it because John could be very dangerous."

Fred Hasty's cross-examination wasn't gentle. Why, he demanded, once they were all in custody, didn't Becky tell the police that Maree had confessed to her? Why had she not told any of the investigators about this over the past five months?

"You've never told any law enforcement officers that, have you?" he asked.

"I have not been asked, Mr. Hasty," was the best answer she could give.

After the defense rested, the prosecution called several rebuttal witnesses, one of whom was Julie Baldwin. She completely contradicted much of Becky's testimony. No, she said, Becky had never told her she'd been threatened by Ronny, and she'd never seen Ronny Akins drunk or under the influence of drugs—except on that morning in October of 1973 when he was taken to the hospital.

"You know," she said, "I wouldn't call it drunk. He was almost unconscious then, groggy, that kind of thing."

By late Friday, both sides had made their closing arguments, and just past 8:30 the case went to the jury. They reached a verdict in only an hour and 25 minutes. At 10:20, the parties were called back into the courtroom, and the jurors took their seats.

The spectators were silent. Ronny's parents held hands as Judge Morgan addressed the jury foreman.

"Would the foreman please rise? Mr. Smith, have you reached a verdict?"

"We have, Your Honor," William Smith answered.

Morgan turned to Becky. "Will the defendant please rise?"

Becky and Vane Hawkins stood, their eyes locked on the twelve people in the jury box.

Judge Morgan looked at the district attorney. "Mr. Hasty, would you accept and publish the verdict, please?"

Hasty took the slip of paper from the foreman and glanced at it. His face showed no reaction. In an emotionless voice, he read aloud, "As to Count One, we the jury find the defendant, Rebecca Akins Machetti, guilty as charged. February 28, 1975, William Thomas Smith, Jr., Foreman. As to Count Two, we the jury find the defendant, Rebecca Akins Machetti, guilty as charged. February 28, 1975. William Thomas Smith, Jr."

Becky's only reaction was to briefly close her eyes. But her daughters went cold with shock, and Sara Zuber appeared to have aged several years in only minutes. She was barely able to hold back her tears as she led her granddaughters out of the courtroom. The girls followed like sleepwalkers. Even though they knew she'd arranged two murders, they never really expected Becky to be convicted. The three made their way through the quiet nighttime streets back to their hotel, believing that the jury would retire for the night.

However, the jury's work wasn't done. The judge directed the prosecution and defense to present their arguments and witnesses concerning the sentence. As he'd said he would, Hasty argued for the death penalty. Hawkins asked for mercy. At 11:07, the jury received that portion of the case and resumed their deliberations.

At 1:00 A.M. Friday morning, March 1, they returned to the courtroom.

Judge Morgan first turned his attention to the few spectators left in the seats. "Thank you for your continued courtesy and cooperation. Please let us have no demonstration, however the verdict may read." He again asked the foreman to stand. "Have you reached a verdict?"

"Yes, we have, Your Honor," Smith answered.

Once again, Fred Hasty took the paper from the foreman and read aloud: "1 March 1975. As to Count One, we the jury find the following statutory aggravating circumstance to exist in this case: The offender committed the offense of Murder for herself, for the purpose of receiving money or any other thing of monetary value, and we recommend that the defendant be punished by death. William Thomas Smith, Jr., Foreman."

The verdict was the same on the second count. Becky stood very still, showing no emotion.

"Any objection to the form of the verdicts, Mr. Hawkins?"

"No objection to the form. No, sir, I think they are correct."

"All right now. Would you bring the defendant forward now, please, Mr. Hawkins?"

Hawkins and his client left their places behind the defense table to stand a few feet in front of the judge's bench.

"Mrs. Machetti, is there anything you wish to say to the Court before the Court pronounces sentence?"

"No, sir."

Morgan then passed his sentence: "It is considered, ordered and adjudged by the Court that you, Rebecca Akins Smith, a/k/a Rebecca Akins Machetti, be taken from the Bar of this Court, to the common jail of Bibb County, Georgia, where you shall be safely kept and confined until you shall be moved, when you shall be delivered to the State Board of Corrections of the State of Georgia for electrocution, as provided by law, between the hours of ten o'clock in the forenoon and two o'clock in the afternoon on the 15th day following the filing in the Trial Court of the remittitur from the Supreme Court of the State of Georgia, and may the Lord have mercy on your soul."

Rebecca Machetti was the first woman sentenced to death in Bibb County since Anjette Lyles in 1958. Observers in the courtroom were shocked to see Becky smile when her sentence was read.

As soon as he could find a telephone, Hawkins called the hotel to give Sara and the girls the bad news. Sara was inconsolable. She spent the night crying and pacing the floor. Valerie and Vanessa wept right along with her. In spite of the turbulent, sometimes frightening lives they'd led with her, Becky was still their mother. Now they knew they'd lose their only remaining parent to the electric chair.

The next morning, Sara took the girls back to Athens. Along with the grief and anger at the death sentence passed on Becky, she was fearful for her granddaughters' safety. Vicki was gone, and Sara was afraid that Valerie and Vanessa might try to follow her. Although Valerie never admitted she'd helped her sister run away, Sara suspected she had. The first thing she did when they got home was have the window in Valerie's bedroom nailed shut.

Chapter 22

Nothing had worked out as Vicki had planned. Soon after arriving in Miami, she'd gone back to their old neighborhood and found the man who'd taken their belongings. But five months hadn't softened his attitude a bit. He still demanded a storage fee. So, she gave up the idea of ever getting back her family's things and bringing her sisters back to Florida. She now turned her attention to keeping a roof over her head.

During the months after leaving Athens, Vicki worked odd jobs, scrabbling for money and living any way she could. She'd tried to keep in touch with her sisters, but Mama Sara had refused to take her calls. She wrote them letters, but the girls never got them. The only way Valerie ever knew her sister had written was by retrieving the torn-up letters from the trash. She and Vanessa pieced a couple of them together as well as they could, but parts were still missing and they only got snippets of information from them. One of the letters provided the information that Vicki was working for a television station and had a nice apartment. On another scrap, they found a telephone number. Valerie carefully tucked that information away.

On March 26, 1975, Vane Hawkins filed notice of appeal for Becky Machetti and also filed a pauper's affidavit on her behalf. Both Machettis remained at the Bibb County Jail while their appeals played out, and Becky discovered an interesting way to pass the time. She initiated correspondence with a variety of people, writing and receiving nearly forty letters a day.

Through the letters, she sought and found support in numerous areas. And she was delighted that many of the letters she received contained money for her defense.

Becky's correspondence also resulted in a growing number of visitors. One afternoon, a deputy brought a well-dressed man to Ray Wilkes's office. He introduced himself to the chief deputy as a representative of a television program called *The Baptist Hour*.

"I know visiting hours are on Sunday, but I need to see Rebecca Machetti today. And they tell me you're the only one who can give me permission."

Wilkes invited him to sit down. "I'm not sure you need to see her."

The man explained he'd been corresponding with Becky. "She's ready to profess her faith and be baptized. It's important that I see her now, baptize her, and record this for our program."

Wilkes frowned. "I don't think you know who you're dealing with. I don't think you really want to see her."

The man became insistent. He mentioned civil rights, freedom of religion, and started quoting the Constitution. About that time, a Catholic priest walked past the office, and Wilkes called out to him.

"Father Healy, could you come in here a moment?"

Wilkes and Healy had known each other for several years, their paths often crossing at political and charitable events. Healy came in and was introduced to the man from *The Baptist Hour*.

"Father Healy," Wilkes said, "would you tell him what you know about Rebecca Machetti?"

Healy smiled and said in his rich Irish brogue, "Oh, yes. Dear Rebecca. She's going to be confirmed today in the

Church."

At that, the television man slammed his notebook shut and left without another word.

John Maree finally had to face the consequences of his actions on a rainy Thursday in April 1975. He stood before Judge Cloud Morgan and pled guilty to the murders of Juanita and Ronny Akins. Present were Fred Hasty and Don Thompson from the District Attorney's Office, Maree, and his attorney Willis Sparks.

The state recommended life in prison, and Sparks indicated he and his client were in agreement with that recommendation. Hasty did tell the court he believed that John Maree had been fearful of the Mafia and Rebecca Machetti, and that he didn't consider Maree to be a "full partner" in the crimes.

"He got away from the Machettis when they got back to Florida," Hasty said. "And he cooperated with the police and testified against his codefendents."

Any hope of a light sentence would have evaporated as soon as Maree saw the judge's expression. Morgan wasn't an easily influenced man, and he wasn't swayed by Hasty's picture of Maree as being frightened into committing the crimes.

"I'm not too much impressed by your contention that you were frightened into it, frankly. I don't put much credence in that. As a human being you had an obligation not only to refuse to participate in it, but to expose it and prevent it. I am more impelled by considerations that have been mentioned, that you have cooperated once you were apprehended."

The judge acknowledged that the Machettis would probably not have been convicted without his testimony. "And I think it's a real factor that must be considered, that you testified, that you made a clean breast. There's also the possibility of having made a clean breast of even such a horrible crime as this, Mr. Maree, that having confessed your guilt, you may be in a position to rehabilitate your life. You have a family. I wonder how that family will ever be able to react to you. I don't know.

"You are a human being and I feel for you as a human being, but I am just outraged by the crime, Mr. Maree."

Morgan then took the state's recommendation and sentenced him to two life sentences to be served concurrently.

Maree only spoke two words. "Thank you."

John Maree soon left the Bibb County Jail and was taken to the first of several state prison camps where he would serve his sentence. In May, Ray Wilkes wrote Allen L. Ault, commissioner of the State Department of Corrections, expressing concern for John Maree's safety. Wilkes knew that in the prison system, an inmate who testified against his codefendants could have trouble. Ault wrote back, assuring Wilkes that every effort would be made to protect Maree from harm.

Valerie's and Vanessa's feelings for their mother were ambivalent. While they wanted to be removed from Becky's cruelty and drama, she *was* their mother, and that wasn't an easy bond to break. Their grandmother encouraged those feelings. Under her supervision, they wrote regularly to Becky. Mama Sara always read their outgoing letters before mailing them. She also insisted on reading those that they received from Becky. Once a week, they spoke to Becky on the telephone, and Sara took the sisters to Macon once or twice a month to visit her in the jail there.

It was impossible for Vanessa and Valerie to assume a normal routine and act as if everything were fine. Their grandmother still had angry outbursts, frustrated by the situation. She was also worried about what the girls might do when they weren't with her. Because of that, they were rarely allowed to go anywhere without her because she feared they might run away. After the winter quarter ended, she withdrew them from public school and hired a teacher to tutor them at home.

It wasn't a peaceful household. Valerie and her grandmother had screaming arguments, and little Vanessa just cried every time she got in trouble. The girls were no different than other teenagers, pushing the limits and challenging authority. But these normal adolescent behaviors were intensified by their history. They'd been removed from a parent not once, but twice. They were living with people they didn't know well and were haunted by the fact that their mother had killed their father.

Vicki Akins returned to Athens once during this time. She tried to see her sisters at the Zuber house, but Mama Sara refused to allow her in the door and an argument ensued. Hearing the commotion, the other girls ran to see what was going on. When Valerie tried to push past her to get to Vicki, Sara slapped her across the face.

"They hate you," Sara told Vicki.

"My sisters don't hate me," Vicki shouted. "They don't hate me."

"They do hate you." Sara called to Vanessa, "Come over here. Tell her you hate her. Go on. Tell her!"

Vanessa started crying but Sara wouldn't give up. "I said tell her you hate her."

Finally, Vanessa turned to her sister and whispered, "I hate you, Vicki."

Vicki left the house then and never went back.

Valerie and Vanessa had good and bad days with their grandparents. Sometimes they almost seemed to get along, but the peaceful moments never lasted. By the end of May, Valerie was worn out emotionally by the nearly constant conflict. More and more she blamed Becky for their situation. When her mother called the house Sunday night, as she'd done every week since her arrest, Valerie refused to talk to her. This triggered a terrible scene between Valerie and her grandmother. The two barely spoke after that.

John and Sara were at their wits' end. They discussed whether Valerie might be better off in a girls' home. Valerie even wondered that herself. She was miserable. She stopped eating and announced she'd rather die than stay in their house. Finally, her step-grandfather persuaded Sara that the best thing for all of them would be to let Valerie go.

Once the decision was made, Sara didn't hesitate. The next morning she put her seventeen-year-old granddaughter on a bus to Miami. Valerie hadn't been allowed to take anything with her, so she boarded the bus empty-handed. She had no money, no purse, and no luggage. Still, she wasn't unhappy. She felt she was free for the first time in her life and was sure that only good things lay ahead for her.

The bus sped along back roads and interstates, stopping to take on and discharge passengers. But when they stopped in Byron, just south of Macon, a police officer climbed aboard and walked down the aisle until he stood in front of Valerie.

"Are you Valerie Akins?" he asked.

"Yes, sir."

"You'll have to come with me. We've got a lookout for you for theft."

He led her off the bus and into the station as she tearfully protested she hadn't done anything. There, they were joined by a second officer who explained that her grandmother had reported she'd run away and stolen jewelry and money from her.

"But I didn't. I don't *have* anything." To demonstrate the fact, she even turned out the pockets of her jeans. She told them the whole story, and finally one of them made a telephone call to the Athens bus station. The person he spoke with verified that an older woman had come in that morning, bought a bus ticket for a blonde teenaged girl, and put her on the bus to Miami.

The men felt terrible about the misunderstanding. They took Valerie to Burger King and bought her lunch. Back at the bus station, the officers got her a seat on the next bus to Miami and gave her $10. When she was finally moving south again, Val broke down and cried with relief.

Valerie arrived in Miami twelve hours later and stepped into a strange and frightening world. The bus station was loud and busy and filled with people who scared her to death. She found a pay phone and called the number she had for her sister.

When she arrived at the bus station an hour later, Vicki was furious.

"What are you doing here?" she demanded.

Val explained what had happened. She'd expected her sister to welcome her, but Vicki told her she shouldn't have come. Her letters had painted pretty pictures of her life, but they'd been lies. She didn't work at a television station and she didn't have a nice apartment. She and three other girls shared a cheap, crowded apartment in a seedy section of town. They worked at anything they could to make it from day to day. Vicki knew this was no place for her sister.

But even under these circumstances, it was good to see family again. And she really had no choice but to take Valerie in. So, Vicki did the best she could for her sister, making sure she had a place to sleep and food to eat.

Surprisingly, things weren't too bad. The girls began to think this might work after all. Vicki wrote to her father's parents and let them know where she and her sister were living. She told Valerie she could enroll in North Miami Senior High School in the fall.

"I just have to get guardianship of you," Vicki told her.

Chapter 23

Appeals are automatic after death penalty sentences, and both Becky's and Tony's attorneys were hard at work in that regard. But other people were working just as hard to see that their sentences were carried out. In July of 1975, Ronny's parents, Thelma and Raymond Akins, wrote to Governor George Busbee requesting his help: "Lord only knows the anguish and heartache that parents and family go through unless they have experienced an ordeal such as ours. If these people are paroled in a few years, they are very capable of killing again. Please help us all you can."

Other legal matters were also underway. The settlement of Ronny Akins's estate was time-consuming and acrimonious. As the legal guardian of the two younger girls, Sara Zuber expected to receive their insurance money. Their Social Security survivor benefits were already coming to her, and she had received Vicki's as well until the girl's eighteenth birthday. But Ronny's parents weren't convinced that the inheritance from his estate should go to Rebecca's mother. They hired Emmett Goodman, the attorney who'd represented Ronny in his divorce.

One of the first things the lawyer did was contact Vicki in Miami. She surprised them all by agreeing to come to Macon and meet with the family to discuss her father's estate. She didn't hesitate, even when Goodman advised that the police also wanted to speak with her.

Valerie wanted to accompany her sister, but the two weren't sure she would be safe. Val wouldn't turn eighteen for another six months, and they were afraid Mama Sara would try to force her to go back to Athens. Vicki, however, had no doubts about returning to Georgia. Her mind was made up, and this time she was going to tell the whole truth. She was tired of lying and would take whatever consequences came of her past prevarication. And this time she was not going to have to go back on a bus. She and Valerie managed to scrape together enough money for a round-trip airplane ticket.

On July 24, 1975, the same day the Apollo 18 astronauts splashed down in the Pacific, Vicki Akins arrived in Macon. She arrived at the courthouse just before 5:00 P.M. Although it was getting late in the day, the 90-degree heat still beat down on the city, and she was glad to get into the air-conditioned building.

They were all waiting for her in the sheriff's office conference room. Her Akins grandparents; two of her father's brothers, Walter Randall and William; Emmett Goodman; and Durward Mercer, the court-appointed administrator of Ronny Akins's estate sat around a big wooden table. Chief Investigator Harry Harris and Bibb County Assistant District Attorney Donald Thompson were also present.

They exchanged the usual greetings and Vicki took a seat. She was a little nervous, remembering that she'd lied to two of these people in the past, but she was ready to do this now. It was time to tell the truth. At their urging, she told about Becky's first attempt on Ronny's life. Then, for the first time, she related what really happened on the weekend of the murders. Harris and Thompson listened with satisfaction as she corroborated everything they'd already believed about the killings of Ronny and Juanita Akins.

With that behind her, Vicki moved on to the main reason for her visit. She explained that she wanted to get custody of Valerie and that she would need the Social Security benefits to take care of her, enroll her in school, and eventually into college.

"What about Vanessa?" Mercer asked.

"I think Val would be better off with me, but Vanessa should be with her grandparents," she said, nodding at Thelma and Raymond.

"Do you believe this strongly enough to assist me and cooperate with me in perhaps trying to get another guardian appointed for these two children, other than Mrs. Zuber?" Goodman asked her.

Vicki looked at him for a long minute, then said, "Yes, sir, because I don't like the way she's treating them."

Vicki claimed that Mrs. Zuber hadn't ever used the Social Security benefits for the girls and that she deprived them food and clothing and gave them only a $5-a-month allowance.

"If Mr. and Mrs. Akins had control over this money, do you feel that they would oversee it properly?"

"Oh, yes, I'm sure they would."

When asked about the inheritance, Vicki said, "My grandmother said that we would get, like, $5,000 a piece. And she said some of it had to go to the lawyer. And the rest of it would have to go to her because—for taking care of us."

Before saying goodbye, Vicki's grandparents offered their home to her and Valerie, but Vicki wasn't ready for that kind of commitment to people she hardly knew.

Vicki returned to Miami the next day. She didn't know what would happen with her father's estate. Her life to this point had taught her to expect the worst. Now, she couldn't help comparing life in her cramped apartment with what Valerie would find with her grandparents. Vicki knew what she had to do. She and Valerie talked a long time about what was best, and Val reluctantly agreed to go live with the Akinses. Their dream was still that the three of them could live together, but it couldn't happen right then.

As the summer was coming to an end, Vicki and her grandparents made arrangements for Valerie's return to Athens. On a hot August day, Val boarded a plane in Miami and flew to Atlanta. During the flight, she prayed hard that her grandparents—people she'd only seen a few times in her life—would welcome her and love her.

When she walked down the jet bridge and entered the terminal, the whole family was there—grandparents, aunts and uncles, and cousins she didn't even know she had. For a heart-stopping moment, nobody moved, then her grandmother stepped forward and hugged her. One by one, the others did the same, embracing her and introducing themselves. There was her uncle Randall and his wife Linda, her uncle Bill and his wife Reba, and a sweet woman who was introduced as her Aunt Peggy, but who was actually her father's cousin. For the first time in a long while, Valerie felt like she was home.

The Akins household on College Station Road was quite a contrast to what Valerie had experienced with the Zubers. The small brick ranch, located only a couple of miles from the sprawling University of Georgia campus, was full of love and laughter. Although only Raymond and Thelma and, now, Valerie lived there, the rest of the family was in and out all the time. Instead of returning to Clark Central that fall, Valerie was enrolled in Athens Christian School. She'd never have expected it, but Valerie thrived at the strict school. The combination of love and discipline made her happier than she'd been in years.

The dispute over Vanessa Akins's custody was bitter. After months of fruitless negotiation and a hearing at which Valerie testified, Mr. and Mrs. Akins were awarded custody of Ronny and Becky's youngest daughter. However, Vanessa wasn't happy about the outcome of the case. She didn't want to move to the Akinses' home and was very angry that she had been ordered to live there. For the first couple of weeks in her new home, she wouldn't speak to anyone. But she gradually began to respond to the warmth and love that was being offered to her.

Her grandparents enrolled Vanessa in the Athens Christian School where she, like her sister, flourished. Here in Athens, the girls had opportunities they never would have had in Miami. Their grades were good. They made friends easily and were both able to take senior trips to Europe.

Chapter 24

By the end of 1975, the initial appeals processes for the Machettis had run their courses. On January 6, 1976, the Georgia Supreme Court affirmed both convictions, and their executions were scheduled for fifteen days from the date the remittiturs were received by the trial court.

But people who understood the workings of the legal system knew that this didn't mean they'd really be executed in two weeks. It was simply the signal to begin another round of appeals. It's likely that neither defendant really believed they'd ever be executed.

At that time, the implementation of any death penalty was uncertain. In 1972, a Georgia death penalty case had been heard by the United States Supreme Court. The defendant in the case, a black man named William Henry Furman, had been burglarizing a house when the homeowners surprised him. He'd tried to run, but tripped and fell, and the gun he was carrying accidentally discharged. One of the residents of the home was killed. Furman was convicted of murder and sentenced to death.

However, the Supreme Court ruled that, in Furman's case, the death penalty was cruel and unusual punishment. They also found that, in Georgia, the death penalty was imposed arbitrarily and was biased against black defendants. That decision forced Georgia and several other states to reconsider and reconstruct their laws in that area.

The last week in June 1976, Georgia's new death penalty statue was reviewed by the Supreme Court and ruled constitutional. When, shortly after that ruling, Tony Machetti's next appeal, based largely on the points in the Furman case, reached the Supreme Court, it was denied.

The longer she lived with the Akinses, the more removed Valerie became from her mother's influence. Her life was now relatively happy. She'd never before had the opportunity to get to know her paternal grandparents. It broke her heart to realize that it had taken her father's murder to bring this about. She no longer wrote to her mother and wanted no more contact with her. But she couldn't remove herself from the reality of Becky's conviction and the appeals that followed.

One of those appeals was pending when, on July 21, 1976, Valerie wrote to the Supreme Court, asking that they not overturn her mother's conviction.

"Mrs. Machetti (my mother) is a dominating woman and has the idea that she can con anyone into anything. She killed my dad and his new wife. She thought she could get Dad's insurance money after he died and she wanted it to gamble and to buy liquor with.

"She said that if I ever told anyone the truth about the things she did to my dad that she would get rid of me, too. Well, sir, she did kill my dad, so what's to stop her now.

"You see, sir, I hate her. To me my mother has been dead for quite a while. I hope she gets electrocuted real soon. Tomorrow wouldn't been soon enough. Don't let her fool you gentlemen.

"If she were to get out, my grandmother and grandfather, myself and my little sister are in big trouble. She hates us. Please push the death penalty to insure law abiding citizens like us safety from people like her."

Valerie graduated from Athens Christian School that

year and began attending the University of Georgia in the fall of 1976. An indifferent student, she had no idea what she wanted to do with her life. She went to classes because that was what was expected of her, but she had no clear goals at the time. More and more, her thoughts turned to Vicki, who'd been her best friend as well as her sister. She missed her terribly.

After his latest appeal was denied, the Bibb County authorities made arrangements to have Tony Machetti moved from their jail to Reidsville State Prison to await his scheduled October 26th execution. On Thursday, October 14, he and Becky were allowed a brief visit. Then, Chief Deputy Ray Wilkes and Investigator Robbie Johnson led Machetti, handcuffed and with a waist chain, out of the jail. Tony still sported a full, bushy mustache and wore oversized glasses. He blinked in the bright sunlight. It was a warm, clear day, and the first time he'd been outside in almost two years.

During the two-and-a-half-hour drive, the two lawmen chatted about the news of the day—the upcoming presidential election, in which Gerald Ford would face Georgian Jimmy Carter, and the swine flu epidemic that was expected later in the year—but their prisoner was quiet. His defiance and arrogance were gone. This trip was a stark contrast to the last one when Wilkes accompanied Tony and John Maree from Florida back to Georgia.

Even with the new execution date set, the appeals went on. Attorney Sidney L. Moore Jr., of Decatur, petitioned Governor George Busbee to delay the execution, citing constitutional questions about the legality of the death penalty. Tony's case was attracting enormous attention. If the execution took place, he would be the first person executed in the United States since 1968.

Moore had taken the case without concern for being paid—fighting the death penalty on all fronts possible was his passion. And he knew you could fight the system not only through legal means, but also through the court of public opinion. The Georgia Committee Against the Death Penalty scheduled a rally in support of Anthony Machetti for Saturday, October 23, only three days before Tony was scheduled to die. The rally was to be held near the state capitol and a large crowd was expected. However, some of the enthusiasm was dampened when Governor Busbee signed a ninety-day stay of execution on the 21st.

On a chilly Monday, November 1, the Supreme Court finally issued their decision in Becky's case. Her conviction and death sentence was upheld. The next day, Jimmy Carter was elected president of the United States.

The law enforcement community in Macon wasn't concerned with the Machettis right then. They were dealing with their own problems. Sheriff Jimmy Bloodworth resigned and pled guilty in Bibb County Superior Court to two charges of accepting gifts in violation of his oath of office. In November, the governor appointed Ray Wilkes as sheriff. It was a position he would hold for many years.

The dispute over the distribution of Ronny Akins's estate dragged on, with the parties all refusing compromise. Finally, in frustration, Durward Mercer filed suit against the insurance companies and Ronny's former employer on behalf of the three girls, demanding payment. A jury trial was held during the first week of January 1977. Philip S. Brown represented Valerie, James McLaughlin represented Vicki, and O. L. Crumbley represented Vanessa.

On January 10th, the jury returned a verdict in favor of the sisters. After court costs and attorneys' fees, each girl was awarded $10,039. Valerie and Vicki both signed away their rights to the money and had the checks made over to Raymond and Thelma Akins. The Akinses, in turn, wrote Vicki a check for $1,500. Vanessa's share was held in trust until the dispute over her custody was resolved in Clarke County. Vicki returned to Florida, where, later that year, she married a man she'd been seeing for several months.

Mary Ann Oakley was an Atlanta attorney only two years out of law school when she took on Becky Machetti's case. A long-time opponent of the death penalty, she felt she had to do what she could to save this woman from execution. Oakley appealed Becky's death sentence, arguing that the jurors might have thought the death penalty would never actually be carried out since Georgia's old death penalty law had been struck down.

While the new appeal was making its slow way through the system, on January 14, 1977, Judge Cloud Morgan denied Becky's motion for stay of execution. He also denied a petition for declaratory judgment and a motion for a new presentencing hearing on the grounds that the court lacked jurisdiction and that the motion and petition were without merit. The next day, Oakley filed notice of appeal of Morgan's ruling.

Becky Machetti never seemed to run out of complaints. At one point during this time, she claimed that the food she was being given in the Bibb County Jail was damaging her health. She declared she was suffering from kidney disease and was required to take diuretics and maintain a low-sodium diet of fresh vegetables and fruits.

In response to her client's complaint, Oakley wrote to Sheriff Wilkes, demanding that jail personnel provide proper food and medication to treat Becky's illness. Her diet improved, but in April, she complained of chest pains and declared she was having a heart attack. She was taken to the Medical Center, where she was examined, given an injection, and returned to jail. It's possible that this was an anxiety attack brought on by the news the week before that the Georgia Supreme Court had turned down her latest appeal.

With her appeal denied, Becky was again resentenced and, on April 29, was moved to the Women's Correctional Institute at Hardwick to await execution.

Becky wasn't shy about approaching anyone for help. On July 31, 1977, she wrote Governor George Busbee. Written in old-fashioned language in neat script, her letter began in an oddly familiar manner: "I trust you are well and I hope my letter does not jolt you. I wish I knew why I was writing it, but I am not clear as to my motivation. I only realize I am impelled to write it."

She mentioned the many letters that had been sent to him on her behalf and declared that a few had especially touched her. She described in great detail the suffering—mental and physical—that she'd endured during her incarceration and then demonstrated that she had now abandoned Tony. "I have endeavored to separate from those guilty of this dastardly crime totally. I have almost succeeded. I only have one tie left. A legal technicality—my marriage."

She declared her innocence several times, then veered off into a religious vein. "Nothing is impossible with our Creator. And, Gov. Busbee, He knows the truth! I have tried, oft times most unsuccessfully, to forgive, love and pray for all who seem to be glad of Bibb County's triumphant condemnation of me. But I still try! I knew the night I was sentenced that I would still be alive and trusting my Lord long after the downfall of those who sought to crucify me!"

She alluded to graft and corruption in Bibb County and said the sheriff, district attorney, police chief, several detectives, and many more were "guilty of crimes of such a severity even the state capital should have rocked."

Finally, on page four, she arrived at the reason for the letter. "I realize the grave responsibility you assumed at the helm of leadership, and that you continue to strive to be the best leader you can be. I commend you, I respect your position and I feel for your immense and wide spread concern for this great state...but I am praying daily to the Holy Mother and Her Son Christ Jesus that the grave injustice suffered by one of your native-born citizens will be so impressed upon you that you will be lead [*sic*] by such conviction that you will seek to correct this."

Becky ended her letter on another familiar note. "God bless you and those you love. I sincerely hope and pray your mother-in-law soon is well. Please give my letter your utmost scrutination [*sic*] and ponder it. I am totally sincere, honest and hopeful."

She signed it Ms. Rebecca Ann Machetti.

~~~
~~~

As more appeals were filed in both cases, Becky kept herself occupied by writing letters. She wrote to people all over the world, was active in groups fighting capital punishment, and started her own prison ministry.

She also gave interviews to book, magazine, and newspaper writers. Pictures taken of her at the time show a pretty woman with brunette hair styled in a bouffant flip and a bright smile. She proclaimed her innocence and declared she had been mistreated at the Bibb County Jail, where, she said, she'd suffered migraines, skin rashes, and a stroke. She even professed to be a member of Mensa, an international society for exceptionally bright people. The primary requirement for joining Mensa is having a high IQ. However, when that organization was contacted, they had no record of Becky under any of her various names.

The last woman executed in the United States was Elizabeth Ann Duncan. In 1962, Duncan died in California's gas chamber for the murder of her daughter-in-law. In 1977 and 1978, Becky Machetti was the only woman on Georgia's death row and one of only five women under sentences of death nationwide. This fact alone brought her a great deal of attention.

The anti-death penalty movement was one of the largest and strongest in the world and generated a constant flow of letters in support of Rebecca Machetti. In 1978, Governor Busbee received one such letter from a woman named Frieda Groffy from St. Niklaas, Belgium. In somewhat awkward English, she wrote: "We the undersigned, a Belgian Action Group for Indian America, are shocked to find out, that in a great country like the U.S.A. who pretend to respect Human Rights and Human Dignity, a woman like Rebecca Ann Machetti, mother of three children, with a blanco crime sheet, could be send to Death Row, for a murder case she couldn't possibly have committed, while she was 700 miles away from the crime-spot. It was proved—she pleaded non guilty. During her proces she was brought under the influence of heavy sedative medication. For all these fact's we have good reasons to believe that the simple fact she is part Cherokee-part Italian had a lot to do with this grave, cruel sentence."

More than forty signatures were attached to the letter. It appears that the organization had little grasp of the law and hadn't done much in the way of homework, since Becky Machetti was neither Cherokee nor Italian. They had, however, referred her case to Amnesty International.

Within a year of her marriage, Vicki Akins's first daughter was born in early 1978. That summer, after Vanessa graduated from high school, she and Valerie went to Florida to meet their new niece. It was good to be back with Vicki, and, in many ways, Florida still felt like home. So much so that, after a short time, Valerie and Vanessa decided to stay in Miami.

Unfortunately, the family they'd left in Athens saw this move as the girls' abandoning them. The couldn't understand why Valerie and Vanessa would choose to stay in Florida. For the sisters, this began an estrangement from most of their father's family that would last for many years.

After several months living with Vicki and her family, Valerie and Vanessa moved out on their own. Vanessa attended a community college, and Valerie, who'd dropped out of the University of Georgia the previous winter, began taking business education courses at Miami Lakes Technical Education Center. At night, she worked at the Caterpillar Tractor Company.

~~~

George Busbee was reelected governor in 1978 and Becky wrote to him again: "First of all congratulations on your recent victory!" Then she launched into a series of complaints about the Georgia Women's Correctional Institute in Hardwick. She'd been assaulted by the former chaplain, she claimed, and then been harassed because she'd reported it.

"Were you aware that mail tampering by a few employees went on until other arrangements were made?"

She asked that Busbee send someone to talk to her. "SIR, I AM NOT GUILTY AND WHEN THE TRUTH DOES FINALLY COME OUT WON'T YOU AT LEAST HAVE IT NOT ON YOUR CONSCIENCE IF YOU HELP ME?"

Busbee's polite return letter assured her he'd forward her complaints to David Evans, commissioner of the Department of Offender Rehabilitation.

Tony Machetti's case had been taken up on appeal several times, but none succeeded. On Tuesday, February 6, 1979, he appeared again before Judge Cloud Morgan for another resentencing. After setting the new execution date for February 26, Morgan asked Machetti if he had anything he wanted to say.

"I wasn't guilty then," he told the court, "and I'm not guilty now."

Once again, appeals were filed and the sentence was delayed.

Becky lost another appeal as well, and her execution was now scheduled for September 14, 1979. Attorney Mary Ann Oakley petitioned the United States District Court for a stay
~~~

of execution, contending that Becky had been denied a fair trial because of ineffective counsel and pretrial publicity. She also claimed that Becky had been given "personality altering drugs" before and during her trial and that these drugs prevented her warm, sympathetic nature from showing. She accused then Chief Deputy Ray Wilkes of keeping her client in isolation for a month as punishment for her not answering his questions the way he wanted her to.

Judge Wilbur Owens agreed to take her request under advisement, but he warned that the public was growing tired of seeing sentences delayed over a long period of time.

On September 1, Judge Owens stayed Becky's execution indefinitely to allow the federal court to review the conviction.

While she waited for a decision, Becky continued her voluminous correspondence. In the spring of 1980, thanks to the efforts of numerous people worldwide, she was rewarded with an Apostolic Blessing and a signed color photo from Pope John Paul II.

In June of that year, Becky wrote once more to the governor, again declaring her innocence and accusing the "barbarians" at Hardwick of threatening her life. On June 9, Busbee responded by saying he'd received her letter and asked an attorney on his staff to investigate the status of her incarceration. "I am sorry you feel that you have been unjustly convicted on this charge, but understand your case is currently on appeal and trust the Judiciary to render a just and reasoned decision in your case based on all the circumstances surrounding your arrest, trial and conviction."

Although the governor's letter was little more than a polite response, Becky took it as a sign that he was on her side. On June 12, she wrote in an almost flirtatious manner: "Dear Gov. Busbee: You are a doll! I have yours of the 9th and appreciate your time and energy! Thanks!" That was followed by paragraphs of flattery and prayers for his soul. She closed saying she expected a miracle. "Watch the days to come! God bless, Excellency! Sincerely."

She was even more flamboyant and less restrained in her next letter to him. "Dear Gov. Busbee, I pray God is blessing you!" She told him she'd been in touch with the Justice Department, FBI, Postmaster General, Federal judges and lawyers, and that she felt he should know what was going on.

She was evidently less pleased by the actions of David Evans, commissioner of the Department of Offender Rehabilitation. "I like you! I level with you! I pour out my heart—And I keep right on. And I do not blame you—but just who runs Ga? David Evans? He doesn't! You do! And the Constitution is over you all."

Becky told him to expect to hear big things about her case very soon. She said twelve foreign governments were intervening diplomatically on her behalf. "God takes care of his own in due time." She finished with: "Hey, come on. Be a Christian and see that Jesus' commandments are followed. Nothing would please me more than to state one day you were the best Gov. & best friend I had in a sin trodden state. Is it wrong of me to seek charity & compassion from you or is that verboten?

"I *still* believe all in Ga are not rotten. I still believe in you."

Chapter 25

John Maree spent time in several prisons. In 1980, he was in the Hall County Correctional Institute in Gainesville. He'd earned trustee status and, during the fall of that year, was assigned to work at the local Georgia State Patrol post. He wasn't happy with the arrangement, feeling that the menial chores of cleaning, making beds, and cooking for the troopers were somehow beneath him. In letters to friends, he complained that this work did nothing to promote his rehabilitation or teach him a useful trade. But it did provide him with free time outside for breaks.

"Weather here has turned cool and expect frost," he wrote to a friend on October 25. "Trees are very beautiful with bright orange, brilliant reds and soft yellow being the most prominent. The squirrels are very plentiful and full of mischief. All getting ready for the winter ahead."

Maree had begun a correspondence with Milledgeville attorney James M. Watts. He wanted Watts to try for a special parole for him and believed that former Bibb County Assistant District Attorney Don Thompson would be willing to speak to his truthfulness and would lend his support to the request. However, Watts suggested waiting until after Christmas to put the request to the board.

Maree wrote that he was concerned about his own safety since it was known he'd testified against Tony and Becky. He was especially worried about how his fellow prisoners would react if death were the final outcome of the appeals that were going on for Tony and Becky. His hope was to be moved to a halfway house or a restitution center where he'd have to deal with as few people as possible.

Maree was given a Thanksgiving leave that year—from 6:00 A.M. November 27, 1980, to 6:00 P.M. November 29, 1980. He spent the time in a small town near Athens with a family he'd met through a prison ministry program. The holiday was cool and rainy, but Maree thought the weather was fine because he was out of prison for the first time in six years.

The day before Maree started his Thanksgiving leave, US District Judge Wilbur Owens denied Anthony Machetti's application for a writ of habeas corpus. That cleared the way for the next round of appeals to move on to the Fifth Circuit Court of Appeals in New Orleans.

A United States magistrate denied Becky's latest attempt to have her conviction set aside on March 24, 1981. Ironically, on that same brisk spring day, jury selection began in the Macon trial of a man named Pless Brown Jr. He was charged with the murder of Don Thompson, the assistant district attorney who'd been so involved in the Akins murder investigation. Thompson had been killed when he surprised two burglars in a friend's apartment in East Macon. Brown's codefendant, Jimmy Lee Horton, had been convicted of the crime in February and sentenced to death. Brown, too, would be convicted.

In November, the Eleventh Circuit Court of Appeals in Atlanta upheld Judge Wilbur Owens's rejection of Tony Machetti's petition. That action moved Anthony Machetti to the top of the list of the ninety men awaiting execution on Georgia's death row. There were three others whose appeals were in the advanced stages—William Anthony Brooks, Alpha Otis Stephens, and Guy Mason—but Tony's case was the furthest along in the system.

Atlanta attorney Robert Glustrom was now representing Machetti, and, in April of 1982, he asked District Court Judge Wilbur Owens to extend the stay of execution he'd issued before Tony's last appeal had been heard. Owens denied the request, making no secret of the way he felt. "I don't think Mr. Machetti is entitled to another day in court. He committed this horrible crime and his day has come." That ruling resulted in Machetti's execution date being rescheduled, and he was sent to the state prison at Jackson to await the carrying out of his sentence.

The news for Becky was more encouraging. On a hot June afternoon, the three-judge panel of the Eleventh Circuit Court of Appeals ruled that women were underrepresented on Rebecca Machetti's jury. The jury list for her trial was only 18 percent women, but the population of Bibb County was 54 percent women. A Georgia law that provided women could opt out of jury duty by simply notifying the court that they wished to do so had been struck down as unconstitutional some months after Becky's trial. While the court didn't proscribe any specific ratio, it did require that the makeup of the jury more closely resemble the population.

As a result of the ruling, Judge Wilbur Owens issued a writ of habeas corpus for Becky. This left the Bibb County District Attorney's Office with four choices—set her free, schedule a new trial, ask the full Eleventh Circuit Court to consider the case, or appeal the decision to the US Supreme Court.

Willis Sparks, who had recently been elected district attorney, took several days to make a decision. After conferring with Georgia attorney general Mike Bowers, he decided to request a reconsideration by the entire court. His decision meant that Becky could now relax a bit. It would take several months for the circuit court to hear her case, and the odds were good that they'd agree with the three-judge panel.

Meanwhile, Tony was running out of appeals. His attorneys filed a habeas corpus in Butts County, where Jackson State Prison was located, claiming there was new evidence in the case. The request for a hearing was denied, but appealed. In September, the Georgia Supreme Court ruled that a hearing had to be held in Butts Superior Court. Judge Sam L. Whitmire presided over the procedure on Monday, November 8, 1982.

At that time, Machetti's attorneys presented their new evidence—an affidavit from Fred Hasty, stating he had offered John Maree sentences of life imprisonment in exchange for his testimony against the Machettis. Hasty further stated that he'd told Maree that if he didn't testify against them, he'd seek the death penalty against him, too. Hasty also stated that although Don Thompson and Ray Wilkes knew about the deal, he never informed any of Machetti's attorneys.

Willis Sparks was called as a witness for the state and testified that he didn't know of such an arrangement between his former client and Hasty.

Machetti's attorneys contended that the state's deal with Maree kept their client from getting a fair trial. They also claimed that Georgia's death penalty law was applied "arbitrarily, capriciously, and in a discriminatory manner."

But Judge Whitmire wasn't convinced that any of the information presented constituted "new evidence." The next day, he dismissed the petition. As expected, that ruling was appealed.

~~~

The full Eleventh Circuit Court upheld the three-judge decision on Monday, January 10, 1983, and refused to reinstate Becky's death sentence. The ruling effectively granted Becky a new trial. Willis Sparks obviously couldn't prosecute after having once defended one of her codefendants. So a special prosecutor would have to be appointed.

John Maree applied for parole in both 1981 and 1982. He was denied both times.
~~~

Chapter 26

An arctic cold front ripped through Georgia on 50-mph winds in January of 1983, leaving 10,000 houses in Macon without power. But schools, businesses, and the courts continued to operate. And, on that frigid Wednesday morning, Judge C. Cloud Morgan appointed Joe Briley as special prosecutor for Becky Machetti's second murder trial. Briley had been district attorney in the neighboring Ocmulgee Judicial Circuit for some years, and Morgan was familiar with him. He had also acted as special prosecutor for the last of Tony Machetti's appeals the year before.

When Briley accepted the appointment, he knew that the reindictment and trial of the defendant would take a great deal of time and research. So, he requested assistance to prepare for the case, and, in April, Bob Boren, a sergeant in the Investigations Division of the Bibb County Sheriff's Office, was pulled away from his other duties to work as Briley's investigator. It was a coincidence that Boren had been the deputy left on overnight guard at the Akins crime scene in 1974.

Sgt. Boren had mixed feelings about his new assignment. He was honored to be chosen. After all, Briley, a legend in Middle Georgia, was famous for eccentricity, courtroom brilliance, and winning. But Boren was accustomed to being out in the field, tracking down felons, and making arrests. He didn't think this new job was going to be very exciting.

That impression was reinforced when he was given a tiny office on the second floor of the Bibb County Courthouse.

His new workspace was a windowless cave jammed with boxes of all the records on the Akins investigation. Every time he went to his desk, he felt like he was going into a closet.

A third person was named to assist Boren and Briley. Tim Sceviour, a Long Island, New York, native, was a third-year law student at Mercer University. Tim would be responsible for most of the legal research.

But in spite of Boren's misgivings, the three men made up a team that, from the very beginning, seemed to click. And it was just that—a team. Briley was open and down to earth. He often asked the two younger men for their opinions and really listened to what they had to say.

They began with a thorough review of the case itself and the first trial. It didn't take long for the new prosecution team to realize one key fact: they needed some corroboration of John Maree's testimony. And there was only one place to get that—from Becky's daughters.

Valerie Akins was living in an apartment in Hialeah, Florida, and still worked the 3-to-11 shift at Caterpillar Truck. She was, for the most part, satisfied with the life she'd built for herself. She had a good job and a handsome boyfriend named Manny. In the mornings, she took business classes at Miami-Dade College, and she played softball whenever she could.

Valerie learned about her mother's new trial when a subpoena arrived in the mail for her to testify before the Bibb County Grand Jury. A sense of dread settled on her. She'd thought the whole awful experience was in the past, but here they were dragging it up again. She was angry that the courts would allow such a thing to happen and furious that her mother was getting a second chance. After all, Becky hadn't given Ronny one. The first thing she did was call her older sister.

Vicki had had a second daughter in 1980, and she and her family were living in Ocala, Florida. Her reaction was much the same as Valerie's. Not only did she not want her mother to have a second trial, she didn't want to return to Georgia, especially right then. Her husband was seriously ill, and she needed to be with him. Even if they found someone to care for him in her absence, she still had the responsibility of her children. Any trip she took to Macon would, out of necessity, have to include her five-year-old and three-year-old daughters.

Only Valerie and Vicki had been subpoenaed to testify. Vanessa had left Florida in 1980, and neither of her sisters had heard from her since.

The prosecution team was determined to have the Akins girls testify before the grand jury. There were numerous telephone calls and letters between Briley's staff and Valerie and Vicki. The men promised both girls that they'd make it as easy as possible. They'd be protected the whole time and wouldn't have to worry about a thing. Valerie was particularly impressed with Tim Sceviour, who was very kind to her and her sister. Bob Boren also spoke with the girls at length. He was well aware of how hard it was going to be for them.

Valerie soon grew accustomed to receiving calls from the prosecution team, both at home and at work. She'd made her employers aware of what was going on, and they never complained about the time the calls took away from her job. The sisters, now twenty-seven and twenty-six, were no longer children. Even though they were nervous, they were determined to testify truthfully this time.

Valerie and Vicki traveled to Macon and appeared before the grand jury. It was as quick as they'd been promised. They told the truth and returned to Florida.

On Monday, May 2, 1983, Rebecca Machetti was reindicted for the murders of Ronny and Juanita Akins. Eleven days later, Becky was brought from Hardwick Prison to the Bibb County Courthouse. Dressed in a red blouse and beige skirt, she was led by deputies to the defense table in Judge C. Cloud Morgan's courtroom.

Two local attorneys, Rick Cook and Bill Gifford, had already been appointed to defend her. Gifford was a former United States Attorney while Cook had made his reputation in private practice. He was well known in Macon and had represented, among other celebrities, the Allman Brothers. When asked by the judge if she was satisfied with her attorneys, Rebecca said she was.

"I found out that you appointed them," she told Morgan in an almost flirtatious tone. "I think you have extremely good taste."

Minutes later, her attorneys waived formal arraignment. Special Prosecutor Joe Briley announced that the state would again be seeking the death penalty, and Judge Morgan set the trial date for June 20. Less than an hour after it began, the hearing was over.

The week after her arraignment, Becky's lawyers filed sixteen motions, among them the demand that the prosecution be forbidden to ask potential jurors their feelings about capital punishment and a request that Becky be released on bond. Finally, they asked for a change of venue, declaring that their client couldn't receive a fair trial due to the extensive publicity the case had received in Macon.

On May 26, Morgan ruled on some of those motions. He denied bond for Becky but approved several defense motions concerning jury matters and discovery. And he set a special June 14 hearing for arguments about a change of venue.

As part of their case preparation, Cook and Gifford conducted what they called a "random telephone survey" in Bibb

County. They phoned 250 people, 100 of whom agreed to participate in the survey. Of that number, about forty were registered voters and, therefore, eligible to serve on a jury. About half of that number believed Rebecca Machetti was guilty.

The lawyers presented their findings at the motion hearing on June 14, arguing that this clearly demonstrated that their client couldn't receive a fair trial in Bibb County. Then they had Becky address the court herself. She announced that she'd conducted her own survey among 450 of the other women inmates in the jail and discovered the general consensus was that she was guilty. However, she told the court, that opinion changed when they got to know her.

The prosecution argued that the results of such a tiny survey didn't prove there was a great deal of inflammatory opinion on the street. They dismissed Becky's statement out of hand. And Judge Morgan agreed. The motion for a change of venue was denied.

June 20 was unusually hot for so early in the summer. Temperatures were expected to top 90 later in the day. People reporting for jury duty dressed in their lightest summer clothing. In the *Macon Telegraph*, Rebecca Machetti's second trial shared front-page space with stories on local property-tax reappraisals and President Reagan's upbeat assessment of the recovering economy.

There had been quite a lot of publicity about this second trial, and the crowded courtroom reflected the public's interest. In a conservative pink and gray striped dress, Becky sat quietly at the defense table, making and reading over notes. Ronny Akins's three brothers were there, sitting together behind the prosecutors. However, Valerie and Vicki were still in

Florida, waiting to fly to Macon as soon as Briley called them.

Judge Morgan convened court at 11:00, and a panel of 135 prospective jurors was sworn in. The judge had granted a defense motion that they each be questioned separately and, after being chosen, that the jurors be sequestered.

It was slow going. Many of the prospective jurors were familiar with the case, and quite a few had already made a decision about Becky's guilt or innocence. Some of those called were connected in some way to the case or the defendant. One man had attended one day of Becky's first trial. One woman had met her through a jail ministry. Yet another knew her in the early years of her marriage to Ronny. Finally, a man who had been employed by Hart's Mortuary was working the night Ronny and Juanita Akins's bodies were brought in. Jury selection continued through Tuesday and into Wednesday.

Morgan adjourned court early Wednesday afternoon. It was becoming obvious that selecting an impartial jury in Bibb County was going to be very difficult, if not impossible. Thirty-three of the fifty-one jurors who had been qualified at that point knew that Machetti had already been tried and convicted of the murders. The judge knew that knowledge would make it very difficult for them to be objective. And any conviction from such a jury pool could easily be overturned on appeal. On Thursday, he announced he was granting the defense motion for change of venue. He left it up to counsel to come up with an alternative location.

Chapter 27

Vicki and Valerie were disappointed when they got the news. They only wanted the ordeal to be over. The change of venue meant more waiting for them—it could be months or even years before the trial was held.

Briley and Cook met and considered several locations—Columbus, Jesup, Jonesboro, and Madison were all possibilities. But they finally decided on Lawrenceville in Gwinnett County, forty miles northeast of Atlanta, because that circuit could accommodate the trial that summer. And everyone involved wanted to take the case to court as soon as possible. The trial was scheduled for July 18 and Becky was returned to Hardwick.

Everyone involved in the Machetti case—the witnesses, judge, and attorneys—would go to Lawrenceville. The only things that Gwinnett County would provide were the courthouse, the jury pool, and security.

A few weeks before the trial, Joe Briley, Bob Boren, and Tim Sceviour went to Gwinnett County. They settled in a motel near downtown Lawrenceville and began preparation for the upcoming trial. They were assisted by Gwinnett County District Attorney Bryant Huff.

Huff was a colorful local figure. His conviction rate as district attorney was legendary, but it was his interest in hoboes that had garnered him national attention. On more than one occasion, the dapper, silver-haired attorney had taken time off and actually ridden the rails across the country. He'd even appeared on *The Tonight Show* to talk about his adventures.

During the day, Briley and his team worked in the county courthouse. Briley and Huff spent countless hours reviewing the facts of the case and strategizing about the presentation of the evidence. In the evenings, Briley and Boren worked in one of their motel rooms. The prosecutor liked working from memory. They'd construct a list of questions for each witness. Briley would study it, then get up and "question the witness."

On Thursday, July 14, Becky was brought from Hardwick to Lawrenceville and booked into the county jail. A local reporter happened be there at the time, and Becky willingly talked to him, describing at length how she'd been framed. She also did her best to charm the folks at the jail, telling them what a nice place it was.

Becky wasn't the only new prisoner in the Gwinnett County Jail. John Maree was already in residence, waiting to testify against her one more time.

On July 18, the trial began in the old brick courthouse on the square in Lawrenceville. Judge C. Cloud Morgan took the bench in one of the two high-ceilinged courtrooms on the second floor. Becky arrived, escorted by Gwinnett County Deputy Bobbie Aaron. She wasn't cuffed and was dressed in a long-sleeved, striped cotton dress, tied at the waist with a fabric belt. Her dark hair was cut short and neatly styled.

Prosecutors and defense attorneys questioned prospective jurors for almost seven hours that day. Becky sat quietly at the defense table, speaking every now and then to Gifford or Cook. Bryant Huff shared the prosecution table with Joe Briley for much of the day, helping with jury selection. Since there'd been little pretrial publicity in Gwinnett County, finding qualified jurors was much easier here.

The witnesses all arrived in Lawrenceville just as the trial started. They'd been told that the proceedings could drag on into the next week and were advised to bring enough clothes for that possibility. Alan Barfield drove up from Macon and checked into a motel Tuesday morning. He had recently married, and his wife, Debbie, joined him that afternoon. They had an early dinner and went swimming in the pool that evening.

Bobby and Ann McElroy left their home before sunrise Wednesday for the drive to Lawrenceville. By the time court convened that morning, they were sitting in a small witness waiting area behind the courtroom.

The McElroys were startled when a deputy led Becky Machetti up a flight of stairs from the basement holding cells right into their waiting area. She wore large, black-rimmed glasses and carried a Bible in one hand. As the two walked past the witnesses and into the courtroom, Becky gave Bobby McElroy a faint smile.

That morning, a jury of seven men and five women was sworn in, along with two alternates—one man and one woman. Minutes later, Joe Briley stood and made his opening statement, introducing himself and explaining why they were hearing a Bibb County case here in Gwinnett. He then laid out the case he expected to present. The main difference between this trial and the one held in 1975 was that the prosecution would be calling Becky's daughters as witnesses.

Bill Gifford followed Briley and presented the opening statement for the defense. Gifford claimed that Becky had no knowledge of the murders. They were planned and committed, he said, by her husband, Anthony Machetti, and his friend John Maree.

The prosecution case followed the same path it had in 1975. Briley built the story logically, starting with the discovery of the body and questioning of witnesses. Alan Barfield testified to his trip to Florida the weekend of the murders. His wife, Debbie, was able to sit in on some of the testimony that day since she wasn't a witness. It was the first time she'd ever seen Rebecca Machetti.

"She's one mean-looking lady," Alan told her on the drive home that afternoon. "I want you to remember what she looks like and, if you ever see her, get away from her."

Both McElroys took the stand to tell about the green Gremlin they saw entering and leaving their subdivision on the night the Akinses were killed. And Ann McElroy testified to later picking out John Maree from a photo lineup. The couple was surprised that their appearances on the witness stand lasted only ten to fifteen minutes. They were on their way home by 5:00 that afternoon and back in Macon before dark.

During the questioning of the witnesses, Briley would pace around the courtroom. Occasionally, he'd stop and look over Bob Boren's shoulder at the list of prepared questions. When his direct examination was coming to a close, he'd reach up and kind of pull his hair. That was Boren's signal to check that everything had been covered. If Boren pulled his nose, Briley would return to the prosecution table and check the notes.

The first day of testimony went just as the prosecution had hoped. However, by the end of the day, the jurors were getting restless. The state hadn't introduced any evidence to this point that connected Rebecca Machetti with the murders. But, that was about to change.

Vicki Akins's life was incredibly stressful just then. Her husband was still ill and she'd recently broken her leg in an accident. So, she had to fly to Atlanta in a cast with her two young daughters. It was a difficult flight, but things improved a bit when she met Valerie at the Atlanta airport. At least her sister would help with the kids.

A uniformed Gwinnett County deputy was there to pick them up. As they walked out to the waiting marked car, the women were surprised to discover that it was hotter in Atlanta than it had been in Florida. Vicki got into the front passenger seat, the better to accommodate her cast-covered leg, and Valerie and the two children climbed into the back seat. It was a uniform car, used more often for transporting prisoners than for delivering witnesses to the courthouse. There were no door or window handles in the back seat, and a plexiglass shield separated them from the occupants of the front seat.

Vicki's oldest daughter didn't like it a bit. She was frightened by the whole experience, and now, seemingly trapped in the back seat of a police car, she decided that they'd been arrested. She began crying and eventually became so upset that she started throwing up. There was little Valerie could do to help. Since there were no window cranks in the back seat, she couldn't open a window for ventilation. The smell was almost overpowering. Fortunately, this happened just as they arrived at their Lawrenceville motel, and within minutes they were outside the fouled vehicle.

The girls were checked into the motel under an assumed name. That was a relief since, more than anything, they didn't want to hear from their mother. The sisters and the children shared a room.

The star of the Thursday morning session was John Maree. Unlike Becky, he wasn't dressed in street clothes, but wore a white jail uniform with a blue stripe up each leg. John was relaxed as he arrived at the courthouse. Hands cuffed in front, he joked with the deputies who escorted him from the jail. He'd done this before and knew that he could get through it with no problem.

His cuffs were removed before he was taken into the courtroom. On the witness stand, he appeared at ease and almost comfortable. Just as he had in Becky's first trial, he told the crowded courtroom about his and Tony Machetti's trip to Macon and the murders. And he calmly and convincingly described Becky's planning of the murders and how she approached him with the offer of $1,000 to drive the car from Miami to Macon.

On cross-examination, Cook tried to portray Maree as a freeloader. He accused him of scheming to kill Ronny to collect the insurance through his relationship with Vicki. He also suggested that she was involved in the murders. But Maree never wavered. Although the jury might have seen him as a self-serving criminal, it appeared they also believed what he said.

After lunch, it was time for Valerie and Vicki to make their appearances. Valerie went first. Her heart was pounding as the deputy called her name, and she stood up to follow him. They entered the courtroom from a rear door, and she walked to the witness stand, acutely aware of her mother at the defense table only a few feet away. Briley positioned himself between Valerie and Becky as much as he could, trying to protect her. But throughout her testimony, Becky continued trying to make eye contact with her daughter.

Telling how she and her sister had held her father down as Rebecca tried to smother him was almost unbearable. Although she cried only occasionally, tears were always just below the surface. Joe Briley asked why, after the divorce, she and her sisters hadn't gone with their father.

"Because she wouldn't let us."

"How could she stop you?"

In a shaky voice, she said, "She could. Because she told us we had to go with her and she told us if we tried to go with him, she would tell the police what happened and we would be put in jail, too."

"For what?"

"For helping to try and kill Dad."

"Did you always do what she told you to do?"

"Yes, because we were scared."

"What were you afraid of?"

"That she would kill us, too, or try to."

He then guided Valerie on to tell about her mother's second marriage to Eldon Smith.

"Why did he change his name to Machetti?"

"I was told that he wanted to get in with the Mafia in New Jersey."

"Who told you this?"

"My mother did. She said that in order to get into the Mafia—they wanted him to be a hit man—he had to have an Italian name. And then if he had killed somebody and gotten away with it, scot-free away with it, then they would accept him into the Mafia."

"Did your mother want him to be in the Mafia?"

"Yes, she did. That was the reason for all the name changing and everything." She explained how she and her sisters were expected to change their names, too.

"You didn't have a choice?"

"We weren't asked if we wanted our names changed. We were told our names were going to be changed."

"Did you always do everything she told you to do?"

"Yes."

"Why?"

"Because we were afraid of her." She knew, as an adult sitting here in the courtroom, that her answers were hard to understand. None of these people could know what it was like, but she tried to make them see. "She would threaten that she was going to separate us. And after she tried to kill Dad, we knew if we didn't do what she wanted, if she had tried to do it to him, she would try to do it to us, too."

Then she told about the weekend of the murders and how Becky had brought her and her sisters together and told them that Tony and John had gone to Georgia to kill her father. She explained that she didn't put much stock in it, since her mother was always saying stuff like that. Now she wished she had.

Rick Cook cross-examined her and asked about her testimony in front of the Bibb County Grand Jury in 1975. She had to admit she'd lied when she denied any knowledge of the murder plan. He pointed out she was under oath then and now. She repeated that she had been terrified of her mother.

He then had her identify the letters she'd written to Becky when she was living with her grandmother, Sara Zuber. Valerie agreed she'd written them.

Then, he went back to the first attempt on Ronny's life. "Was that the first time something like that had happened?"

"As far as—with us involved, yes."

"Did you lead a pretty normal life up until that point?"

"Other than fights, which all people have, pretty much."

"Up until that incident, where you held your father's feet, had you lived a pretty normal life?"

"Yes, I would say that."

On redirect, Briley asked about that normal life. "You said that life was pretty normal at your house. Tell us how normal it was. Tell us how your mother treated you and your father. Tell the jury. They need to know."

Valerie took a deep breath. "My mother wore the pants in our house and we acted like we had a million dollars. My mom was always buying stuff and my dad wasn't making enough to pay for everything. They were always fighting because something was always being brought new into the house."

"Why were you so afraid of her?"

"It was some kind of power she had over us and..." How could she make them understand? She just shook her head. "Other than tell us that she would separate us, I don't know what it was."

"You weren't whipped, were you?"

"More times than not—"

"How?"

"When we were young, with the belt. My dad never hit us, but then my mom would hit us when he wasn't home."

"What part of the belt were you whipped with?"

"The buckle part."

"Did that seem normal to you?"

"Yeah, because it had always been like that. You know, we had black eyes and we would tell the kids at school that we had fallen against a door or fallen down the stairs."

Valerie explained they never told their father about the beatings because they knew their mother would just beat them again.

When she finally left the stand, Valerie was drained. She was weak and exhausted, but there was also a spark of pride inside her. She'd finally told the truth!

Next was Vicki's turn. If possible, she was even more nervous than her sister had been. But she hobbled to the stand on her crutches, determined to do what was right this time.

Just as her sister had, she testified to the first murder attempt. When Briley reached the part about Eldon Smith changing his name, Vicki said, "My mother didn't like the name John Smith. She wanted him to change his name. She always told me he was a member of the Mafia and that his name should be Italian because Smith was not a Mafia name."

She stuttered every time she tried to say "my mother" and at times sobbed almost uncontrollably. Every time she looked at her mother, Vicki became more obviously upset. Becky stared at her daughter with bleak eyes and no expression. Finally, a deputy went to stand between the two so that the witness couldn't see her mother.

In testifying to the events the weekend of the murders, Vicki told the court that Machetti and John Maree returned early Sunday morning about 5:00 A.M. But after the arrests, she said, Becky ordered her to tell a different story. "My mother told me to say about one o'clock or thereabouts, five after one."

Her testimony agreed with her sister's about the divorce and the matter of custody.

Cook got to his feet, an expression of disbelief plain on his face. He asked if she continued to love John Maree after the murders.

Valerie took a shaky breath and told the truth. "Even though he killed my father, I was so in love with the guy."

Then, he began showing her letters she'd written to her mother while in Athens and asking her to identify them.

Unlike Valerie, who'd meekly admitted to writing the letters with no explanation, Vicki grew a bit combative. "Do you know why I had to write these letters?" she asked the defense lawyer. "My grandmother used to make us sit down and write her letters."

Cook asked her about her first testimony before the grand jury, but Vicki didn't remember any of it. She also said she didn't remember anything said in the letters she'd received from Maree.

Then, he asked if she recalled changing her name to Machetti.

"Yes, sir. I changed my name. *She* changed all our names."

"Did you accept your new name?"

"What was I going to do, not accept it?"

Cook tried to get her to say she knew about the insurance policy on her father's life that was in favor of her and her sisters, but she maintained she wasn't aware of it until after his death. He asked if her mother had told her to stop seeing John Maree, and Vicki said she had but that she kept seeing him even after her mother had forbidden her to do so. Then Cook asked, if she was so afraid of her mother, why did she defy her and see Maree behind her back.

Vicki's answer was heartbreakingly simple. "I thought John was going to be my escape."

When she was finally released from the stand, Vicki left the courtroom without another glance at her mother.

Next, Emmett Goodson testified about first meeting his client Ronny Akins.

"When he came into my office on the first meeting, he had scratches on his face and bruises and he told me a story about what had happened to him."

One of the photographs taken by Ronny's brother was introduced, and Goodman testified that it was an accurate depiction of the way he looked on that day.

Goodman said Ronny had explained that a peace warrant had been taken out against him and that the hearing was scheduled for later that week.

At this point, the defense objected on the grounds of hearsay. But the court ruled that Goodman could testify to what Ronny had said in that hearing. So, once again, the court heard the story of the first attempt on Ronny Akins's life.

Briley asked if Rebecca was present at that hearing and Goodman said she was.

"Did you see any marks on her like you saw on him?"

Goodman nodded as if he were pleased that the question had been asked. "No, I didn't. That was one of the things that was specifically pointed out in court. There was no marks whatsoever on her in any way at all at the time the peace warrant was—there was other testimony, people who had seen her during that time, as I recall, that saw no marks either and she did not have any that day."

Late Thursday afternoon, Joe Briley and his team decided they'd done everything they could to ensure a conviction and rested for the state.

Friday morning, it was the defense's turn to present evidence. Their case lasted only a few hours, and Becky's testimony was the centerpiece. Just as she had in her first trial, she attempted to refute much of what had been said about her. She denied ever trying to smother her husband. She also denied any connection to the murders. She insisted that Tony and Maree had returned home around 1:00 A.M. the morning after the murders.

When asked about the name change, she dismissed it. "Machetti was an old family name my husband wanted to take."

Her daughters had no desire to wait for another jury to reach a verdict. As soon as testimony was over and they were released, Valerie, Vicki, and her children were taken back through the record-breaking heat to the airport. They were back home before sunset that day.

Closing arguments were made and the case went to the jury late Friday afternoon.

Just before 11:00 A.M. on Saturday, word came that a verdict had been reached. The principals reentered the courtroom. Becky seemed to be in high spirits, talking and laughing with counsel and her supporters. Then the jury filed in and the foreman announced the guilty verdict.

Once again, the prosecution and defense moved into the presentencing part of the process. Briley put up no evidence. He believed that his witnesses, especially Valerie and Vicki, had convinced the jury that Rebecca Machetti was a cruel, heartless person who deserved to die. He did, however, make an eloquent argument for sentencing her to death, describing Becky as "pure evil."

The defense called eight witnesses, including Becky's mother and stepfather, other family and friends, her former attorney, Mary Ann Oakley, and a woman who'd met Becky while conducting a prison ministry. They all testified that she was a kind, loving person who couldn't have done the things she'd just been found guilty of doing. They pleaded with the jury to spare this gentle woman's life. Becky sat, solemn and sad, throughout the testimony.

The jury once again left the courtroom to deliberate and, early Saturday night, returned with the sentence—two consecutive life sentences.

Rick Cook and Bill Gifford were pleased.

"After nine years," Gifford told reporters, "justice has been served."

He and Cook both believed that because she had already served more than eight years, Becky would now be eligible for parole.

Briley felt like he'd made the case he wanted to but believed he understood why the jury decided what they did.

First, it was an old case. And murder cases lose their sense of immediacy as the years pass. Second, juries are uncomfortable giving the death penalty—particularly to a woman—and this jury, he knew, believed that two life sentences, to be served one after the other, would guarantee that Becky would be in prison a very long time.

And that belief did play a big role in determining the sentence. When jurors learned that Becky Machetti might be eligible for parole immediately, they were astonished.

"With two life sentences not running concurrently, our impression was that she could not be paroled now," one of them said. "That was our intention. We did it deliberately."

The families of the victims were furious, and Becky's daughters were shocked and terrified. Valerie and Vicki had finally managed to do the right thing. In spite of their lingering fear of their mother, they'd stepped forward and told the truth. Now, they were faced with the very real possibility that Becky could be out of prison soon. Valerie was sure she'd never be safe as along as her mother was alive and free to find her.

Becky Machetti's attorneys were right. Now that she was no longer under a death sentence and had already served nearly nine years, she was eligible to be considered for parole.

As soon as her trial was over, Becky's attorneys requested that the State Board of Pardons and Paroles consider their petition for parole. That request began a months-long process of compiling records of the case, her time in prison, and conducting what was called a social investigation. They interviewed Becky, her friends, relatives, and those people who'd associated with her while she had been in prison. The board was also bound to consider any communications they received on her behalf.

Chapter 28

Tony's Machetti's appeals continued. Several hearings were held in Butts County, Georgia—the location of the prison—and the state prevailed each time. On March 1, 1983, the Georgia Supreme Court reversed a Butts County Superior Court decision, which had earlier dismissed Tony's petition, and sent the case back with instructions for that court to hold a hearing on his claim of prosecutorial misconduct. So, two more hearings were held, but they did nothing to further Machetti's cause. On August 5, 1983, the Superior Court in Butts County issued an order rejecting his claim. Four days later, Judge Cloud Morgan rescheduled Tony's execution for August 25.

But his attorneys never gave up. Additional appeals and petitions for stays of execution were filed on Machetti's behalf, but none of them were successful. During August and September, Judge Morgan twice resentenced him to death, setting dates that came and went. But on December 2, 1983, the Eleventh Circuit lifted their stay, and Judge Morgan set a new execution date of December 15. In response, Tony's attorneys petitioned the State Board of Pardons and Paroles for clemency, claiming that he'd been led astray by his wife, Rebecca.

Under the Georgia Constitution, only the board has the authority to commute a sentence. As they considered Tony's petition, they had three options: commute Tony's sentence to life, grant a ninety-day stay, or send him to the electric chair.

The board had been provided with copies of his appeal

and supporting paperwork the previous week, so when they convened on Monday morning, December 12, they already had some understanding of the case. They spent most of the day discussing it, and, when they adjourned that afternoon, they promised to have a decision by 10:30 the next morning.

At that time, the Board of Pardons and Paroles rejected Tony's petition for clemency. In announcing their decision, they declared that there was no doubt that Tony was a willing and active participant in the murders. They refused to stop the execution.

Since the United States Supreme Court had reinstated capital punishment in 1976, nine men had been executed in the United States, but none in Georgia. The last execution in the state had been in 1964.

Then, on Wednesday, December 14, the US Supreme Court, by a vote of six to three, turned down an emergency request to stay Tony's execution.

Tony Machetti's deathwatch had already begun Tuesday morning, December 13, 1983, the day before the Supreme Court turned down his emergency request. He was moved from maximum security at the Georgia Diagnostic and Classification Center at Jackson to a building at the back of the prison complex where the electric chair was housed. There, he was put into a holding cell next to the death chamber. He was monitored at all times by two guards. The cell was equipped with reading material, a television, and a radio.

Tony was allowed two fifteen-minute phone calls a day. He could also have visits from immediate family, his attorneys, and clergymen. Richard Wise, a Catholic priest from Jonesboro, spent most of Wednesday with him, conducting mass for him Wednesday afternoon.

Late that afternoon, Tony made his last telephone call to Catherine Fitzgerald, his ex-wife, in Tyrone, Pennsylvania, telling her he was ready to go if his last-minute appeal didn't work. The two had been married in 1953 and had one son, Larry. They were divorced in 1965.

Tony had married and divorced a second woman before marrying Becky back in 1974. But when he found himself in prison, Catherine was the one he turned to. They'd begun corresponding soon after his trial, and he'd told her numerous times over the years that if he ever got out of prison, he'd be returning to Pennsylvania. On that cold Wednesday afternoon, he told her that the last thing he would do on earth was say a prayer for her. As the conversation was ending, she said she loved him. He said he loved her, too.

Tony didn't request any special food during his deathwatch, eating the regular prison meals of one meat, two vegetables, bread, dessert, and tea. Wednesday night was cold and clear, with temperatures dipping below the freezing mark. There were no protesters outside the prison demanding that his life be spared. And he and Reverend Wise passed the long dark hours watching old movies on television, eating sandwiches, and talking about any- and everything.

Assisted by a second priest, the Reverend Nick Navario, Richard Wise conducted mass for Tony in the hour before dawn. It was becoming apparent that there would be no stay this time.

"Well," Tony said after the mass, "the Lord's going to get another one. I'm not going to be in this world much longer."

Over the course of his imprisonment, Tony had evolved from a murderer into a quiet, Christian man. Thursday morning, he was calm and resolute and had accepted the fact he was going to die. He told the priest he was confident he was going to heaven. "I won't have a mansion, I guess, but I'll be tending somebody's garden."

Just before daylight, one anti-death penalty demonstrator showed up. By eight o'clock, he was joined by twenty or thirty others just inside the prison gates. They were all required by prison security to wear green ribbons to identify them and their cause. Nearby, on the other side of a barbed-wire barrier, about a dozen pro-capital punishment demonstrators gathered, wearing blue ribbons. Both groups were, in turn, watched, questioned, and photographed by the press, who had to wear yellow ribbons.

The witnesses had arrived at the prison before the protesters. Their ranks included several members of the media, including Oby Brown from *The Macon Telegraph*. Bibb County District Attorney Willis Sparks was there along with Sgt. Bob Boren.

A few months earlier, Ray Wilkes, who was now the sheriff, had approached Boren and asked if he wanted to witness Tony Machetti's execution. Remembering how he'd guarded the scene the night of the killings and all the work he'd done on Becky's second trial, he felt it was something he needed to do.

"Yes, I would," Boren had said. "I'd like to see the full circle of justice consummated."

One of Tony's attorneys, Robert Glustrom, also attended. He didn't talk to the others and sat by himself.

The witnesses were escorted into the death house by prison authorities and took seats in a small, darkened room where chairs had been set up for them. A large glass wall allowed them to see the room where the empty electric chair waited. The execution was scheduled for 8:00 A.M. Just minutes before that, Warden Ralph Kemp entered the death chamber. He announced that there had been no stays and the execution would proceed as scheduled.

Tony Machetti's entrance was low-key. He was dressed in the usual white prison uniform with blue stripes up the legs. Surrounded by guards and followed by Reverend Wise, Tony seemed small and insignificant. His glasses had been removed, of course, and his head shaved. The only familiar feature that remained was the bushy mustache.

He didn't have to be urged, but walked quietly across the tiny room and took his seat in the white wooden chair. The guards began wordlessly fastening wide leather straps across his body.

"Hey!" Tony said at one point, "There ain't no point in pulling them so tight!"

When asked if he had any last words, Tony's voice was steady. "My final statement will be read by Father Wise."

As Tony watched, Wise read from the Bible. "We know that when the earthly tent in which we dwell is destroyed, we have a dwelling in heaven." He then offered a prayer. "Father, I abandon myself into your hands. Do with me what you will. Into your hands I commend my soul." Then he made the sign of the cross.

"Thank you, Father," Tony said.

Wise nodded. He gave one last look at Tony, then left the room.

Electrodes were attached to the condemned man's body, and his head was strapped hard against the chair. Finally, a cloth mask was placed over his face. Through all this activity, Machetti was silent. When they were finished, Tony took a deep breath.

In an adjoining room behind a one-way mirror, three prison employees waited. They had all volunteered for this duty. In front of them was a board with three buttons, only one of which was connected and would turn on the electricity to the waiting chair. No one, including these three men, would ever know who pushed the live button. At a signal from the warden, the three buttons were pushed simultaneously.

Two thousand volts of electricity shot through Tony Machetti's body. His muscles convulsed, but there was no sound. Five minutes later, the current was cut off and three doctors entered the chamber. Each one examined Machetti, and all declared he was dead.

In the observation room, the witnesses now left their chairs, waiting to leave. They milled about, reluctant to meet each other's eyes. There was an air of something like embarrassment. They were all relieved when a guard came to lead them out of the death house and across the prison yard to the gates.

An hour later, Tony Machetti left the prison, too, in a hearse. He was buried in a location somewhere in Georgia that was never disclosed to the press.

There was no rejoicing in the Akins and Knight families after Tony's execution. Instead, there was only a sense of profound sadness at all the deaths that Rebecca Machetti had set into motion.

Chapter 29

Both John Maree and Rebecca Machetti petitioned the Board of Pardons and Paroles numerous times, and, on December 23, 1987, John Maree was paroled and went to live in Marietta, Georgia. He had served just over thirteen years for the murder of two people.

However, the board continued to deny parole for Becky Machetti. The fact that she still refused to admit her guilt probably didn't help her cause.

Each time she was considered, the Bibb County Sheriff's Department and District Attorney's Office wrote letters asking that parole be denied. The Akins family and, sometimes, her own daughters also wrote letters asking that she not be released.

So, Becky found other ways to amuse herself by manipulating the judicial system. On November 22, 1988, she filed a bar complaint against Judge C. Cloud Morgan, claiming that he had conspired with her attorneys in her second trial, Rick Cook and Bill Gifford, to keep her from appealing her conviction. She alleged that the attorneys, at Judge Morgan's order, misinformed her that she couldn't both appeal her conviction and apply for parole, so she had signed a waiver of appeal. The complaint was ruled unfounded. She had filed earlier bar complaints against Rick Cook and Bill Gifford with the same result.

By 1993, Becky could find no more attorneys willing to take on her case. The conventional wisdom was that there were no more appeals to be filed. But she wasn't satisfied with that and began confronting the legal system herself. She filed another writ of habeas corpus, this time jointly with a man named Vito Lorusso. Lorusso was purported to be a retired police officer, and he and she had somehow met through correspondence. Becky now referred to him as her husband and told her family that the two had married by telephone.

In the accompanying petition, which she had handwritten, the two alleged that she should be released from custody because:

—the Board of Pardons and Paroles repeatedly refused to free her, but had paroled John Maree, "the on the scene killer,"
—Becky was 800 miles from crime scene and, therefore, couldn't be guilty,
—Joe Briley had joined up with more "good ole boys" against her,
—Ray Wilkes had made everything up in order to search her house for the drug diary,
—and there was no transcript available from the second trial in Gwinnett County because it had been destroyed.

For some reason, Becky now focused on Ray Wilkes as the villain in her case. She accused him and other Bibb County officials of framing her for the murders. In this bizarre document, she insisted she'd been illegally detained in Miami and that Ray Wilkes and Don Thompson had coerced her into signing a "consent to search" by threatening that she'd never see her children again. She claimed that the real object of their search of the Florida house was to locate a "diary that listed names of persons involved in illegal drug trafficking." She claimed that two of the names in the book were of a Bibb County sheriff and a state senator. Although she gave no explanation as to how or why this book might have been in her possession, Becky said it was slated to be turned over to DEA agents on October 17, 1974, but was illegally seized by Sheriff Wilkes two days before that.

The allegations had no legal premise. Even the suggestion that there was no available transcript was in error. The transcript was readily available from the Superior Court Clerk in Gwinnett County. The application for the writ also cited numerous cases as precedent, none of which seemed to be applicable.

"The State of Georgia has not only Illegally taken my freedom away from me, and Unlawfully Imprisoned Me, an Innocent Person, but they have also Committed over <u>120</u> VIOLATIONS of my Civil and Constitutional Rights as follows:

RIGHT TO EFFECTIVE COUNSEL IN A CAPITAL CASE.
INADEQUATE COUNSEL.

DID NOT GET A JURY OF MY PEERS (SELECTION AND COMPOSITION OF SAME).

PRETRIAL PUBLICITY DETRIMENTAL TO MY DEFENSE.

CONVICTED ON PERJURED TESTIMONY OF A CO-DEFENDANT AND NO OTHER EVIDENCE.

THE RIGHT TO BE FREE FROM LOCKDOWNS, ETC., CRUEL AND UNUSUAL PUNISHMENT.

On the last page of the petition, she wrote: "Just how can I be found guilty with NO evidence and NO proven conspiracy. Maree and Vicki and Valerie conspired. NOT ME! NOT ME!!"

There were also odd references to Becky and Lorusso's relationship throughout. "Ms. Machetti and Mr. Lorusso are in love, have formed a common law bond, have resolved to make sure the framing of Ms. Machetti is exposed, and that someone somewhere listens to what the State of Georgia and corrupt law enforcement have done.

"The oldest law known to man is God's Law and there can be no more separation of the truth/God, and the State. Mr. Lorusso pleads before the court that someone listen, and hear the truth of the WOMAN HE LOVES and SHE pleads someone help!"

Valerie Akins was unaware of most of her mother's maneuverings, having done everything she could to distance herself from Becky. She'd made a good life for herself. She was secretary to the vice principal of a local school, had plenty of friends, and shared a comfortable apartment with a roommate.

The one thing she regretted was that she no longer saw either of her sisters. Vicki had been left a widow in the 1980s. She'd moved out of state, changed her name, and remarried, wanting to completely remove herself from the past. The two women spoke by telephone only once or twice a year.

Valerie hadn't seen Vanessa for more than ten years. While she had occasional contact with her Akins relatives and had even recently begun a tentative reconciliation with her grandmother, Sara Zuber, Valerie never really felt like she belonged to any family.

Late one afternoon in 1993, Val came in from work to a mess. Her washer had overflowed and part of the apartment was flooded. She realized her roommate must have left while it was still running. There was water everywhere. The telephone rang as Val was trying to clean it up. She snatched up the phone, still frustrated about the destruction in her apartment.

"Is Valerie Akins there?" a female voice asked.

"What d'you need?" Val assumed it was telephone sales.

"Do you know who this is?"

"No, I don't. I'm kinda busy right now."

"Well, this is your mother."

"Right. What do you need and who is this?"

When the woman repeated that she was her mother, something in her voice was suddenly familiar. Val couldn't speak. She started shaking.

"Aren't you going to talk to me and say hello?"

Val didn't even try to be polite. "No. I'm in the middle of something."

She wasn't pleased that her mother had called her house. Then Becky made matters worse by telling her she was being subpoenaed for a court proceeding.

"You and Vicki better be there."

Val asked how she'd gotten her number. Becky told her that she knew where she lived, the kind of car she drove, where she worked, and what her hours were. She said, "You can run, but you can't hide."

Val couldn't speak for a moment. She'd actually begun to believe she was safe from her mother.

"Your memory is bad," Becky continued, referring to her testimony in the second trial. "You have to come up here and clear my name. You need to remember that it was Vicki who did all the planning with Tony and John."

That made Valerie angry enough that her shaking stopped. "I've already told the truth. It would probably be a mistake for me to come. If I do, I'll tell them you asked me to lie."

"But you have to come. You will, won't you?"

"I will *not* come. Since I'm in Florida, I understand that you have to pay for me to fly up there and put me up in a hotel and give me expenses. Now, if you still want to do that, just let me know."

Becky tried to argue with that, but Valerie stood her ground. Having been subpoenaed to both the grand jury and her mother's second trial, she was sure of her facts.

Finally, she'd had enough. "Don't call me again." She hung up the phone.

It was only then that the fear came rushing in. How had her mother found her? And how did she know so much about her life? For years afterwards, she'd never get in her car without looking in her rearview mirror to see if anyone might be following her.

Through conversations with her maternal grandmother, Val knew which prison was now her mother's home. The next day, she called the warden's office and asked that Becky not be allowed to call her again.

"I don't care what you have to do. I don't want that woman calling here."

When they discovered that it hadn't been a collect call, the prison people did some investigating. About a week later, they called Val back. They explained that the only way they could figure that Rebecca had been able to call her was by convincing a third party to set up a conference call. Valerie assumed that her grandmother must have been responsible for the call and for giving Becky the information about her.

She told the people at the prison that she never wanted to hear from Becky again. They assured her that there would be no more calls from her mother.

The appeal that Becky mentioned to Valerie was originally filed in DeKalb County in February of 1993, when she was in the Women's Correctional Institute. In this petition, she alleged that her attorneys had conspired to frame her by not allowing a key witness, Bill Hendrickson, to testify in her behalf, and that her daughters both perjured themselves during the second trial.

However, before any hearings could be scheduled, Becky was transferred to a prison in Washington County, and her appeal had to be transferred with her. An evidentiary hearing was set by the Washington County Superior Court for July 1.

Becky had tried to subpoena seventeen witnesses but didn't send witness fees and mileage costs to those people outside of Washington County. When they were told they had to pay expenses, Vito LoRusso sent personal checks drawn on a New York bank to those witnesses. But by doing so, he violated the statute that required witness fees to be paid in currency, postal money orders, or cashiers or certified checks. Therefore, all seventeen subpoenas were invalid. Still, some witnesses did appear, including Ray Wilkes and Becky's former attorney Bill Gifford.

It was a strange hearing, with Vito Lorusso acting as Becky's attorney, even though he was not a member of the bar. Gifford and Wilkes both testified, although it was slow going since Lorusso didn't understand the rules of evidence or court procedure. The judge had to correct him time and time again.

Gifford advised that he and his cocounsel had met with the mysterious Bill Hendrickson in a bar and also talked with him on the phone. On both occasions, the man hinted that he could find evidence to clear Becky and asked for money to "go to Florida and put the package together." They declined, deciding he really didn't know anything and wouldn't be a credible witness. Gifford also testified that, at the time, Becky didn't object to their decision.

After hearing all the testimony, the Washington County judge found that Becky's waiver of appeal after the second trial was valid and that denying Hendrickson's testimony didn't constitute error. Her appeal was denied.

Over the years, Becky had written a number of letters to Judge Cloud Morgan, complaining that she hadn't received a fair trial. He always answered them politely, suggesting that she enlist the aid of an attorney in her case. He reminded her that if he hadn't transferred the jurisdiction of her second trial, she might not be where she was—that she might have already been executed. In his last letter to her, in 2000, he explained that he was retiring and that he wouldn't be answering any further correspondence.

Chapter 30

But Becky wasn't through. She scoured the library in the prison for other legal maneuvering she might try. She next filed a writ of *coram nobis* in Washington County Superior Court, and it was transferred to Bibb County, where it was assigned to Superior Court Judge Martha Christian on November 29, 2000.

This filing was basically a writ of error, claiming that Becky had been denied due process. Once again, she claimed that John Maree, Valerie, and Vicki had all lied in the second trial. She contended that her daughters corroborated that she had no involvement in the crime when they testified in 1974 before a grand jury. Therefore, she said, she'd been denied due process and couldn't expect a fair trial where perjured testimony tainted the minds of fact finders.

The final sentence in her petition was pure Becky Machetti, although she was now going by the name of Lorusso: "The winds of justice demand your petitioner be afforded an opportunity to prove her innocence and clear violations to her constitutional rights. Wherefore your petitioner so moves this Court. Respectfully submitted, Rebecca A. Lorusso."

Bibb County District Attorney Howard Simms filed the state's response to her allegations on February 9, 2001. He stated that a writ of *coram nobis* is treated by the state as an extraordinary motion for a new trial based on newly discovered evidence, but that Becky's petition contained no new evidence. There was nothing in it that wasn't presented or known at the time of trial and requested that it be dismissed.

By this time, Becky had persuaded Atlanta attorney John A. Roberts to assist her. He filed her answer, stating that the petitioner should be allowed liberal rule interpretations because of the length of time of her incarceration (almost thirty years). He claimed that dismissing the petition without a hearing was unduly harsh. But his argument failed, and Judge Christian did dismiss it.

Becky and Vito weren't about to give up. They abandoned the courts for another route. They contacted *The Geraldo Rivera Show* about the case, and the television people were interested. They were so interested that they called Val's home every day for a week. They even located Vicki and repeatedly telephoned her. Both women refused to have anything to do with the show, even when the callers offered to fly the sisters first class to New York, put them up in a four-star hotel, and see that they ate in first-class restaurants.

"Your mother is expecting to be paroled and she wants to clear the air. She'll be on a big screen and you two will be talking to each other," one of the television people told Valerie.

Valerie couldn't imagine anything she would want to do less than that. "I don't want to be on your show," she said, not for the first time. "Just stop calling me." But they persisted until she finally installed an answering machine so she could screen her calls. After about six weeks they gave up.

Chapter 31

In May of 2003, Valerie Akins married. She and her husband settled in South Florida and, for the first time since her father's death, Valerie felt like she once again belonged to a family.

Sara Zuber, who had been widowed for a number of years, passed away on December 7, 2003, at the age of eighty-five. Val and her grandmother had achieved a sort of peace by that time; they'd almost become friends. She was making plans to attend the funeral until she was told that the prison officials were going to allow Becky to go to the service. Valerie didn't dispute that Becky had every right to be there, but she couldn't go if it meant seeing the woman who'd killed her father and nearly ruined her and her sisters' lives.

However, on the morning of the funeral, her grandmother's son, Jody Zuber, called and told her that Becky wasn't going to be allowed to go after all. Unfortunately, it was too late for Val to get a flight to Athens in time for the service.

But Becky's family was not left in peace after her mother's death. Sara Zuber's entire estate was the small, split-level house on Camelot Drive in Athens. Ordinarily, the house would have been sold and the proceeds divided between Sara's only heirs, Becky and her half-brother, Jody. But that wasn't to be.

Becky decided that she and Vito should own the house outright, reasoning that when she was paroled, she'd need a place to live. She made life so miserable for Jody, filing demands and lawsuits, that he finally signed the property over to her rather than have to put up with any more legal shenanigans. Lorusso moved into the house soon afterwards and remained there until 2006.

It was during the summer of that year that Vito Lorusso died of a heart attack in the house. His body was taken to a local funeral home and Becky was contacted in prison. Although she first demanded a lavish funeral service, the fiscal realities of such a ceremony soon made her scale back on her plans. In the end, there was no service. Vito Lorusso was cremated, and, at her request, his ashes were sent to Becky in prison.

Chapter 32

As the years passed, the Akins sisters reached out to each other, gradually rebuilding their relationships. Vicki raised her family in the north Georgia mountains. Valerie and her husband remained in Florida, but the two women occasionally visited each other's homes. Vanessa married and established her own life in Missouri. The girls have never had any further contact with their mother.

Becky's health was deteriorating. By 2010, she required a wheelchair to get around. On June 30 of that year, she was paroled and sent to a halfway house in Middle Georgia. At first, she used the wheelchair all the time, but she gradually managed to walk on her own. In a few months, she was walking without any assistance.

Soon after that, she was allowed to move into the house on Camelot Drive in Athens. She was required to report to a parole officer monthly. The only other condition of her parole was that she have no contact with her children or any of Ronny Akins's family members.

Becky lived there without incident for several years, but her health continued to deteriorate. Her parole officer started visiting her home once a month rather than requiring Becky to come to his office.

Then, in December 2019, on one of his monthly visits, the man found Becky lying on the floor in her house. It appeared she'd lain there for a day or two, unable to get up.

In the local hospital, she was diagnosed with dementia and blindness. Her condition was stabilized and she was moved to a nearby nursing home. And there she remains. She doesn't communicate well, so no one knows what she remembers of the turbulent, violent life she led.

EPILOGUE

Telling a story like this one requires many interviews and extensive research. As I plowed through fifty years of newspapers and court documents, I found the account of the 1955 deaths of Coy Turpin and his three-year-old son Michael in Athens, Georgia. The official finding by both the police and the coroner was that it had been a murder/suicide. Such a tragic event had to be included in this family's story, even if I wasn't sure of the implications. So I used it as the prologue.

In the course of my investigation, I discovered no facts that could contradict the official conclusion. However, at the time and through the decades since, there have been plenty of rumors surrounding the case. It was no secret that Becky Turpin despised her younger brother. She wasn't hesitant about sharing her feelings about the boy. Not surprisingly suspicion turned to her at the time of the deaths.

No one had seen her at the house that day, but it wouldn't have been difficult for Becky to be there around noon. Like many students at her high school, she often went home for lunch. It was an informal arrangement. Students simply left and returned on their own. There was no procedure for signing out or signing back in. Becky could have gone home, slipped in the house, and returned to school with no one seeing her.

But did she? There's certainly no evidence to suggest that Becky had anything to do with the killings. Like most cops and former cops, I'm very suspicious of coincidence. But all I have is suspicion.

I do know that the deaths of Coy and Michael Turpin was a shattering event for the family. It had to have had an effect on sixteen-year-old Becky. Was it disturbing enough to affect her future behavior to the point of turning her into a killer? Or is it possible that Becky herself murdered her father and brother? There are no answers to these questions.

During the editorial process of readying this book for publication with Mercer University Press, my editor, along with a couple of other people who know about these things, pointed out that the deaths of Coy and Michael should be resolved. I couldn't agree more. Unfortunately, that is something I'm unable to do. I simply don't know what happened on that November day in 1955. All I can do is leave to you, the reader, to draw your own conclusions.

Index